Twenty-Five Doors to Meditation

Zhunti Buddha
(see page 34)

Twenty-Five Doors to Meditation

A HANDBOOK FOR ENTERING SAMADHI

by
William Bodri
and
Lee Shu-Mei

SAMUEL WEISER, INC.
York Beach, Maine

First published in 1998 by
SAMUEL WEISER, INC,
P. O. Box 612
York Beach, ME 03910-0612

Library of Congress Cataloging-in-Publication Data
Bodri, William.
Twenty-five doors to meditation : a handbook for entering samadhi / William
Bodri, Lee Shu-Mei.
p.   cm.
Includes bibliographical references and index.
ISBN 1-57863-035-5 (pbk. : alk. paper)
1. Meditation—Buddhism.   I. Shu-Mei, Lee.   II. Title.
BQ5612.B63   1998
294.3'4435—dc21   97-51639
CIP
BJ

Typeset in 10.5 point Bembo
Printed in the United States of America
04 03 02 01 99 98
10 9 8 7 6 5 4 3 2 1

TO Mahakashyapa, who patiently waits,
and to Rahula, Pindola, and Kundupada.

TO all the world's students who wish to cultivate,
and who ardently seek the path to enlightenment.

Contents

List of Illustrations

Introduction

The purpose of this book is to introduce a wide variety of cultivation techniques to people who are searching for an appropriate spiritual practice. From the wide selection of techniques within, there are sure to be one or two methods which will interest any aspiring practitioner. Thus, any of these techniques can serve as the initial basis of spiritual practice.

The very first requirement of the cultivation path is to accumulate merit, for without merit it's impossible to succeed at the task of self-realization. But to succeed in enlightenment, you must also devote yourself to some form of spiritual practice, for otherwise you can't possibly attain Tao. The formula for progress in spiritual cultivation, which is valid for all other forms of endeavor as well, is Method + Effort + Time + Experience = Result. Thus you can expect the positive results of self-realization only after you put time and effort into following a proper cultivation technique (*sadhana*).

From your familiarity and experiences with an initial form of meditation practice, your understanding of cultivation principles will naturally grow, and from this progressive increase in wisdom and experience, your practice can be adjusted accordingly. In this way, matching experience with wisdom and theory, over time you make tremendous progress on the cultivation path. So with effort, experience, time, and practice you will definitely achieve substantial spiritual results.

It's often said that there are 84,000 different afflictions in one moment of the mind, and so there are also 84,000 various methods of cultivation practice, called "dharma doors," that you can use to appropriately address these vastly different afflictions. The biggest problem in our lives is that these mental afflictions continually arise and give us no peace, thus blocking the path to attainment. Hence all the genuine cultivation methods in existence are aimed at quieting your thoughts, and when thoughts stop we attain a state of mental stillness or cessation called *samadhi*.

Samadhi is not a state of mental dullness or torpor, for within samadhi your mind remains clear, open and aware. It's an experiential realm where clear awareness and mental quiet are conjoined, for within samadhi the mind experiences such one-pointed concentration that the busy extraneous thoughts which normally bother us totally drop away. This is the initial stage on the path to spiritual development: a state of mental quiet within which our miscellaneous random thoughts seem to disappear. Sometimes we call this state of quiet "emptiness," which is just a synonym for the absence of our discriminative monkey mind.

The samadhi of mental quiet marks just the very beginning stages of spiritual cultivation, for the ultimate attainment of self-realization requires that we develop transcendental wisdom as well. Transcendental wisdom, or *prajna*, is that discriminative but completely nonintellectual awareness that empowers us to perceive the true nature of the mind. Samadhi is just a stage of quiet and calm: it's still a phenomenal realm even though we say it's empty. When you attain samadhi, however, this emptiness of normal mentation allows you to realize how to detach from clinging to your mental experiences, and this is the necessary lesson we need to learn so that we can use our wisdom to turn around and perceive enlightenment.

The cessational aspect of samadhi is also important because it's through samadhi that we can purify and transform our physical bodies, and that's when all our spiritual powers and *kung-fu* (mind-body attainments) come out. On the spiritual path, both these aspects must be mastered—we must purify both our bodies and minds in order to reach the highest levels of attainment. But ultimately, prajna-transcendental wisdom is the factor we must rely upon for identifying and learning the enlightenment way. Without prajna-wisdom, you cannot awaken to enlightenment. Prajna-wisdom enables you to recognize the true mind.

Now, if people start practicing a particular cultivation method but don't understand the principles involved, they're likely to get lost on the path of spiritual cultivation. Unless one's beliefs are based on wisdom, practice without understanding is equivalent to being superstitious. Hence developing prajna-transcendental wisdom is all important, and to cultivate self-realization everyone must develop samadhi since samadhi is the means by which we realize our prajna.

In other words, samadhi is the pathway to cultivating spiritual wisdom; from within a quiet mind, you can develop the spiritual wisdom that lets you recognize the true mind and succeed on the path of cultivation. You can perform all the religious ceremonies you like and attend all sorts of spiritual services, perform a wide variety of meritorious acts, exercise your intellect in all sorts of ways, strictly follow religious injunctions and codes of conduct, and even memorize reams of religious dogma. These can all be extremely worthwhile activities, but no matter what you do, *there is no such thing as true spiritual progress unless you attain samadhi and prajna*. All these other activities are just expedient means designed to guide you to this goal.

Some methods of arriving at samadhi begin with the mundane realm of reality and apply various techniques to arrive at a state where discriminative thought disappears, where the mind is calm and still—what we call empty or void. Some methods begin by cultivating this emptiness directly. Some cultivation practices involve form; other methods involve formless doors to samadhi. Sometimes a method will involve adding burdens to the mind in order to get rid of mental chaos, other methods will involve subtracting burdens to arrive at an absence of internal mental chatter. Certain methods will involve cultivating one's *jing* (seminal essence) or *chi* (vital energy or prana), while other methods will involve cultivating one's *shen* (spirit). Some methods will investigate the insubstantial nature of worldly appearances, while others will abandon phenomena altogether and work solely on investigating the formless mind which is able to perceive phenomena.

There are cultivation methods which focus on elements within space and time, and methods which focus on elements outside of space and time. Some cultivation methods deal with tracing the senses back to their ultimate source, and other methods focus on mastering various realms of consciousness. But all these different cultivation methods, if they are genuine spiritual techniques, are equally aimed at giving rise to samadhi, and then to transcendental spiritual wisdom.

In cultivation practice, you first bring about a state of quiet mental cessation, or samadhi, and then use your wordless insight to look into that state of mental calm which you produce. Then you'll be able to see that both "existence" and "nonexistence," which are our terms for the two states of mentation and emptiness (the no-thought state of samadhi), are both dualistic realms that appear in the bright, formless, clear mind of voidness which extends everywhere. We blind ourselves through fixing it in one location because we're so attached to our body, but the true mind extends everywhere. Because it's everywhere we say it's empty and formless or void. Being empty it encompasses all things. When you can identify *that* state, which is the true one that knows, then you will begin to truly climb the ranks of spiritual practice. But to get there you have to practice mental cessation and internal contemplation (prajna-wisdom), and these two have to be matched in practice.

Now, there are not only a tremendous number of approaches available in cultivation practice, but there are an infinite number of samadhi realms you can attain as well. However, all these possible samadhi realms can be classified into nine large nondenominational stages. The first four ranks of samadhi attainment are called the four basic concentrations, namely the first, second, third, and fourth *dhyana*. The next four samadhi include the samadhi of infinite space, the samadhi of infinite consciousness, the samadhi of infinite nothingness, and the samadhi of neither thought nor no-thought. Finally, there is the "Arhat's nirvana," which is a state of liberation, free from the realm of birth and death, and which is only accessed through the Buddhist path of wisdom cultivation. The first four dhyanas are called Form Realm samadhis, and the next four absorptions are called the Formless Realm samadhis. This is because the four dhyanas still involve various mentalities of subtle form, but the four formless concentrations have for the most part abandoned gross form and thus are involved with great states of emptiness. For a short description of these samadhi, we've included brief details and references in the appendices of this book.

Though there are nine basic samadhi, each of these have further subdivisions, accounting for the numerous realms that people can experience in their cultivation practice. For instance, when people reach the realm in which they experience that "the universe is pure consciousness," or that "God is everywhere," they are not yet enlightened but have simply attained the samadhi of infinite consciousness. Sometimes one reaches a realm that can only be described as pure bliss without coarse thought; this corresponds to the third dhyana. Sometimes one can reach a mental realm that can only be described as endless empty space, and this is the samadhi of infinite emptiness that some people mistakenly take as enlightenment. Then there are the countless samadhis you can obtain by tuning your *chi* or *shen* to match with some particular state in the same manner that you would adjust the frequencies on your radio.

The characteristics of these various realms are very profound, and in this book we are only providing the initial indications for how to enter these stages of attainment. As a general rule, the amount you can ultimately achieve through your cultivation efforts and the extent of your ultimate progress will correspond to two things: the merits you accumulate on the path, and the depth and devotion of your cultivation practice efforts.

No book can possibly summarize all the various means for attaining samadhi. This book, for instance, is simply an introduction to the wide variety of methods in existence. In fact, to explain each method in detail would require an entire book for each method in turn, which is why we've designed this text for your own initial efforts at self-study and as a handbook for meditation teachers who need a textbook for leading discussions. While we can only introduce the rudimentary principles behind some of the world's most popular cultivation techniques, nonetheless we've provided many references for further study. There are sure to be one or two methods here that will suit your individual temperament and personality and be appropriate for your own cultivation practice. If you follow these practices according to the proper principles, samadhi and dhyana are sure to result.

Upon learning of a method for developing samadhi, it has always been a practitioner's responsibility to test its effectiveness in body and mind through personal practice and experience. Shakyamuni Buddha, for instance, would recommend different methods to students based upon their qualifications and potential, but the students still had to test out the techniques and adjust their practice or even change their practice based on their personal results. It's like going to a doctor for a prescription and returning for a further adjustment of the remedy. People have different illnesses so not everyone can use the same medicine, and even after you take a medicine, you might have to come back and have your prescription altered a bit. Thus, since everyone has different capabilities and attainments, not everyone will benefit through employing the same cultivation technique, or sadhana, and not everyone should practice in exactly the same way. You have to test each of these cultivation methods to see which one is appropriate to you, and you must use your wisdom in practice to maximize their effectiveness. Each method will be either more or less useful because each embodies a different degree of karmic affinity to your own personal situation.

In one famous lesson found in the *Shurangama Sutra*, Shakyamuni Buddha asked several of his students to recount the various dharma doors they used to attain samadhi. The various techniques that the students reported were widely different, showing that different people, because of their different karma and different innate capacities, can benefit by using vastly different cultivation practices. Twenty-five of Buddha's students volunteered twenty-five different "dharma doors," or cultivation methods, by which they had achieved some level of attainment, the wide variety of which are illustrative of almost any sadhana practice and its application.

For instance, in scanning the sutra we learn that there are various dharma doors to samadhi and prajna-wisdom that focus on the six sense data:

- Kaundinya attained samadhi by meditation on sound;

- Upanisad attained it by meditation on the impurity of form and on the impure nature of the physical body;

- Bodhisattva Fragrance-adorned attained it by meditation on contact with smells (fragrance), through which he achieved cessation-contemplation;

- The Bodhisattvas Bhaisajya-raja and Bhaisajya-samudgata by meditation on taste, the process of discriminating among flavors;

- Bhadrapala through meditation on touch;

- Mahakashyapa through meditation on (the emptiness of all) dharmas.

Other cultivation methods for samadhi and wisdom are based on the five sense organs:

- Aniruddha, who was blind, attained samadhi by meditation on the organ of sight and learned how to perceive not with his eyes but with his mind;

- Kshudrapanthaka attained it by meditating on the organ of smell (the nose), while cultivating the breath to a state of emptiness;

- Gavampati by meditation on the organ of taste, turning taste back to its knower;

- Pilindavatsa by meditation on the body, whereby he success-fully abandoned the conception of a body;

- Subhuti attained samadhi by meditation on the mind;

There are also methods for attaining samadhi and wisdom based on the six consciousnesses:

- Sariputra attained samadhi by means of sight perception;

- Samantabhadra Bodhisattva attained it by meditation on ear perception.;

- Sundarananda attained it by meditation on the perception of smell. He fixed his concentration on the (olfactory) base of his nose while cultivating the breath to cessation;

- Purnamaitrayaniputra by meditation on tongue perception;

- Upali by meditation on the perception of tangible objects, for he mastered control of his body in learning to observe disci-pline;

- Mahamaudgalyayana by meditation on the faculty of mind.

Finally, meditations on the seven elements can lead to samadhi and transcendental wisdom:

- Ucchusma, who was burdened with sexual lusts, attained samadhi by meditation on the fire element, employing the skeleton-method visualization in conjunction with kundalini cultivation;

- Dharanimdhara Bodhisattva attained samadhi by meditating on the earth element, contemplating the identity of his body with the earth element spanning the universe;

- Candraprabha Bodhisattva attained it by contemplation on the water element and its pervasive nature;

- The Bodhisattva of Crystal Light attained samadhi by contemplation on the wind element that is embodied in all kinds of movement, including the arising of thoughts;

- Akasagarbha Bodhisattva attained samadhi through a meditation on boundless space;

- Maitreya Bodhisattva by meditating on the element of consciousness-only;

- Mahasthama meditated on the element of perception to attain samadhi, which he achieved through Buddha-mindfulness.

Due to this wide variety of techniques, whether or not a method is appropriate for your own practice can only be answered through personal testing; devotedly cultivating a method for awhile is the only way to determine whether it is suited to your needs. As a warning, a method you abhor may very well be the one best suited to your needs, since bad karma tends to oppose our efforts to cultivate practice and transform karma in a positive way. Cultivation always has a positive effect on changing negative karma for the better, and thus resistance and obstacles will always arise when we sincerely start to cultivate. Conversely, a cultivation method you love may also prove ineffective despite your personal preference, for it may draw you into a realm of torpor, indulgence, self-satisfaction or laxity. Hence you are best advised to try a variety of cultivation techniques. In fact, we strongly feel that everyone should try the following meditations:

- the practice of cessation and contemplation practice called shamatha-vipashyana (chapter 4);

- watching the breath (chapter 6);

- the white skeleton visualization practice (chapter 5);

- the Zhunti mantra (chapter 7);

- Kuan-Yin's method of listening to sound (chapter 3).

The nine-step bottled wind method of breath retention (chapter 10) should also become a daily part of everyone's cultivation routine, like brushing one's teeth, and all people should be taught this method for health reasons whether they are meditators or not. While the practice of breath retention and internal cleansing in the nine-step bottled winds practice may not ultimately result in spiritual progress, it will definitely lead to better health and increased longevity for every practitioner.

When people cultivate a particular spiritual practice correctly, certain phenomena are sure to arise that will manifest in accordance with the practitioner's stage of accomplishment. A discussion of such mind-body changes, or *kung-fu*, is beyond the scope of this book, but the reader is referred to *Tao and Longevity: Mind-Body Transformation, Working Toward Enlightenment,* and *To Realize Enlightenment,* by Nan Huai-Chin, for extensive information on such transformations. These works, published by Samuel Weiser, contain the best information available on this topic. In time, we hope to produce a further work on "Measuring Meditation" or "The Various Stages of the Spiritual Experience" that will also address these various phenomena and the stages of the path as described by the world's different cultivation schools. In the meanwhile, we've indicated further helpful reading in the appendices.

We hope this short work will lead to further understanding and advances in your current cultivation practice, or open the doorway to cultivation practice if you aren't already involved with some particular meditation technique. We also hope it reveals the highly scientific, non-denominational, and cross-cultural nature of the path. The techniques within this book represent most of the basic doorways for attaining samadhi, and we cannot emphasize enough that samadhi and prajna-wisdom are the crux of spiritual development. But since our primary purpose in writing this book is to help people ultimately reach Tao, we must also point out time and again that samadhi is not Tao, but just a stepping stone on the path.

After a person attains samadhi, he or she must still cultivate prajna-transcendent wisdom or the fruit of ultimate attainment will always stay out of reach. One who attains samadhi but doesn't cultivate transcendental wisdom is like an individual who decides to make a trip to a fabulous palace but gets sidetracked by all the pretty scenery along the way. If he ends up playing in the gardens of samadhi, he'll lose his way and never reach his ultimate destination. The greatest samadhi is absent of both samadhi and mundane mentation and that's why it's called great. That's Tao, whereas the various samadhi are simply experiential realms of rarified mentation. So if you keep thinking that samadhi is the path, but don't cultivate the wisdom that is letting you realize or be aware of the samadhis, you'll never be able to truly experience the Tao.

Thus our best wishes are extended to you for your ultimate success in cultivating both samadhi and wisdom. We hope that this book helps you attain the fruit of the path in this lifetime.

1

Union with Child Light to Realize Mother Light

There are two types of light in the universe called "mother light" and "child light," respectively. "Mother light" is the invisible, formless basis of light that can give rise to physical light, and physical light is the light we can see or measure because it has form or appearance. The images of the physical world we see with our eyes—including brightness, darkness, shades, and colors—are the light with form that cultivation schools term "child light." While child light is visible, the true mother light is not something we can see with our eyes, because it is fundamentally formless. Cultivation science says that our true self-nature is akin to this mother light, but its formless radiance is something we realize with the mind rather than something we perceive through the senses.

To see any form of child light requires that we use our eyes. Because our eyes possess this inherent capacity to see, we can view all sorts of colors and phenomena—such as brightness, form, movement and depth. But the thing that ultimately enables our eyes to see all these appearances is not a type of light, and the path of cultivation is the search to find that one thing that is ultimately, foundationally behind all our seeing and knowing. We call this thing the "true mind"

Figure 1. The first Indian Zen master, Mahakashyapa, resides sealed within this rock face on Chicken Foot Mountain in China, waiting for the coming of the next Buddha Maitreya. Zen master Mahakashyapa abides in samadhi within, practicing the method of union with Mother light. Hence he is often known as the "drinker of light" or "eater of light." Photograph courtesy Bill Porter.

because it is the ground state of awareness, and we call it the "fundamental nature" because it's our true essence of being, the one that stands behind all our knowing and awareness states.

Now the method we'll introduce for cultivating the seeing of light is different from the methods used in Taoism, Hinduism, yoga, or Tibetan esoteric Buddhism. These other schools all have various cultivation practices for seeing light, but they substantially differ from this one. Our method starts by utilizing our eyes in looking at natural light, and it doesn't matter what form of natural light we employ. We can use the sunlight, the light of the moon or stars, or even the artificial light from light bulbs. Unlike other cultivation practices that rely on specific forms of light, in this method we can use any source of light that comes our way.

This cultivation technique starts by having you look straight ahead in front, with your eyes facing the light and without moving your eyeballs. To be able to do this requires some kung-fu, because you have to allow your eyes to point straight ahead without tiring, and they must remain relaxed without movement. At this moment, whether the eyes are open or closed, an image of light will always appear to the eyes. For instance, in the daytime we say the light is bright, but when you close your eyes the degree of brightness is indeed decreased but you aren't seeing absolute blackness; you're just seeing dimmer light. This is true even in the night time, for there's never a perfect absence of light. It's always just a situation of dimmer light.

With your motionless eyes now facing the light, relax your body and mind and just stay in that state. Let your body and self merge with the light, no matter what type of light you're seeing, and gradually forget your body. In time, the light you see will extend to fill the universe and it will seem as if there is no such thing as space or time. No matter how the light changes, there should be no other realization than "I am the light" and "the light is me." Practicing in this way, emptiness, light, and you will merge into one. This is the basis behind the New Testament saying "God is Light," but Tibetan Buddhism and Hinduism also recognize this stage of spiritual recognition.

This, however, is still a child-light scenario belonging to the realm of form since it still emphasizes the light that eyes can see, and you are still depending on the mind of discrimination in this practice. When you can realize "I am light," you're still at the stage of conception and ideational consciousness wherein you know and comprehend things at an intellectual level. But the thing that enables us to comprehend light and its fundamental energy is not a light with form, nor does it belong within the domain of consciousness. That's the thing we want to recognize.

When you reach the stage of ultimate, fundamental no-form, you already forget about the knower, the knowing, and the object to be known. You forget about what you see, the process of seeing, and what fundamentally enables you to see. This is a state of true no-form. This is when the mother light and child light conjoin—the light of formlessness and form come together so that there is no discrimination whatsoever, which is the samadhi of true wisdom. In this practice, you merge your prajna knowing developed through the path with the primordial wisdom which has always been there, and the child light merges with the mother light. This is how one should practice if they wish to cultivate the child light as a path to Tao.

2

Zen, the Method of No-Method

Zen is considered the highest of all possible cultivation schools in existence because it doesn't rely on any method at all—it just directly points to the true nature of the mind. In terms of the pathway to Tao, it is neither an adding nor subtracting method of cultivation; Zen doesn't rely on any artificial techniques. In Zen you don't add anything to the mind in order to attain samadhi, nor do you try to subtract anything from the mind. In other words, with Zen practice you neither accept nor reject your thoughts in trying to attain samadhi, but you simply let them come and go without clinging. Since there's no effort involved at all, except for the effortless fundamental watching or knowing that is always there, Zen is therefore called the method of no-method.

In Zen, as in Tibetan Mahamudra, you simply ride the function of awareness and turn it inward, reflecting it back to its source, to perceive the fundamental essence of this knowing. Some refer to this process as "resting," since it means "dropping the busy mind" or "letting everything go," while the function of knowing continues to stay. Thus in Zen, the mind is perfectly open and aware, yet mental busyness naturally comes to a rest. Some people mistakenly consider this a particular form of cultivation technique, but since awareness is a perfectly natural process that's always there, where is there any special method or any artificial contrivance? Whether we know something or don't know something, our true mind knows that we know or don't know, so awareness always shines. In cultivation, it's the root source of this awareness we must find.

Our minds are forever visited by chaotic and confusing thoughts, so in Zen we treat these thoughts like hotel guests that come and go without prolonging their stay. If you give them no service but simply watch them without adding any energy to the situation, in time all the guests will depart and you will arrive at samadhi. The Zen master Chia-shan said, "The dragon carries the ocean pearl in its mouth, paying no attention to the fish swimming by [the mental realms which arise]." Hence if you continue to shine effortless awareness on your mind's activities and the experiential realms that may arise, without becoming involved in these multitudinous phenomena, you will naturally scale the various ranks of samadhi and attain self-realization.

In Zen practice, you never hold onto any mental realm or phenomenon that arises because of your cultivation, nor do you ever identify any stage of progress as being the ultimate attainment. If you fixate on any state as being "it," you're already out of Zen. Once you think that any stage of progress is real, you've already produced an illusion that masks the true nature. For instance, even thinking about emptiness creates a thought of emptiness, and the thought is actually an impurity that will mask any stage of emptiness you may have already achieved. So the method of practicing Zen is that of simply shining awareness on all the mental realms that arise, and in time they will naturally depart without staying, like clouds dispersing in the open sky. Then you'll be left with true emptiness, and the awareness of knowing that state. But since that emptiness is also an object of your knowing, it's not the true self. Hence you have to turn around and see what gives rise to this knowing. Progressing with this exercise of wisdom, you will eventually arrive at fundamental mind, which is the fundamental nature.

Every thought and every type of mental realm, including the various samadhi, have to depart because nothing stays—death will certainly come to thoughts as it does to all other phenomena. Only one thing remains unmoved during all these transformations—the true self, which is the ultimate source of awareness. You can go east or go west, but that one thing has never moved, has never left, and has never gone anywhere; it's just that the experiential realm within it has transformed. Thus it is that Zen Master Pao Chih said:

If you only learn to cultivate unmindfulness at all times while you're walking, standing, sitting, and reclining, then you may fail over time to leap over to true Reality only because your strength is insufficient. But if you continue practicing in this way for another three, five, or ten years, you will surely awaken to Tao in the end. It is because you cannot practice in this manner that you set your mind on the academic study of Zen and Tao, but this is irrelevant.

Thus we say that "the mind can give birth [engender thoughts] without abiding anywhere." There's nothing wrong with thoughts themselves, it's just that you shouldn't cling to them. In fact, the mind should not dwell in any experiential realm. Furthermore, we must note that on this road of practice it's very easy for your breath to combine naturally with your thoughts so as to transform the physical body and bring about all sorts of kung-fu. Thus Zen has all the esoteric changes and stages of attainment described by the world's other cultivation schools, but makes no fuss about any of these matters. It ignores such phenomena because they're transient manifestations, just like any other, which are always in a process of transformation, and thus Zen discards any preoccupation with these states and proceeds directly to the true nature.

In the other schools, however, people end up getting attached to prana, chi channels, chakras, astral bodies, and all sorts of other experiential realms with the result that hardly anyone makes it to enlightenment. Making no fuss and paying no attention to these things, most

Zen practitioners tread the straight path to Tao, whereas other practitioners get lost along the way.

The Fourth Zen Patriarch said to Fa-yung:

> The hundreds and thousands of gates to Tao are all ultimately in the mind; the subtle virtues as numerous as river sands all lay in the source of mind. All aspects of discipline, samadhi, prajna, and the manifestations of various spiritual powers are all inherently there; they're nowhere else but in your own true mind. All your mental afflictions and obstructions caused by habit energies are originally empty and void. All the causes and effects of mundane existence are like dreams and hallucinations . . . So in true cultivation you just let your mind be free. You do not perform contemplative practices, and you do not promote efforts to make your mind clear. Don't arouse the emotions of greed or anger, and don't fall into sorrow or worry. Flowing unhindered and unobstructed, be free in all ways, however you might be. When there is no doing good and no doing evil, then in all your activities and circumstances, everything that meets your eyes will be the inconceivable function of Buddhahood. It is blissful and sorrowless, so we call it Buddhahood.

3

Kuan-Yin's Method of Listening to Sound

 The most famous cultivation technique in the *Shurangama Sutra* is the method reported by the Bodhisattva Kuan-Yin, who used hearing to realize the self-nature. Using hearing, he was able to enter samadhi and ultimately attain complete enlightenment. Manjushri, who is the Buddha of Wisdom and teacher of the other Buddhas, said that this technique surpassed all the other dharma doors in existence. Describing this technique in full would require a level of sophistication beyond this text, but the basics of this practice can certainly be introduced.

A cultivation saying runs, "Whoever hears the sound of water without using the sixth consciousness for thirty years will achieve Kuan-Yin's all-pervading wisdom." So in this practice, you let sounds come to your ears without trying to distinguish them. Remaining natural, relaxed, and detached, you spontaneously know what the sounds are without trying to recognize them or deliberate their meaning. Eventually you will find you can hear quiet as well as sounds, and will discover that they are both the same thing—sounds and silence are both objects of hearing, they're both phenomena. Sounds, and the state where they're absent, will still exist but will start to seem more and more separate from yourself. Since now they have less to do with you, they won't bother you so much anymore and you can detach from them both to enter into samadhi.

A famous individual who used this technique was the Chinese Zen monk Han-shan, who practiced Kuan-Yin's method of hearing on a bridge next to a noisy torrent of water. Han-shan reported that at first the noise of the water was quite audible, but in time it could only be heard when his thoughts arose, and not when they ceased. Then one day, his practice improved such that he did not hear the sound of the water any longer; sounds and noises vanished completely.

When describing this method in the *Shurangama Sutra*, Kuan-Yin said:

> I entered into the stream of the self-nature of the sense of hearing, thereby eliminating the sound of what was heard. Now proceeding from this stillness, both sound and silence ceased to arise. Advancing in this way, both hearing and what was heard melted away and vanished. When hearing and what is heard are both forgotten, then the sense of hearing leaves no impression in the mind. When sense and the objects of sense both become empty, then emptiness and sense merge and reach a state of absolute perfection. When emptiness and what is being emptied are both extinguished, then arising and extinction are naturally extinguished. At this point the absolute emptiness of nirvana became manifest, and suddenly I transcended the mundane and supramundane worlds.

In this method, you listen to and gradually detach from both sound and silence. When there's no sound, we call this silence, and we conventionally say there is no hearing. But that doesn't mean that the nature of hearing has ceased. It's simply that the function of hearing now recognizes a state of no sound, or silence. Since the nature of hearing can ascertain the state of sound and no sound, it's easy to use this method to realize the nature of duality and then to detach from both existence and non-existence. That's the method of practice.

Both quiet (stillness or silence) and un-quiet (sound or disturbance) are phenomena, so tying oneself to either extreme is wrong. That's why the state of samadhi (mental quiet) isn't Tao either, even though you need to practice samadhi in order to awaken self-realization. For instance, if you don't detach from the phenomenon of silence, you'll never find out what's hearing silence. *Thus the quiet one recognizes in samadhi is not Tao*, and the task you must perform is to return the hearing to hear the self-nature.

To progress past the quiet calm of samadhi through continued cultivation efforts, you must also practice prajna-wisdom. All the various methods of cultivation first get you to the point where the mind is calmed and still, but *this doesn't qualify as perfect penetration* to the vast source of the mind. It's just a phenomenal realm of quiet, another false creation of the mind. To attain Tao you must shine awareness on this state, without engaging in some form of mentation, so as to go further and achieve some genuine realization. That's the practice of prajna-wisdom.

As Kuan-Yin said, you must cultivate to the extent that your awareness of samadhi and the state of samadhi both become extinct. Then it is *real* samadhi. Proceeding in this manner, you will eventually reach enlightenment. What is Kuan-Yin's method? It's withdrawing your energy from a focus on the outside, turning the function of hearing around to return it to its source. Hearing returns to listen to its self-nature, and through this method you can penetrate through all the various obstructions to achieve ultimate enlightenment.

4

Watching Thoughts:
Cessation and Observation Practice

Many of the world's cultivation techniques are based on the principles of cessation and contemplation practice, also known as shamatha-vipashyana, in order to generate samadhi. For instance, the Chinese Tien-tai cultivation techniques, Confucian introspection, Tibetan Gelugpa meditation on the mean, the Hindu yoga practices of observing the mind, and orthodox Buddhism's emphasis on right views are all based on the principles of cessation and contemplation, or stopping and observation (wisdom or insight) practice.

The basic method behind cessation-contemplation practice involves using some mental exercise to stop the flow of random thoughts, and then turning one's awareness within during the state of mental stillness you produce to contemplate the mind (the state without thoughts). This is not only a means for attaining samadhi, but a way to police one's thoughts and normal behavior.

The detailed explanations of this method can be found in Chih-i's *The Greater Cessation and Contemplation* and in Tsongkhapa's *Lamrim chenmo (Great Treatise on the Stages of the Path to Enlightenment)*.

However, for brevity's sake, the basic practice of watching thoughts to attain cessation and contemplation can be abbreviated as follows:

1. First, sit comfortably to relax your body and your respiration. We call this first step the "preparatory practices," or physiological adjustments, for tuning the physical nature. Basically, you want to situate yourself so as to lessen any physical disturbances or distractions. Then after your body is calmed, you start quietly observing your inner thoughts and emotions. In other words, you simply watch your internal psychological functions as if you were a third-person observer. This third person doesn't interfere with what's going on, or participate in the activities they're observing. He's like a great host at a banquet who can accept everything that's going on around him. He just stays there watching, neither rejecting nor clinging to anything; he simply sits there silently observing, without becoming involved.

2. You continue watching your internal process of mentation until you reach the point where you can clearly observe every thought and idea that appears in the mind without any vagueness or ambiguity. Naturally, you are not tightening your body or mentally straining during this practice. Rather, you always remain relaxed while clearly observing your internal mental processes. After a while, you will eventually be able to distinguish that the process of mentation has three parts: a preceding thought that has gone, a thought that has not yet arisen, and the immediate, clear, radiant state of present mind. With continued watching, the separation of these three states becomes quite evident.

3. With continued observation, you progress a bit further and next realize that the past, present, and future thoughts never stay. Since they don't stay they can never be grasped, hence we say that fundamentally they have no basis. This observation of the appearance and disappearance of thoughts is called "observing birth and death," for the coming and going of thoughts is a ceaseless, never-ending process of arising, and then disappearance or decay. This is the realm of birth and death, and while you attach to this realm you cannot achieve liberation. That's why people who focus on their in-breathing or out-breathing never make progress in the Tao, for they must learn to focus on the state of stillness between the breaths which is outside the realm of coming and going.

By observing this stream of birth and death, you will gradually learn how to detach from the mental processes and you will become more familiar with the false mind of consciousness. In other words, you will be able to drop the illusion that our mental process is a fundamental reality. Rather, you will gradually see that all mental states are ungraspable, transient phenomena that come and go without end, and they're more like insubstantial bubbles of foam or particles of dust that have no fixity of nature. Because of their ceaseless birth and death and the gap inbetween, what we normally imagine as a continuous continuity of thoughts is actually an illusion, like the unbroken wheel of light we see when a stick of fire is spun in the air. Thus, through this process of inner watching you will begin to realize that our mental state is an ongoing process separate from our true self. The true self is what's watching this play scene, like an internal knower who never moves. If you go from here to the North Pole and back, the scenery always changes, but that inner knower never changes—it never moves. In fact, it never leaves, and has never come either. It just *is*. That's what we're seeking, though on a more profound level than we can explain here.

Now, in watching thoughts without adding any energy to the process, you'll begin to understand how dreamlike our consciousness actually is, because the reality it gives birth to seems to be there and yet the concreteness of this reality isn't real. Phenomena are empty, and yet they are conventionally real, but this conventional reality is also empty. So eventually, through observation with detachment, you'll reach the stage when you can mentally relax while "giving birth to the mind without abiding anywhere."

Through continued observation you will notice that thoughts or phenomena (existence) are born from emptiness (mental silence) and that even the existence of emptiness relies on phenomena. Existence and emptiness are both manifestations of one nature—its single source, our true self—so on the road of cultivation you don't cling to either

15

side. Both sides are phenomenal constructions, or false relativities, so both sides are not real. Hence in shamatha-vipashyana practice, you start to contemplate the mean between stillness and activity. In contemplating the mean, you penetrate to the source.

In practicing this inner watching, you'll get progressively better at becoming mentally free because you'll stop clinging to or rejecting your thoughts, emotions, and sensations. Thus your mental awareness will increasingly open and your ability to function in the world will increase as well, so you'll actually be expanding your awareness while saving a lot of energy that you'd normally waste in useless clinging. Furthermore, your internal state of peace and calm will progressively develop with every increase in clarity. Thus if you keep observing the origin and destruction of thoughts while paying particular attention to where they come from and go to, you'll eventually interrupt the stream of consciousness.

4. With the stream of consciousness disrupted, you will then notice a momentary gap of stillness or silence between all your thoughts. In other words, if you practice this method of inner observation for a long time—by wordlessly watching thoughts without injecting any energy into the thought stream—the process of silent observation will itself disrupt the stream of mentation. The state of mind in the immediate present will gradually open up to reveal a tiny gap of mental quiet, or emptiness; when a previous thought has disappeared and a subsequent thought has not yet arisen, the mind will seem quiet. This mental silence is not a gap of dullness or stupor, nor should it be a forced silence or blankness you create through suppressing thoughts. Rather, it will be a lucid, clear, and open awareness, and these characteristics will gradually unfold as more time is spent in this state.

In other words, after quietly observing your mental processes for quite some time, you will eventually notice a tiny, silent pause between thoughts, which is known as the initial stage of "cessation." If we continue observing this state without effort and shine awareness on it, it will gradually expand further and further. Looking into this gap of silence and observing its nature is the process of contemplation or vipashyana. The gap is a quiet realm similar to emptiness but it still isn't the genuine emptiness of Tao. Nevertheless, this is what we're initially after because we can use this state to begin cultivating prajna wisdom.

5. If you continue to carry over this state of watching the mind (the process of silent detachment and immediate awareness) during all your normal activities—whether walking, talking, sitting, or sleeping—you'll be able to reach the point where thoughts no longer bind you. Gradually their volume will die down, your radiant awareness will expand, and you will be able to enter seamlessly into the real emptiness of samadhi.

In other words, if you keep observing the state of cessation by shining awareness on this state, you will eventually arrive at dhyana. Thus the practice of shining awareness on the silence within is commonly referred to as "contemplating mind." If you continue progressing in this manner by reaching further levels of emptiness and shining wisdom awareness on any state of cessation you reach, you will eventually acquire prajna, or transcendental wisdom. Then you'll climb the various ranks of samadhi and enter into the Tao.

People the world over are always seeking secret or mystical spiritual techniques, hoping they will provide a short cut to enlightenment. There are no special techniques other than the basic principles revealed here. If you turn to the Christian contemplation practices espoused by St. Augustine you'll find cessation and contemplation. If you turn to the Jewish Kabbalah, or the self-remembering techniques of Gurdjieff, or even the practices for moral self-improvement advocated by Benjamin Franklin, you'll find cessation/contemplation practices once again. Most of the world's spiritual practices are based on the principles of stopping (samadhi) and observation (prajna), so if you really wish to master the road of spiritual cultivation, there's no way you can accomplish this feat without understanding the principles of cessation and contemplation, and applying these in your spiritual sadhana.

5

Dazzling White Skeleton Contemplation

When Shakyamuni Buddha organized the many cultivation practices of ancient India into various categories, he differentiated ten great roads of samadhi practice. In these great paths there were several interrelated techniques that he often recommended: mindfulness of the impurity of the body, mindfulness of death, *pranayama* (breathing exercises), and the skeleton visualization practice. These cultivation techniques are usually practiced together because of their self-reinforcing nature.

All beings fundamentally have no self but we experience sufferings and afflictions because we attach to the idea of possessing a self. We often talk about achieving a state of selflessness or non-ego because the idea of a self is actually false and non-existent, but it's hard enough just trying to ignore the physical body and its various sensations. All the obstacles to attaining enlightenment arise because we believe in the existence of a body and a self, but if you can ignore the body and abandon the idea of an inherent ego, then you can achieve Nirvana. This is the standard rule of cultivation for all beings in the universe. If we can get rid of the idea of a body and detach from the notions of possessing a self, we can ultimately reach enlightenment.

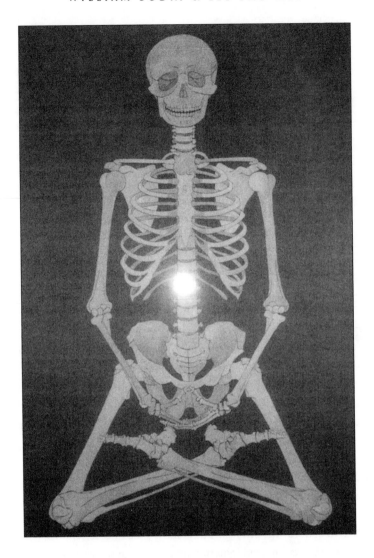

Figure 2. In the white skeleton visualization method, you must clearly envision your own skeleton as shining with a bright white light. The contemplation should always be anatomically correct, starting with the left big toe and visualizing upward. During the visualization, a bright light is optimally visualized between the seventh and eighth lower vertebrae. (Lao Gu Publishing.)

Selfishness is one of the great barriers in cultivation, and since sentient beings often aren't willing to give to others, the first rule of cultivation is to always practice charity. The practice of giving starts to chip away at our ego-centeredness and helps us accumulate the necessary merit we need in order to succeed at cultivation. Thus we must practice two types of giving: internal and external. Internal giving means giving up our thoughts, afflictions, and sorrows, while external giving means offering our wealth, material things, cultivation teachings, spiritual support, and even life to others. Offering wealth and material possessions to others is difficult enough, but offering one's life for others is harder still. Nevertheless this is the basis of the skeleton visualization technique.

In practicing internal and external giving, you will finally be able to escape the net of reincarnation, so in cultivation it's really essential that you cultivate giving and establish a foundation of merit. Thus it can't be emphasized enough that the spirit of giving is an important ingredient of the skeleton visualization practice. Esoteric Buddhism has many pictures showing the "dual practices" of sexual cultivation, and when you see the Buddhas and their consorts in these pictures, they're always standing on skeletons below. This is another important point to remember: those who want to practice sexual cultivation must already be proficient in the skeleton visualization technique, otherwise they won't succeed.

When Buddha was alive, there was no temple or communal shelter for his students. Therefore, he often asked his students to cultivate in graveyards where they were to practice the body-mindfulness and skeleton visualization techniques. In that time in India, graveyards were very dirty places with corpses visibly decaying everywhere, so there was plenty of opportunity to watch the putrefaction of the body and to observe its internal structure of flesh and bones. Hence a proper knowledge of anatomy was important for practicing this sadhana and still is today. In watching a physical body decay and putrefy, the practitioners would also be struck by the dirty, impure, and impermanent nature of the body, from which it was easy to learn detachment and free oneself from sexual desires. Today we use books to look up anatomy, and practice our cultivation in luxurious homes rather than in graveyards, but it seems we hardly achieve any self-cultivation progress at all. However, many of Buddha's students achieved enlightenment in as little as three days because their surroundings were different and they learned how to detach from the physical nature.

When you practice the skeleton visualization technique, you must therefore visualize all the bones of your body shining brightly, starting *with the tip of the left big toe*. It's important to start with this left toe, and then continue visualizing your other bones, proceeding upward until you internally see your five left toes, then your five right toes, and then your feet bones, leg bones, thigh bones, and so on. You gradually proceed higher and higher with your visualization, section by section, until you finish visualizing all the white bones of the skull. Everything must be anatomically correct, and all your bones must be visualized as *shining with a brilliant white light*.

When you can visualize your entire skeleton shining with this white light, then you must imagine you are dead and that all your skin and internal organs soften and putrefy. Using an imaginary knife, you cut up your dead body and offer all your organs, skin, flesh, and blood to all the demons and ghosts to eat and drink. You must regard these other beings as your parents, brothers, sisters, and friends from ages past, and so *with a sincere mind*—without holding back—you *joyfully offer* them your flesh and blood to repay any debts and satisfy their cravings and desires. You must be joyful during this offering of charity, and during the subsequent bodyless state as well, and then this state of joy and bliss can match with the ecstatic nature of the first dhyana. Then you can quickly succeed in your cultivation.

In this technique, when you can completely visualize your whole skeleton as a set of clean white shiny bones, this is one level of success. But it's important not to add any sorrowful emotions to this visualization. Instead, you should be very open and joyful while offering away your body to others, for this will satisfy the desires of any beings that make a claim on you, and quickly settle your debts. By offering your body in this way, all your past sins can be forgiven, and hence you can attain enlightenment quickly.

After you imagine that you are dead and have offered everything away, you visualize your white bones dissolving to become dust until there's no body left at all; there's only the phenomenon of emptiness corresponding to the white bone skeleton samadhi. If you are even partially successful in attaining the skeleton visualization samadhi, you'll be able to see an internal light within your body, and you'll eventually be able to see other people's skeletons, even when they're walking on the street. This is possible because all your chi has accumulated inside, and due to this massing an internal light is generated inside as a friction between the physiological and psychological elements, creating a result similar to that achieved by the Taoist practice of shining awareness within. This meditation can also lead you to achieve the state of inner luminosity mentioned in Tibetan esotericism and the stage of breaking through the form aggregate mentioned in Buddhism. Hence it can even result in the ability to see events at far distances, including other worlds. When you can see other skeletons because of this inner chi luminosity, you'll realize there is no distinction between males and females, the young and old, or rich and poor. Since there are no distinctions, hierarchies, or levels, all beings are seen as equals, and your mind will become even and calm. From this samadhi of equanimity and internal illumination, one can continue cultivating step by step to reach the stage of an Arhat.

Altogether there are thirty-six different versions of the skeleton visualization technique. For instance, you can use the time spent relaxing in bed to visualize that you are just a skeleton of white bones shining brightly, which would be the "skeleton relaxation technique," but you must remember to detach from any physical feelings or sensations which arise due to this practice. This practice quickly restores lost vital energy, and so if sexual desire arises through its usage, one must be careful not to lose one's energies in such activities. In the "medicine skeleton method," you can imagine that only one section of the body becomes a skeleton if that area is sick or troubles you, and then it will tend to get better faster because the focus of attention sends chi to that area. The supreme "Manjushri skeleton method" is another technique that tells us to especially visualize a point of light between the seventh and eighth thoracic vertebrae of the spine when doing the visualization.

Some great practitioners who succeed in skeleton practice become extremely flexible because they can imagine their bones becoming dust (which of course doesn't actually happen, they simply become more flexible). Others quickly purify their bodies and rapidly climb the ranks of the four dhyanas, which are the basic foundational states of true spiritual practice. First they cultivate their chi and one-pointed concentration through this technique, and then their chi transforms into *shen* (spirit), whereby they progressively reach a state of no-thought, emptiness, and, finally, they attain Tao. All this wonderful progress starts with the simple act of visualizing the white skeleton within.

6

Watching the Breath

There are over three hundred different breathing practices you can use in cultivation, called *pranayama* or *anapana* exercises. However, the basic principle behind all these techniques is that you must reach a certain stage of respiration in your practice where it seems as if your external breathing slows to a halt. As the Indian yoga master Patanjali said, "The cessation between the in-breath and out-breath is [true] pranayama." The Hindu *Hatha Yoga Pradipika* also says, "When the breath is irregular, then the mind will be unsteady, but when the breath is controlled, then the mind will also be controlled, calm and one-pointed." Hence in the world's various breathing practices, you are instructed to achieve a stage of relaxation wherein your coarse inhalations and exhalations cease while you remain perfectly relaxed and totally aware. When you reach this state, your true inner breath will ignite, thus initiating the state of *hsi* which signals the beginning of real chi, shakti, or kundalini cultivation.

Why is it possible to use breathing as a means of cultivation? Because the thoughts and breath are related; consciousness (mind) and chi (the body's wind element) are linked. Specifically, mind rides on the breath just as a rider is carried by a horse, so if the breath ceases moving, then extraneous thoughts will settle and stop busying your mind. Just as salt dissolves in water and becomes one with it, so there also occurs the union of mind with the breath when the breath subsides and the mind becomes still; mind dissolves in breath and the two become one during "cessation." This then, using the calming of the breath as a form of approach, is the basis behind many cultivation methods.

In normal activities, most people never realize they are breathing. If their breath and thought can combine, however, not only will individuals become clear about their breath, but they will also become extremely mindful of their other body sensations. Since mindfulness is a cultivation method in itself, the principle of keeping the mind in tune with the breath while remaining relaxed, detached, and aware is found in many cultivation schools and techniques. But in this technique you must not fall into sleepiness or torpor, and your thoughts mustn't remain scattered as in everyday activities. Normally we're always in either one of these two states—torpor or drowsiness, or the excitedness and restlessness of mental involvement. However, you try to abandon these two states when you're practicing observing the breath.

At the beginning of genuine anapana breathing exercises, one just watches the breath. After a very short while, the breath will calm down to become long and soft. As this external breathing dies down to a point of near cessation, the chi of the inner body will start to become more activated. That's because the extreme of yin (stillness) will give birth to yang (movement), which in this case is chi. However, this internal chi is not the same as the external wind used in respiration. Rather, it's the real chi of the body which has tremendous power because it can transform the physical nature and is connected with consciousness. When the expiration finally ceases and the mind quiets down, we then arrive at shamatha. This is the state of stopping or halting found in cessation and contemplation practices.

If you continue relaxing the body and mind, and don't become frightened or tense during this period of cessation, this inner breath will really come to life. Taoists call this the "internal embryo breathing," and it has a tremendous power to develop all the esoteric structures within the physical body. So if you can stay in this state of internal breathing without worrying about the fact that your external respiration has slowed to almost non-existence, then you can transform the body quickly and enter into deep samadhi. We can therefore summarize this entire process as: calming the body and the breath until respiration ceases—perhaps from the process of counting the breaths—and then letting this cessation conjoin with mental emptiness (absence of discriminative thought). At this point the real chi of the body will arise, which is the precursor of kundalini, and one can enter into samadhi.

When you have reached the state of cessation, or shamatha, through this practice, you must begin to concentrate on cultivating the mind rather than the body. This is the stage of vipashyana, which means contemplating prajna-transcendental wisdom. In the Tien-tai school, these two stages of shamatha and vipashyana are called cessation and observation (contemplation), samadhi and wisdom, or *chih* (stopping) and *guan* (observation). In this initial stage, the workings of the mind slow down and seem to stop, like a glass filled with dirty water whose dirtiness settles; if you put the glass down, slowly the dirt and dust inside will sink and settle, leaving clear water, akin to the clarity of samadhi. This is the Mahayana samadhi.

The stages of the four dhyanas are all included in this practice, but in progressive practice you don't pay attention to these as they occur; you don't even think of cultivation stages and states of achievement, but just let them be. Let the mind rest and it will naturally clear itself to become pure and clear, and *this cessation is the correct cessation*. The Zen school describes this state as follows: "Everything is crystal clear, there are no wandering thoughts, no scattered thoughts; it's like 10,000 miles of clear sky empty of clouds." This is true samadhi. What is samadhi? It is that mental state of peaceful stillness and clarity that is not sunk in drowsiness, sleepiness, forgetfulness, lethargy, or torpor, such as when we're sleeping or "blanked out." It is also not restlessness or scatteredness, which is the state of excitedness or movement. Your state of observation will be very clear, crisp, and radiant in this realm, and if you can maintain this state of open awareness and observation without relying on thoughts, then prajna-wisdom will arise.

After you arrive at this stage of mental stability, or cessation, what is it that you observe? What is it that has stopped or ceased? At this stage of achievement we can say you've reached an experiential realm at the edge of mind and matter because your breathing and thoughts have both stopped, and you've entered into a stage of peace and quiet. But the state of cessation, however calm, is still just another phenomenon—it's just the result of stopping, but it is not *that thing* that enables you to stop. It's just a phenomenal state of emptiness and clarity, so it's still a phenomenon, although one which exists in opposition to mental business. What we ultimately want to reach in cultivation, however, is not a mental realm or phenomenon.

That thing which is ultimately at rest, without being a samadhi, is the substance of mind, whereas this stage is just a function of the mind. It's not the mind itself, just one of its activities or projections. Thus, at this point, your stage of stillness is a still a phenomenon arising out of the true mind of Tao. This first step of cessation or shamatha is just the phenomenon of stopping miscellaneous thoughts that are like bubbles that arise and then burst or disappear. So at this stage you simply stop blowing the bubbles any more—and at this stage you've simply enabled yourself to see this process of creation and destruction all very clearly. To know this is prajna-wisdom. All thoughts are originally empty, so they arise from emptiness and then they're gone, returning to their original state. Hence, after this first stage you'll finally begin to know emptiness, which becomes the focus of your observation. You see that the original nature of these thoughts is empty, and so you set yourself to observing the state of thoughtless calm that we call "observing emptiness."

Within this emptiness, there is still something that can be aware and know, and this is what actually gives rise to your thoughts. It's from within this clean purity that you can produce all sorts of experiential realms. Mental realms always seem to exist, but their existence is ultimately unreal and illusory, so at this point you can clearly know and see emptiness, phenomena, and the emptiness of both of them. At this point you can recognize that all phenomena are false and yet in another sense they're also true. But in terms of cultivation, the big breakthrough is when we realize their falsity or emptiness as a result of this or some other spiritual practice. This is why the Hinayana Arhats, when they see that all phenomena are illusory, want nothing to do with them. They think, "I'd rather remain in emptiness."

The Mahayana school, however, teaches that things are illusory and so there is no reason to fear them. It recognizes that the world is a case of "false existence" because conventional reality has no concreteness to it, and at the same time we can call it "miraculous existence" because this wonderful display, absent of any true reality, does indeed have a logical nature. So during cessation you observe emptiness and existence—a set of dialectic opposites we call the real and non-real, reality and non-reality, truth and falsity, existence and non-existence, emptiness and phenomena.

The final state of observation approaches the actual substance of mind where you observe that both existence and non-existence are not real, and yet both existence and non-existence are real. Emptiness (samadhi) and phenomena are both false, and emptiness and phenomena are also both valid. This is *madhyamika*, or the Middle Way, where you see that emptiness and phenomena coexist but you don't abide in either: you perceive both realms, but fall into neither. Yes, you rest your mental realm in the quiet of samadhi, and yes, you allow the phenomenal world (including the physical body) to continually transform but without your falling into any sort of clinging to this realm. That which knows is freely born and freely functions, but it doesn't abide in either of these states. It doesn't dwell.

There's no affirmation or negation or arguing in this state of attainment, there's just the middle way. This is the true path of observation—observing emptiness and phenomena—the middle way of prajna. *And this is also philosophy, science, psychology, and the study of our true ontological essence.* But in our explanation, it's just the step of observation. After you understand this, you proceed to another step called "returning," which means returning to one's original nature, or "original face." What do you return to? This is hard to explain, so a story will have to suffice.

An ancient Zen story relates that in a Zen hall once, a master was sitting in his seat and an old monk yelled from the rear of the hall, "I'm enlightened!"

The master said, "Speak!"

The monk replied, "Nuns are females!"

The master then replied, "Yes, you're enlightened."

There are many Zen explanations like this that have to do with returning. Someone comes to the master and says, "I'm awakened," and the master replies, "To what?" The man then says, "Our nostrils are at the bottom of our nose," and the master confirms his realization. Hence it's very hard to talk about this state of returning. The Zen school uses all these examples to illustrate the matter, but people don't really understand them unless they've already pierced through the ranks of the various samadhi, and none of the intellectual commentators or pop psychologists on the matter has ever done so.

In the *Shurangama Sutra,* Buddha and his cousin Ananda have a discussion on the whereabouts of the mind. Buddha says that if you can return all the phenomena that can be returned to their source of origination, but there is something that can't be returned, it must be you! That's the essence of returning. Drop everything, and if there's something you can't drop, then it must be you. Return everything to its causes and conditions, but if there's something you can't return, that must be the fundamental you.

Buddha taught this anapana cultivation method to his son Rahula, who was able to reach enlightenment in a matter of days using this technique. When Buddhism first came to China from India, this was also the major form of cultivation practice transmitted to the public—watching the breath so as to let thoughts and breath reach a point of cessation in which they combine into one, and then observing the mind. Most people who cultivate the breath in this manner develop all sorts of superpowers, regain their lost vitality, banish their physical illnesses, and end up living extremely long lives. Some can even foretell the time of their death. Hence this is a method of mastering the prana, or wind element of the body. But this method must also be matched with observation, or contemplation, when one reaches the stage of cessation. That's the practice of prajna-transcendental wisdom, the practice of cultivating the mind. If you don't contemplate the emptiness of the mind and of thoughts when you reach this state, you cannot enter into the highest realms of samadhi or attain enlightenment.

Thus breathing practices for following the body's wind element typically lead to improved health, long life, psychic powers, and samadhi. Because mind and breath are linked, they are the basic practices of almost all genuine cultivation schools, such as mantra practices and the specialized breathing practices of the long-lived immortals who can stay in the world for hundreds of years without dying. Therefore they are appropriate for all types of practitioners. But anapana practices constitute only the first stage to samadhi. Only with continued detachment from the results of these practices, through wisdom cultivation that remains aware without getting entangled, can you reach Tao.

7

The Zhunti Mantra

 There are many mantras, from many different spiritual schools, that we can use in our cultivation practice. However, most of these mantras can only be recited according to specific rules and under certain particular conditions. For instance, some mantras can only be used if you are vegetarian (you must also refrain from eating onions, garlic, leeks, and so on, which lead to an increase in sexual desire). Some mantra techniques require that you abstain from all sexual activity. Other mantras are limited in that they cannot be used when you are in a filthy or smelly location (as this drives away the protecting devas), or during a woman's period of menstruation. There are all sorts of various restrictions for mantra recitation, called *japa* in Hinduism, but the Zhunti mantra is free from all such restrictions.

The Zhunti mantra can be used anytime, anywhere, in any situation. It is one of the few mantras that can be taught to others without restriction, and no particular ceremony is needed for its recitation though a special sadhana is available. In this preliminary contemplation (sadhana), you first imagine the universe as a vast region of empty space. From within the stillness of this great void, you next imagine

Figure 3. When reciting the Zhunti mantra, practitioners should visualize a brightly shining tiny moon or dot, or the image of Zhunti Buddha, at the level of the heart chakra (behind the breast bone in the center of the body). This will help open up the energy channel restrictions in this area, without which it is impossible to see the Tao. (Lao Gu Publishing.)

that a great wind slowly begins to stir until a giant revolving wind forms that runs throughout the entire cosmos. The friction of this wind then produces a fire that engulfs the whole universe, and because of this fire element, water starts to congeal and form. The water then solidifies into a solid diamond earth as clear and bright as crystal. From within this diamond earth, you imagine that an eight-petalled, red lotus flower arises, on top of which sits the Zhunti Buddha reciting the Zhunti mantra. This is the Zhunti visualization sadhana. Unlike the mantras of the lower heavenly beings found in many cultivation schools, even without this sadhana this mantra's workings are so powerful and its effects so refined that it functions on a level beyond comprehension.

The Zhunti mantra comes from Zhunti Buddha, who is called the "Mother of the Buddhas" since countless Buddhas have achieved self-realization using this mantra. The ability to lead so many others to enlightenment shows the inconceivable power of this mantra, and since the Zhunti technique has given birth to many Buddhas, Zhunti Buddha is called a "Buddha mother."

At the mundane level, the Zhunti mantra is recited by people who wish to change their fortunes and destiny, as in the story of Yuan Huang of the Ming dynasty. At the supramundane level, it is the chief mantra recited by those who wish to attain enlightenment in this lifetime. The reason for its popularity is that it is one of two mantras capable of opening up a practitioner's heart chakra. This mantra thus enables an individual to quickly realize the great prajna-transcendental wisdom, which is thus responsible for its great effectiveness. Therefore it is even sanctioned in the Zen school, which typically abstains from depending upon any external cultivation crutches other than directly looking into the true nature of the mind. The mantra runs phonetically as follows:

BODHI NAMO SADOH NAH
SAMMIAO SAMPO DOH
JEE-ZHR NAH
DAH-ZHR TOH

OHM ZHURLI ZHULI ZHUNTI SOHA
OHM BRIN

After one million repetitions, the mantra recitation can be shortened to:

OHM ZHURLI ZHULI ZHUNTI SOHA
OHM BRIN

The Vairocana Mantra

This is the fundamental mantra of the primordial Buddha Vairocana, also known as the Great Sun Tathagata. When Nagarjuna first developed the esoteric school in India, its teachings were mainly comprised of mantras such as this one that helps you to quickly transform the physical body. This mantra is especially powerful in bringing about a purification transformation of the physical body's four great elements, and transforming the four elements lays a strong foundation for cultivation success. The mantra runs,

OHM AHH BEE LAH HUNG CHT!

The AHH sound in this mantra represents and acts upon the earth element in the human body; the BEE sound represents and transforms the water element; the LAH sound represents and transforms the body's fire element; the HUNG sound represents the wind element; and the CHT! sound represents emptiness. In practicing this mantra, you are working on transforming all the great elements of the human body, including your chi (prana), energy meridians (nadi or mai), bright points (drops), chakras and kundalini (tumo fire). The normal sequence in cultivation practice is to transform the physical body's wind element

Figure 4. When reciting the Vairocana mantra, it is often helpful to visualize a brilliant yellow or golden flame in the abdominal region at the level of the navel chakra, or the image of Vairocana Buddha, in the tan-tien, center torso of the body, or at the third eye. Tathagata Mahavairocana (Nezu Museum of Art, Tokyo), reproduced from Buddhist Paintings: Japanese National Treasures: Restored Copies by Mihakara Ryusen, *published in 1981 by Kosei Publishing Company, Tokyo.*

(chi) first, then its water element (chi channels), then its fire element (kundalini warmth), and then finally its earth element (bones) because it's the densest and most resistant to transformation. The sequence of progress requires over a decade to complete, but the initial stages are greatly shortened through the use of this mantra.

Vairocana is the primordial, fundamental Buddha of the universe. His perfect and complete enlightenment was achieved endless eons ago, and his practice is so comprehensive that it extends everywhere. If you want to see Vairocana, you need only realize that everything we see, everywhere we go is Vairocana's body and every sound is Vairocana's sound. To match his stage of realization and to see what Vairocana perceives, you can even imagine yourself as a projection of Vairocana as a form of cultivation. When you get Tao, your mind is the same as Vairocana's and all the other enlightened Buddhas, for everyone shares the same enlightened nature.

In reciting his mantra, as with all other mantras, you seek a cessation of ordinary mentation, which Buddhism calls "tying up the sixth consciousness," in order to arrive at the quiet and calm of samadhi. In most forms of mantra practice, you try to tie the mind's inner dialogue to the mantra to get rid of all miscellaneous monkey-thoughts. When you successfully tie the sixth consciousness (ordinary mind of meditation) to a single object of focus, then you can arrive at the mental quiet of cessation after which you must contemplate the state of quiet which you've produced. So by chanting mantras and listening within, and then using wordless insight wisdom to observe the state of quiet you produce, one can quickly attain samadhi.

As to the method of chanting, the internal chanting is usually best, though at times the verbal chanting may be better, depending upon your situation. The choice of method is all up to what skillful means you need at the moment to calm your mind. The *Sandilya Upanishad* states, "The *Vaikhari-Japa* (loud mantra recitation) gives the reward as stated in the Vedas, while the *Upanshu-Japa* (whispering or humming recitation similar to the *vajra* chanting in Tantra) that cannot be heard by anyone, gives a reward a thousand times more than the Vaikhari, but the *Manasika-Japa* (mental chanting) gives a reward a myriad times more than the Vaikhari." When you can perform your mantra recitation, or japa, in conjunction with rhythmic breathing while intently visualizing the form of a Buddha, deity, or bright flame as in kundalini yoga, you can more quickly reach the stage of one-pointedness and transform the physical body into a vehicle more suited for cultivation.

CHAPTER

9

The Amitofo Mantra

This is a very popular mantra, for it is the main cultivation technique of the Buddhist Pure Land school founded by the Chinese monk Hui-Yuan. Before becoming a monk, Hui-Yuan had studied Confucianism and Taoism but found both lacking, so he went over to Buddhism to look for that transcendental something beyond the physical immortality promised by Taoism, and beyond the rules of behavior espoused by the Confucianism of his times.

After his own success in self-cultivation, and noting the difficulties he had himself encountered along the way, Hui-Yuan fully realized how difficult it would be for people in later generations, such as ourselves, to achieve enlightenment. Thus he promoted the simple technique of chanting Amitofo's name and listening to the sound within, because this method could be practiced by every sort of individual— the privileged or poor, the intelligent or the dull, the skeptic or religiously-minded. Because the cultivation method is so simple, it has been predicted that this will be the last of the Buddhist cultivation methods to die out in this world.

To practice the Amitofo mantra, an individual need only silently chant the mantra NAMO AMITOFO or AMITOFO wherever they are, constantly keeping both the mantra and Amitofo in their mind and heart. Sometimes one concentrates on visualizing a picture of Amitofo during the japa practice, but the major basis of this technique is single-minded, pure, sincere invocation. Such devotion is like bhakti yoga, and when practiced in conjunction with breath relaxation, it becomes a type of one-pointed concentration practice leading into samadhi. Success in cultivation does not depend on any outside force, it depends entirely on your own efforts and achievements. However, if an individual doesn't feel strong enough to succeed in cultivation by themselves, this method gives them an outside force to rely upon. They simply chant the name of Amitofo, and ask for his help in attaining spiritual achievement.

Some individuals recite the Amitofo mantra simply because they wish to be reborn in Amitofo's Buddha land after their death, and they carry the hopes of using this more favorable environment (known as the Western Paradise) as a better staging ground for making further cultivation progress. The Zen school, however, takes a different approach to this practice, for the Zen school teaches people to recite this mantra in order to attain samadhi and see the Pure Land in this very life. It teaches that the Pure Land of Amitofo shouldn't be viewed as a physical place, but a state of mind which is forever blissful and pure; your own wisdom knowing is the Pure Land, so you're already functioning in the Western Paradise of Amitofo. When you achieve the true, immediate reality, this is the Pure Land of the human world.

Christianity also tells us that the coming of heaven should actually be experienced in the mind, for as the Gospel of Thomas states: "The Kingdom of God will not come by expectation. The Kingdom of the Father is spread over the earth and men do not see it." Hence by reciting this mantra and listening inward to calm the mind, you can enter into samadhi and attain to this realm; without moving one step, you're already in the heaven of Amitofo. This realm is the same as what Amitofo experiences, and thus in attaining samadhi through the

Amitofo method, you will see what Amitofo sees, which is the Pure Land in every situation at every moment.

When you chant NAMO AMITOFO, the key point is to mantra with the mind and to listen within, not simply to outwardly chant AMITOFO with your mouth and tongue. Actually, mantra recitation, or japa, doesn't really mean reciting with your mind either because the purpose of the practice is to focus your mind, to keep your mind on that clear moment of perfect presence where there is no body, no self, no sound. So no matter which cultivation school you follow or which mantra you use, you should always be physically relaxed during mantra recitation, practicing until the sound disappears and you attain the silence of samadhi.

Contemplating this silence and investigating this clear state that is produced, chanting NAMO AMITOFO will let you realize the message indicated by the mantra: AH stands for a limitlessness without boundaries; MI stands for endless life and endless time; TO stands for unbounded light (the true self-nature); while FO stands for Buddha—someone who is clear, aware, awake, and enlightened. The NAMO in this mantra stands for surrendering to, or giving oneself over to, in the sense of "surrendering to Christ." Hence reciting NAMO AMITOFO is not only a means to attain samadhi, but it's also telling us that the very original substance of our being extends across infinite space as infinite life and infinite light, as does the clear knowing nature of our primordial, transcendental wisdom. The Bible also tells us that "God is light," so there's no distinction between religions when they're talking about our own inherent wisdom; we use the word "light" as an analogous reference to this clear, primordial wisdom-nature, but it isn't anything physical. We also use the words "luminous," "radiant," "clear," and "bright" for lack of a better analogy. Nevertheless, none of these terms refers to a form-based, physical state or phenomenon as the mind is formless.

You should never hold your body in a rigid fashion when reciting a mantra, nor force the chi to the head during mantra practice; otherwise you can inadvertently raise your blood pressure or become nervous due to forcing what should be natural. Neither should you force yourself to continue reciting a mantra if your mind reaches a state of quiet cessation and wishes to rest. After all, that's the precursor state to samadhi that you are seeking. To push yourself out of this state when you arrive is the antithesis of practice!

In mantra practice, you don't actually measure your progress by the number of mantras you perform, but by whether a state of internal quiet is produced. When you achieve this inner state of mental stillness or calm, you must switch to the act of contemplation and observe what it is that perceives this state of silent emptiness. The state of silence actually "floats" in a formless, empty awareness which extends everywhere. That's what you're trying to identify, for it's beyond both the mundane silence we call emptiness and the state of noisy mentation as well. These are both its constructions, and you can only realize this state of formless empty awareness after you turn your attention around and see it within. But you won't be able to accomplish this unless you first attain samadhi.

What's the best way to chant to reach this state of mental cessation wherein you can finally perceive the true nature of the mind? It all depends on your situation at the time; the medicine of the moment depends on your circumstances and situation. But as the *Kularnava Tantra* states in general, "Japa (mantra repetition) is of three kinds. Japa done aloud is the lowest, japa done in low tones is the middle, and japa done mentally is the best." If you are single-minded in your mantra practice, then all sorts of transcendental results are sure to follow.

10

Nine-Step Bottled Wind Practice

 A more forceful breathing practice, that attempts to ignite the body's internal wind element through compression, is the nine-step wind practice introduced by the "Diamond Sow" Buddha into Tibet. This practice, which is also known as the White Brightness practice, relies on the respiratory winds (our external breath) to activate the body's prenatal chi. Once activated, the real chi within the body can transform our *mai* (energy meridian) and ignite the kundalini fire element within. If nothing else, continued proper use of this practice banishes sickness and extends one's life span.

Our bodies are comprised of the four great elements earth, wind, fire, and water, which we must transform during the process of cultivation. Of these four elements, the earth element (such as our bones) is the hardest to transform since it is the densest element of the body. On the other hand, the wind element of the body, corresponding to our chi, is the easiest element to transform because of its flexibility and link to our vitality. So most cultivation paths in the world start with breathing practices since they focus on changing this relatively easy-to-transform wind element. Since mind and chi (the wind element) are interlinked, and since chi and wind are connected, these facts also play a vital role behind the focus of many spiritual cultivation techniques.

By making our respiration more efficient through the forced retention of the breath, which helps open all the tiny capillaries and obstructed mai in the body (the *nadis*), it becomes much easier for a practitioner to reach the required point of respiratory cessation in all their other cultivation practices, such as watching thoughts or watching the breath. In other words, this practice will enable you to become more efficient in your breathing because it will clean the mai and extend the amount of time you can spend between the normal inhalations and exhalations of your breath. Thus it increases the effectiveness of all your other cultivation techniques.

As already mentioned, the popularity of breathing methods in the world's cultivation schools, such as Hindu pranayama, arises from the fact that the wind element of the body is the easiest element of the body to transform. The water element, corresponding to our mai, nerves, and hormones, is the next easiest element to transform. The fire element of the body, corresponding to the kundalini phenomenon, and finally the earth element of the body (corresponding to the bones), are much harder to cultivate. When some masters die, they can transform their physical bodies into realms of light, but they often leave behind bits of hair and nail corresponding to the dense earth element, as mementos for their students.

This entire process of changing the physical nature, for a practitioner who takes no detours and makes no mistakes, takes a minimum of thirteen years of devoted practice. The first one hundred days of practice, wherein one must not lose *jing* (seminal essence) while cultivating a relaxed physical state and emptiness of mind, is called "laying the foundation of transforming jing into chi." This is followed by "pregnancy for ten months" wherein "chi is transmuted into shen." The next three years of practice are called "suckling the baby" wherein "shen is transmuted into emptiness," and the following nine years are termed "facing the wall" because it is a stage of mastering no-thought by cultivating higher stages of emptiness. In the Tao school, these various sequences of cultivating the jing, chi, and shen correspond to attaining the fruit of Hinayana cultivation. One must cultivate past this stage of accomplishment in order to reach the higher Mahayana fruits of attainment, and the realm of perfect enlightenment that is called Buddhahood.

Now, in the nine-step bottled wind practice, there are four phases performed for each of the nine rounds of practice. These four phases are: (1) slowly drawing wind (air) into the lungs; (2) fully filling the lungs as much as possible as if they were a bottle or vase; (3) holding the air inside for as long as possible while remaining relaxed; (4) quickly releasing the air from the lungs, expelling it like an arrow.

One such round is performed three times for the left nostril, three times for the right nostril, and three times for both open nostrils. This makes a total of nine rounds, hence the name of "nine-step" vase breathing practice. The steps of the practice are as follows.

1. Begin by sitting in an upright meditation posture. If the arms can be extended and locked with hands pushing on the legs so as to lift the chest, this is excellent.

2. Visualize that your body becomes as clear as crystal.

3. Close the mouth. Using the index finger of the left hand to close the left nostril, holding the hand as shown (see figure 5a, page 48), press against the left nostril and inhale slowly through the right nostril. The inhalation should consist of a long, gentle, deep breath—as long and deep as possible. Experienced practitioners can maintain this inhalation process for several minutes. During inhalation, contemplate that all of space becomes filled with light, and this brightness is inhaled into the body to dispel any internal poisons, darkness and obstructions. Continue inhaling as slowly and deeply as possible until you are "full" of breath.

4. When the "body vase" or "bottle" becomes full, relax the body as much as possible while holding the breath within. The breath must be compressed, or held inside for as long as possible without being allowed to leave the body, and yet one must use as few muscles as possible for this retention. It is important while restraining the breath to

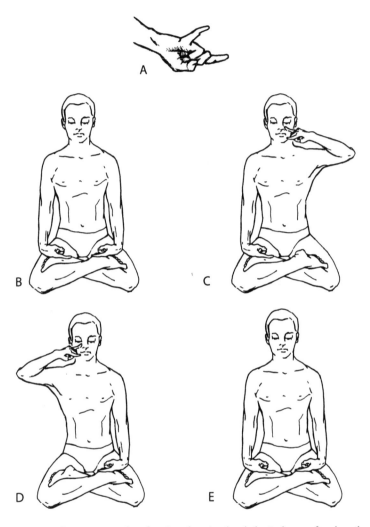

Figure 5. In the sequence of performing the nine bottled winds, you first breathe in and out of one nostril, then through the opposite nostril, and then through both nostrils together. During this time, the arms should be extended and locked so as to lift the chest region, expanding the normally closed spaces between the ribs. This allows the chi to penetrate spaces in the body that are normally closed due to compression.

maintain an upright position without tightening the body so that the wind and chi can open up all the tiny channels in the body that might be compressed during strain. If the body is tightened rather than relaxed, even with force the chi will not be able to pass through certain pathways that are obstructed. Experienced practitioners can hold the breath for several minutes, even as the face turns red, which indicates that the wind element is opening up the body's tiny chi channels.

5. When the breath can no longer be retained, exhale it as forcefully and quickly as possible through the other open nostril. The breath is forcefully shot out of the body with the speed of an arrow to complete one cycle or round. Repeat this exercise of slow inhalation, long retention, and forceful exhalation two more times, for a total of three times. All the while the left nostril is kept closed while the active nostril is the right nostril.

6. Switch hands, so that the right hand now pinches the right nostril closed, and the left nostril is left open. Inhale through the left nostril following the equivalent instructions as before. Repeat this exercise three times for the new nostril. Thus, six repetitions of this exercise will now have been completed.

7. Extend both arms to lift the chest as shown in figure 5e. Using neither hand, inhale slowly through both nostrils, hold the breath within for as long as possible, and then exhale quickly through both open nostrils. Do this for a total of three times. Altogether nine inhalations and retentions are performed, which gives rise to the name of nine-step bottled wind practice.

One can supplement, or expand upon this practice by visualizing the central, left, and right channels becoming filled with light during this bottled breathing technique. During the retention or "compressing" phase of this practice, the air in the left and right channels is envisioned as flowing into and ascending the empty central channel, which shines with a dazzling brilliance. When the breath is expelled, you can also imagine that all sorts of dark and dirty humors are expelled along with it, while clean chi is simultaneously drawn up into the central channel. However, these visualizations are just elaborations of the basic technique. As a further alternative, you might visualize that the incoming air fills out the left and right channels as it comes in, like thin empty balloons which inflate with air, and these are then discharged into the central channel—envisioned as flowing into the central channel during the state of compressed retention.

The important point is to hold the breath for as long as possible, during which time the body is not restrained tightly. One should never employ too much force in restraining the body. *Neither should you try to force any internal circulations of chi.* If the body is held tightly, the chi cannot pass through obstructed regions to open the mai. If one uses force to "guide the chi," what should happen naturally may not happen at all!

After some period of practice, people are generally surprised how little muscle effort is needed to retain the full breath. If people are straining many muscles to hold the breath, they are definitely practicing incorrectly. Nine-step breathing exercises are actually a practice of *using as few muscles as possible (maximum relaxation), to hold in as much breath as possible, as deeply as possible, for as long as possible, and then to exhale as quickly as possible.* People who do not obtain quick results from this practice are violating one or more of these rules.

Another Tibetan breathing exercise related to this one is the vase breathing practice belonging to the Six Yogas of Naropa tradition. In this method, which is very similar to the nine-step bottled wind, a practitioner sits on the flat ground, with legs crossed in a comfortable position, looking straight ahead. The back is held erect, and the two hands are loosely placed on the knees rather than locked in an extension pose meant to spread the intercostal spaces between the ribs.

As before, one then begins the practice by looking straight ahead, drawing in air through the right nostril, gazing to the left, and then releasing the air through the left nostril by exhaling slowly and gently until no more air is left in the lungs. Then you look ahead, draw air in through the left nostril, turn the head to gaze to the right, and slowly and gently release the air via the right nostril until the lungs are empty. Lastly, you look straight ahead and draw in the air through both nostrils, and then release it through both. You repeat this preliminary cycle of inhalation-exhalation sequences two more times for a total of nine breaths, and you never allow the air to pass through the mouth during any part of this practice. If one wishes to embellish this practice a bit further to smooth the chi at the beginning, you can add a prefix by performing the famous Taoist five organ sounds before the start of this routine to help their internal chi reach a state of equilibrium, and to help calm the internal organs and mai.

Now, the heart of the practice begins after the set of nine inhalations and exhalations has been performed, whose purpose was to help calm the breath and open the mai. So you continue in your sitting position with the body straight and erect, and the hands formed into fists with the thumbs inside. Different *mudras* (hand positions) will produce different effects on the body, but this is how you initiate the practice. You then start breathing slowly and deeply, gently pulling the air down to below the navel, which is the region of the tan-tien. You swallow a bit of saliva without opening the mouth and without making a sound, and when the saliva has traveled all the way down to the stomach you press on the abdomen to a point just below where your navel chakra would be. In addition, you tighten the muscles of the perineum and pelvis and pull up from below so that the air seems gently trapped between these two locations; don't use too much force or you'll hurt yourself.

Next you focus your awareness on the region of the navel chakra, which is where the kundalini typically ignites, and you hold your breath for as long as possible in this state, maintaining your awareness all the while on a single point within the tan-tien. This practice is like holding an air ball between two hands, only here you use your mental concentration and a tiny bit of initial muscular pressure to bring about this feeling of compression. Hence we can say the body is filled with air like a vase, or bottle, and when you can no longer hold it inside any longer, you release it slowly through the nostrils without allowing any to escape through the mouth. So, swallowing saliva, you retain your breath while pressing down a bit with the abdomen, while from below, you gently draw in air from the anus and sexual passage to the same site, holding the air for as long as possible.

With repeated practice of either of these techniques, one will be able to retain their breath for several minutes, which will clear the mai and help prepare the body for attaining the stage when it needs little external breathing; the external respiration will cease and all the pores of the body will open. It's even possible to ignite the kundalini shakti in this way. The duration of the retention phase in this technique can and should be gradually lengthened over time, and the number of repetitions gradually increased. *Don't try to be Superman (or Superwoman) and accomplish everything at once,* but start slowly and increase slowly. Initially you need not practice more than once or twice a day—in the morning and evening. Over time, this method will cause the mind to have more clarity, the body to become hardier and healthier, the tiny mai to open up, the muscles to soften, the blood circulation to improve, and it will become easier—when using other methods—for the external respiration to reach and maintain the stage of prolonged cessation. In this stage your thoughts will be lessened and you can enter samadhi.

11

Kundalini Yoga for Opening the Sushumna Central Channel

 There are many forms of cultivation practice that involve concentrating on a single point or esoteric structure within the physical body in order to attain samadhi. For instance, Taoism, yoga, and some Western cultivation schools suggest concentrating on the region of the third eye in order to open up the *jen-mai* (front) and *tu-mai* (back) chi channels. This spot is also the location of the ajna-chakra, which is the top entry point of the *sushumna, ida,* and *pingala* channels of the esoteric schools. Naturally, this accounts for its popularity as a focus point in meditation. By focusing on this region of the third eye, the various cultivation schools hope to bring chi into the body's central channel, and to melt various jing essences in the head (called subtle drops, *bindus, bodhicitta,* or *bodhimind* substances) which bring about the states of physical bliss that accompany the various samadhi.

Some schools suggest alternative points for the focus of concentration: the top of the head, the soles of the feet, or the tan-tien lower belly region called the *hara* in Japanese (females, however, should avoid concentrating on this area). In all these places, practitioners are told to imagine a silvery bright point of light, a shining moon or sun, or tiny

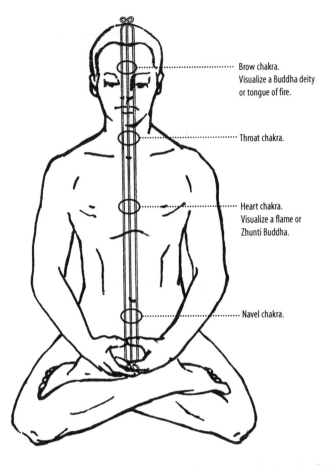

Brow chakra.
Visualize a Buddha deity
or tongue of fire.

Throat chakra.

Heart chakra.
Visualize a flame or
Zhunti Buddha.

Navel chakra.

Figure 6. In kundalini yoga, it helps to visualize the central channel of the body and tiny flames or brilliant tongues of fire at the level of the navel chakra, heart chakra, throat chakra, and brow chakra. For the initial practice, the brow and navel chakras are usually the most important points of concentration as they both provide entry points into the sushumna central channel. In the Zhunti Buddha mantra practice, the point of focus is on the heart chakra. During kundalini yoga practice, which will only bear fruit after you've already sufficiently cultivated your chi and mai, it's particularly helpful if you visualize the navel chakra fire as being incredibly fierce. Hence the Tibet school calls this fire the Fierce Woman that brings about the state of supreme transformation.

radiant flame, and to focus all their concentration upon this image in an effort to make it as stable as possible. The tinier you make it and the more clearly and radiantly you visualize your image, the easier it will be to draw the energies to the point and mass them in the region. So all these images have the purpose of massing the chi at some particular point of concentrated focus; you focus your mind on a point, and then the chi follows. After the chi is drawn to a point and becomes massed within a small area of concentrated focus, it's natural for this state of intensified compression to give birth to a condition of warmth and light, just as the ignition of a flame occurs from the process of friction. So this condition of concentrated massing produces a stage of inner luminosity and inner warmth, which is described in many cultivation schools. This is what we encountered with the skeleton visualization technique.

The Tao school says that when chi sufficiently masses to a point, the inner light will be revealed. It also says that your chi will transform into shen, which in a coarse way is akin to light. Speaking for the Hindu schools of classical yoga, Patanjali says that "through pranayama, the covering concealing the inner light disappears"; by cultivating the breath, a physical inner light will appear as well as the beginnings of spiritual knowing. Tsongkhapa of the Tibet school says that "when meditative stability has been achieved, then the radiance of the light from the inner fire will illuminate the inside and outside of one's body, as well as one's dwelling place and so forth, rendering them transparent." Shakyamuni Buddha described this attainment as breaking through the *skandha* of form, whereby you'll be able to see within your own body, as well as distances far away.

The Zen school doesn't bother with all these details, but simply says that this internal light is brought about as a result of the friction between the physiological and psychological states. So when you sufficiently mass the chi into a small region through the practice of concentrated focus, such as in visualization practices, you can give birth to an internal flame that gives off heat and light. This is the basis of the kundalini yoga practice, which is cultivating the warmth element of the body. First you cultivate your chi and mai, or the wind and water elements of your physical nature, and then you can cultivate the warmth (heat) element of the body which corresponds to the kundalini phenomenon. But you only do this because it will lead to yet other higher transformations, not because it is an end in itself.

How do you get to this state, which also occurs when you master the skeleton visualization technique? By cultivating your jing and chi so that they don't leak, and then throwing yourself into a visualization practice which focuses on a bright point within the body. What's the best image to focus on to bring this about (assuming your mai have already been cultivated, and you haven't been losing your jing through sexual activity)? A brilliant tiny flame, or a dazzling moon, shining silver symbol, tiny deity of lightning brilliance, or whatever other silvery, flame-like image can help bring your concentration to a point. What's the best spot to use as a location of focus for your visualization? Since you can only achieve samadhi if your chi enters the central channel, then the top or bottom entry points of the central channel (the third eye, for instance), or chakra locations within the central channel, make logical points of focus. You don't want to focus on the sexual organs, for the warmth that arises will enervate your jing and stimulate sexual desire, and then you'll likely leak your vital substances through sexual activity when they are necessary for the transformative processes of cultivation. Hence the best area in the lower region of the body corresponds to the tan-tien region of the abdomen, which contains the navel chakra of transformation responsible for the *tumo* fire.

This tumo fire is a concentrated focus of chi which will give rise to warmth and inner light, and the warmth will melt the various subtle drops, or jing substances, that produce physical bliss within the body. The esoteric schools don't tell you this, but the state of bliss comes about because hormones are secreted in the body, and they appear when the body experiences the inner warmth brought about through kundalini cultivation. In other words, the heat element will enervate the water elements of life—our jing, ojas, hormones, bindus, bodhicitta, and so on—giving rise to the sensations of physical bliss. This physical bliss is important because *it helps engender concentration,* so the purpose of the tumo fire is to activate the substances that are responsible for physical bliss. From within this bliss you must generate samadhi. When you have both the samadhi of nonconceptual emptiness and physical bliss conjointly, you want to blend the two realizations. With continued proficiency in this practice and ever higher levels of achievement, you'll be able to eventually see the Tao and enter the path.

In general, single-minded concentration on any part of the body can lead to one-pointedness, and concentration on a specific location will send chi to that region because the chi and mind are interconnected like a man and his shadow or a rider and his horse. However, although you can practice mental focus on a variety of spots to bring about the calm abiding of samadhi and various states of body bliss, it doesn't necessarily mean that your chi will have entered your central channel. To attain the highest samadhi, you actually want to produce a state of warmth that melts the bodhimind substances inside the channels that produce ecstasy, and from this state of ecstasy or bliss will arise a state of consciousness beyond conceptuality, which we call emptiness or samadhi. That's the point of mental cessation, and it comes about when the body is experiencing physical bliss. Thus the esoteric school claims people should focus on the top or bottom of their central channel in their visualization practice, or the chakra locations in between (such as the throat or heart chakras). The reasoning is that if you focus at the top or bottom of the channel, it will draw chi into the central channel, and if you visualize the chakra locations along the channel from within its inner diameter (a crucial point of distinction) this will also draw the vital energies into the channel.

Now as a background, concentration on any part of the body will definitely give rise to the sensation of internal wind at that location, which most everyone mistakes for chi. But the real chi of the body is not this internal wind; rather it is the prenatal energy warmth that we call kundalini or shakti, which can ascend through the body's energy channels, giving rise to samadhi. You can't actually force the kundalini to arise; you can only bring about a state of mental cessation and quiet wherein it will rise automatically and naturally, for the extreme of yin (stillness) will give birth to yang (the kundalini force will awaken). Hence the real purpose of visualization practice is to bring about the one-pointedness of samadhi concentration, rather than to specifically awaken the kundalini. Generating kundalini is not the end in itself, *it is just a convenient means of practice.*

Of course, the awakening of the kundalini, or cultivation of the body's warmth element, happens naturally as a result of the process of cultivation, but people get mixed up about what they're trying to do, and take the production of phenomenal realms as the purpose and point of the path. They don't view these realms as transient scenery which have no ultimate significance in themselves. Hence these phenomenal forms and stages too easily become a focus of misguided fixation whereas the guidelines of cultivation tell us to abandon any fixation with form, including the illusion of possessing a body or identifying with experiences. Unfortunately, most people who use these practices lose sight of this principle and end up clinging to the various phenomena they produce. That's a major problem inherent within the esoteric schools, so we recommend that you take heed of this warning.

Now the technique in the Hindu and Tibet schools is to try and generate this cultivation stage of the warmth element, or kundalini fire, directly. Thus they tell meditators first to visualize the physical body as being hollow or like an empty shell. Next you must visualize the body's central channel, known in Sanskrit as the *sushumna*, in Tibetan as the *avadhuti*, and in Chinese as the *zhong mai*, in order to encourage the wind to enter inside. The concentrated visualization produces a massing of chi, and then heat and light, and you're concentrating on the region most relevant to the arising of samadhi. So the purpose of visualizing the channels has the intent of quickening cultivation progress by drawing the energies into these channels rather than letting the process happen naturally, for kundalini is inherent with life. Thus we can say this is an artificial or forceful path, rather than a naturalistic path—one knows the results of what should happen through the process of cultivation, and tries to bring those results into the causation process itself to speed up the entire path of transformation. Furthermore, one concentrates on states of feeling rather than detaching from the physical nature and cultivating prajna-wisdom directly. Thus, this process can be either good or bad; it can either quicken your progress or bring poison into the path.

In the one-pointed visualization techniques you might employ for this purpose, the left channel is always envisioned as white, the right channel is envisioned as red, and the central channel is envisioned as radiant blue. During kundalini yoga visualizations, however, the central channel is visualized with the color of a brightly burning flame. This brightness encourages a corresponding increase in the intensity of the fire element, and also encourages the bodhimind substances to melt and descend within the channel width. When the substances melt because of the tumo heat, then you can experience the blisses of the samadhi. As to the emptiness realms of samadhi, these are all states of one-pointed concentration, and so you can only achieve the relevant channel visualizations if you master these stages of emptiness.

Once again, the entire purpose of these yogic techniques is to draw the chi into the central channel because from a biophysical point of view, *if the chi doesn't enter the central channel, then you cannot attain samadhi.* On the other hand, if you do succeed in bringing the chi into the central channel through visualization and breath retention exercises, then you will experience a profound samadhi. Hence, one of the ways of describing the preliminary path of cultivation is to speak of the goal only in terms of bringing the chi into the central channel, and in essence this is what the form-based esoteric schools do. Yoga, esoteric Buddhism, and Taoism all have this form-based focus on the path, which can be very misleading if one is not careful. That's why Tibetan monks must study for many years before they are typically introduced to such techniques. Be careful!

Now in kundalini yoga, you try to visualize the central mai and ignite the inner heat at the navel chakra. Then you attempt to control the vital energies you arouse by visualizing tiny flames, bright points, moons, and so on, envisioned within the central channel at various chakra locations. If your practice and merit are sufficient, this will bring the energies into the central channel and arouse the experiences of physical bliss. As we stated, the tinier you can envision the flames, and the more clearly (radiant presence) you can do so, the easier it will be to draw the energies inside the sushumna channel. Then the experience of physical joy and bliss will arise, together with a mental realm that appreciates emptiness during these states, and together this will transform the body and lead to profound states of mind. When the energies enter into the central channel, you can experience samadhi and give rise to prajna-wisdom, which the Tibetan schools call the innate wisdom of Mahamudra.

As we saw in the Zhunti Buddha visualization procedure, the entire process is based on a definite, logical sequence of generation. As in the Zhunti sadhana, first there is a great universal wind which gives rise to a great universal fire, and this great cosmic fire gives birth to the water element. As the *Taittiriya Upanishad* says, "From space [emptiness] came air [wind]. From air, fire. From fire, water. From water came solid earth. From earth came living plants." So as an analogy, if you cultivate the chi (wind) correctly, the kundalini fire (state of hsi) will be initiated, and from the wind element as the basis, the fire element will next arise. The activation of this heat element will in turn cause the hormones or jing (water element, or bodhicitta, bindus, and so on) of the body to descend, and you'll be able to experience the various blisses of the different samadhi. As the Tao school says, "If the jing doesn't descend, you cannot experience bliss." So in cultivating the inherent warmth of life, the water forces of life will become enervated and bring about physiological change.

Thus the purpose of meditating on the inner heat yoga is to induce special blisses, and from these, access to the emptiness realms of meditation. It gives rise to a special type of internal heat that melts the jing substances (activates special hormones), and they descend to produce the sensations of bliss. As the *Hevajra Tantra* would symbolically say, "Candali [the kundalini] blazes at the navel, Ham [the bija sound seed of the crown chakra] is burnt and the moon [bindus, or endocrine secretions producing bliss] melts." Orthodox Buddhism talks of four different blisses that transpire, corresponding to the four dhyanas, and classical yoga has the vitarka-samadhi, vicara-samadhi, ananda-samadhi and asmita-samadhi blisses. These are all the same basic experience. The Tibet school also has four bliss states, but its own description of these blisses differs slightly from those found in these other schools. That's because the Tibet school wants to distinguish itself as possessing a special type of practice: it wants the practitioner to try and generate the four blisses of the four dhyanas and then have the mind access the prajna-wisdom experience of emptiness in these states. That's the special difference of the Tantric schools in that its methods emphasize the physical attainments.

After your meditation period, you try to consciously cultivate mindfulness of this union of emptiness and bliss, and stamp all the events and objects that occur with this seal of emptiness-bliss. The various cultivation schools don't say this clearly, but this is the meaning of the world appearing in the form of a dream, or touched with special radiance. Everything that appears will seem to arise with the presence of an illusion because it's both blissful and empty, and naturally you can only access this experience if your chi and mai have been transformed. If you can keep to this state in your daily activities, your samadhi will become strong and stable, an even greater bliss will grow over time, and you'll create a strong foundation for your practice. That's the practice of co-emergent emptiness and bliss, and if you can't bring it into your everyday experience, then it's just a meditative achievement with no ultimate importance other than being a profound experiential realm. You have to let go of these experiences and cultivate emptiness and prajna-wisdom to awaken to the Tao; cultivating samadhi or co-emergent emptiness-bliss is not enough. You have to be able to answer who it is that's experiencing all of this.

Following the descriptions of Tibetan esotericism and Indian yoga, when the heat of the tumo fire cultivation melts the bodhicitta substances, and the chi is brought to the top of the head at the crown chakra, the first "bliss" is generated. When the substances continue flowing, and descend to the region of the throat chakra, the second bliss, known as the "supreme bliss," is aroused. When the substances continue flowing and collect at the heart chakra, the third bliss, called the "special bliss," arises. When the substances (chi and bodhicitta) flow to the navel and collect there, the fourth bliss, known as the "innate bliss," arises. The Tibet school says that these four Joys, Blisses, or Ecstasies should be produced and matched with four Empties. These are actually connected to the emptiness attainments of the dhyana concentrations we find in orthodox Buddhism. The esoteric school doesn't tell you this clearly, but this is what it's actually doing. You are also taught to access these states as the chi ascends upward through the body as well, so you should not affix any particular dhyana attainment to any specific chakra.

All the methods of the Tibet school are based on mastering the tumo fire of kundalini as the foundation for this process of transformation, but mastering the kundalini heat is just a "generation stage" yogic technique corresponding to the *prayogamarga* (preparatory) practices in Mahayana Buddhism. It doesn't mean you've actually seen the truth path of cultivation, or have "seen the Tao." The kundalini phenomenon isn't anything significant in itself, *but is just a convenient means of practice that corresponds to purifying the body's fire element,* from which certain sequences of transformation can continue. So it's still a very low stage of attainment, and is simply a preparatory practice on the path rather than the path of cultivation itself. You have to be particularly clear about this point, and the overall relevance of kundalini yoga: it's simply a technological tool that you use in the quest for higher mental attainments, and in using it, you must refrain from getting bogged down through attachment to feeling states and physical sensations. To progress in this form of practice, you have to give rise to kundalini after cultivating your chi and mai, but you must never become attached to the various phenomenal realms produced.

There are many methods for getting the kundalini "tumo fire" to ignite, but it will never happen unless you first cultivate the chi and mai, or wind and water elements of the body. If you think you can immediately jump into cultivating this state of hsi (kundalini arousal) at the beginning of your cultivation, you're just kidding yourself. Hence all the schools have various preliminaries to this stage of attainment, such as stressing the necessary moral foundation of virtue, discipline, merit and various physical purification exercises. Pranayama is a particular preliminary adjunct to this practice, because the forceful retention of the breath can often lead to the initiation of an inner warmth similar to the kundalini phenomenon.

After you've purified the body to some preliminary extent, which means you've transformed your chi and mai (energy channels), and the warmth element starts to arise in the area of the tan-tien (perhaps through mantra practice, anapana, or other methods), then you can imagine the chi entering the central channel with some degree of success. If a practitioner's mai (the nadis) are already clean to some degree, perhaps from nine-step vase breathing practices or one-pointed visualization exercises, then this exercise may produce some positive results. But one must be wary of form attachments that may arise through this type of practice, or in believing that thought visualizations can actually open the chakras and mai—as is often mistakenly assumed in chigong and the New Age schools.

Kundalini yoga is a practice of inner focus and imagination to get the chi to collect and thereby arouse the inner heat element (tumo fire, kundalini or shakti) so that it fiercely blazes with strength. To get a proper hold on arousing the inner fire, you can start by visualizing the hollow central channel, which is thinner than the thinnest hair imaginable. You visualize that it stands brightly shining in the center of the body, stretching from the perineum to the top of the head, and you imagine that it blazes with a brilliant dazzling light. Of course there are many variations of this basic practice, such as envisioning the left and right channels on its side, and their points of intersection, and of changing the color of the central channel to that of a brightly burning flame. These are all variations that you have to try yourself. The most important site at the start of the practice is to place your awareness at the point in the region of the central channel where the ida, pingala and sushumna join, which can be at either the third eye or the lower opening in the abdomen of the body. Then you can visualize the four chakras, or four chakras with little flames, and fix your mind on this visualization until you can see them clearly. The idea is to concentrate until they appear stable and radiant, for this is establishing one-pointed concentration.

A practitioner can always modify the meditation, after some proficiency, by imagining the central channel as lengthening to the farthest reaches of the universe, becoming as thick as a column, or having energy swirling around inside it clearing blockages, like a twister or tornado climbing upward. These are all designed to help clear and draw energy into the central channel, *but you have to meditate only from within the center of the channel, otherwise the vital energies will not be drawn in.* At the same time, to the basic visualization you must remember to add the image of tiny, concentrated, brilliant flames in the region of the heart, throat, head, and tan-tien (navel chakra), which should be especially envisioned as containing a fierce blazing fire within. Sometimes you focus on imagining a blazing fire in the region of the tan-tien to arouse the inner heat so that it can enter the central channel, which enables the bodhimind substances to melt and descend. Other times you can focus on the third eye, or the heart chakra to help loosen its restrictions.

When you're doing visualizations at the various chakra locations you envision the brilliant tongues of fire at the center of the central channel, because that's what draws the energies into the heart chakra and gives rise to the realms of samadhi. Rather than use little flames, some schools suggest using various Sanskrit syllables, Buddhas, or deities at the chakra locations. Whatever you use, it's just a provisional form of skillful means without any aspect of holiness. Whatever works for you, use it! Thus the *Vijnanabhairava Tantra* says, "Wherever the mind finds satisfaction, let it be concentrated on that." However, in this case, it should be a brightly shining object because chi flames will ignite at that point.

Various types of heat will in time be produced through this process. For instance, there's the inner heat that arises within the central channel and the heat that arises outside the central channel. There's the heat produced within the depth of the body or near the surface of the body, inner heat that arises slowly, and tumo heat that arises quickly, inner heat that seems thick, and inner heat that seems thin. In all these cases, the first type of experience is superior to the second. So in time these visualization practices on the chakras and mai (if you are also proficient at forceful vase breathing techniques and have some degree of discriminative emptiness—one-pointed concentration, or mental halting), will cause the inner tumo heat to arise within the body, which will coincide with various physical transformations and the appearance of various experiential realms.

This is the basic practice of kundalini yoga, as well as the relevant theory behind this particular road of cultivation practice. It's not the only road of practice, nor is it the foremost road of practice. In fact, the Zen school doesn't believe in following this artificial method of practice because *if one simply relaxes the body, watches the breath, and allows the mind to unite with the breath, the central channel will open naturally*, giving rise to samadhi! It's true! Unfortunately, this method is so simple that most people don't believe it, yet this is the quickest way to open the sushumna central channel. If you practice following the breath, you'll also experience all these stages, but the path will be fraught with less trouble and danger. In trying to force these things into manifestation, there's always the danger of overexertion, which can lead to certain mental and physical imbalances. So never push yourself with this type of practice.

Thus we can understand that of all the cultivation schools in existence, Zen is commonly recognized as the highest, since it directly points to the true nature of the mind without artificial contrivances or techniques. The Tao school and School of Esoteric Buddhism are ranked second on the list, cessation-contemplation practices are ranked third, and yoga fourth. But the Taoism and Esoteric Buddhism ranking refers to the *true* schools of Taoism and Esoteric Buddhism, which are akin to Zen. As practiced today, these schools have simply become fourth-rate collections of yogic techniques.

CHAPTER

12

Bardo Practices

 This book contains cultivation techniques to be practiced while an individual is alive. However, if you know the proper techniques, there are certain cultivation practices you can follow immediately after you die, when you're in the intermediate transition phase between death and rebirth. The Tibet school has many teachings on this topic, but it's impossible to cultivate these practices unless you are familiar with the techniques before you die. Otherwise, without this prior familiarity, you'll simply continue to be pushed along by the winds of karma in the afterlife, and will not be able to use this opportune time (when you're finally free of the constraints posed by the coarse physical body) for cultivation. The intermediate period between rebirths is called the "bardo stage" and the cultivation practices for this period of time are called bardo stage yogas. In actual fact, however, *any intervening period is a bardo stage and can become the subject and focus of cultivation efforts.*

In terms of bardo intermediate states, we must note that there is a silent period of resting between any two periods of dissimilar activity. Whether it is between two thoughts (cessation and contemplation practice), two breaths (pranayama practice), between waking and sleeping, dreaming and nondreaming, or between death and rebirth, the transitional state between two different phases always entails a minor period of resting. This gap of stillness can serve as an entry point by which we can realize the true nature of the mind. In fact, one of the reasons there are so many cultivation methods in the world is that different techniques are designed around different types of these intercessional periods. For instance, the bardo state between sleeping and waking is the basis of the dream yoga practices, the silent gap between thoughts is the basis of Tien-tai cessation and contemplation practice, and the pause between respirations is the basis of pranayama breathing practices. All these practices focus on periods of cessation when the mind is momentarily at rest. If you can extend the amount of time you stay in that state while maintaining your awareness, this open but silent awareness can eventually converge into samadhi. If you apply wisdom to observe the state produced, then you can increase your stage of cultivation and eventually enter into the Tao.

At the initial stages of cultivation, the periods of cessation we've cited are all states where it's possible to drop, even though it's only a short while, the "sixth mind" of ordinary conscious meditation. That's the busy consciousness of mental chatter we usually refer to as "mind." During all these transition periods, however, our mental activity is greatly diminished and ordinary mentation seems absent. Thus these are periods where we can attain mental peace because thoughts are still. Since fundamental awareness always exists, we can use our knowing awareness during these intercessions to try and realize the true nature of the mind. Capturing this idea of bardo contemplation, the *Tantraloka* symbolically states, "Do not worship the Lord during the day. Do not worship the Lord during the night. The Lord must be worshipped at the meeting of day and night." In other words, the transitional state is the period of cessation when it is "neither one nor the other," so this is where you should focus your cultivation.

We typically refer to these intercessory gaps as being empty, but "intercessational periods" are simply lower stages of mental activity. For instance, when we hear sounds we identify them as such, and when we don't hear any sound, we call it silence. But actually, sounds and silence are both forms; silence is just the sound of no disturbance. However, there's that one thing above both sound and silence that can comprehend their true nature. It's this one that we are seeking, and the focus during the bardo gap of silence is to realize its true nature. Thus the various bardo meditations involve making use of the temporary experiences of minor stages of emptiness in order to progress toward true emptiness. Hence, concentrating on various gaps is just a means of abandoning excessive external pollution, giving the mind time to introspect, to turn around within and realize its true body.

As to the famous bardo yoga practices for the period between death and rebirth, these belong to a specific form of cultivation technology which is very similar to kundalini yoga. The problem in our ordinary lives is that we're always preoccupied with our bodily sensations, and so we can't enter into samadhi because of our clinging to these distractions. One way to defeat this type of clinging, or playing with sensations, is to practice imagining you're dead. Even though our mind is formless and extends everywhere, it's extremely difficult to get rid of the view of possessing a body, and the Zen school goes out of its way to point out that you really need great wisdom to let go of this perspective. This is why imagining you are dead and letting go of your thoughts and sensations is one very important way to practice while you're still alive. But when you really die and have not yet gone on to rebirth, there is yet another way to practice.

Shortly after death, every being is free of the restrictions of the body and will momentarily experience the formless "clear light" that accompanies the fundamental state of reality. If you can realize the clear light, this is the same stage as "seeing Tao." The chance to realize the clear light is always there, but you can only notice it when your mind is free of obstructions, as happens during the bardo periods. Because it's the fundamental nature of reality, then when you're finally free of the confines of the body (before you assume a new body) and subject to less distraction due to this transition, you might be able to realize it. That's why, in preparation, people practice discarding their thoughts and physical form during the normal process of cultivation because it's then easier to access this realization. In fact, the clear light also appears every time we're just about to wake up from sleep, and so it's also the focus of the Tibetan "clear light of sleep" practices which ask you to concentrate on the heart chakra. While they're related, the bardo state clear light of death practices are different from this form of cultivation, but both aim at helping you awaken to the original nature of the mind, which is called "clear light" because of its open clarity and emptiness. Naturally, this "clear light" isn't referring to a physical light at all.

When you die, you can use your more subtle, intermediate body, which is composed of chi like the body you seem to possess in dreams, to cultivate the clear light when it appears. If you have the requisite merit and are familiar with the after-death bardo practices, as long as you have previously achieved some level of accomplishment in your meditation practice and are not frightened during this period, then you may be able to "see Tao" at this point in time.

The detailed instructions for this form of practice are too lengthy for inclusion within this book but can be found in the *Tibetan Book of the Dead* and various other Tibetan works which greatly expound upon this technique. The basis of practice is to perceive that realm of primordial formless awareness that Tibetans call the clear light, which corresponds to neither existence nor nonexistence. Although the full teachings of bardo yoga are lengthy, the stages of death and the accompanying bardo practices that are relevant to the path of cultivation can be summarized to some extent as follows.

The first element to start dissipating upon death is the chi of the earth element. When the earth element starts to dissipate, your arms and limbs will begin to feel heavy, as if you can't move your body anymore. It's a very dull, indistinct feeling because you're losing the sensation of the earth element, due to the fact that the earth element chi is dissipating. Similarly, for people who die because of sickness, their bodies will slowly lose their weight and mass, a forewarning of this element's dissolution. But when the earth element is really leaving, your power of sight and vision will start to diminish, objects may seem to appear as if they're in the distance or, as we often see in the movies, the eyes will slow their flickering and become dull and lifeless.

These are just the initial stages of death, and you can still recover at this stage. But next the water element in the body starts to dissipate, and a very sticky sweat secretes from the body along with other bodily fluids. At the same time as the water element is diffusing, your power of hearing will also diminish, so you won't be able to hear sounds clearly anymore; sounds will seem as if they're coming from far away. Next the sphincter muscle will release and the last bowel movement will occur. The urine will pass out of the bladder, and the individual will also release their seminal or sexual fluids. Then the individual will enter a state of unconsciousness or semiconsciousness where everything seems chaotic and moving about. The individual will no longer be able to recognize the meaning of different objects but will be caught in their own mental world. Thus they won't be able to recognize the people about them or even the names of visitors and family members.

Now, the loss of urine and feces shows that the downward moving chi of the body is dissipating, but the upward moving chi also wants to leave the body, so phlegm will begin to form in the throat during this process. In fact, when the water element is dissipating, the mouth will become dry and the individual may not be able to speak clearly anymore or will only be able to mumble indistinct sounds. Because the upward moving wind is dissipating, one's breath will also become extremely shallow and will only reach to the throat rather than to the bottom of the lungs. Thus many people will seem as if they're choking, or struggling to breathe and speak, which is the upward flowing wind undergoing the state of dissolution. At this time the sixth consciousness of discrimination is still there, but it's operating in a very restricted state.

When the individual goes through this choking phase, the last bit of the water element is leaving the body. Soon the wind element will also leave, and at that time the individual will take his or her last breath.

But at this current point in the process, the perceptions of the outside world will have stopped and the individual will rest in his or her own thought-world separated from the input of the senses. This state has often been described as a yellowish or shadowy state of mind, or the road to Hades. After this stage, the heat and wind elements will then begin to leave the body.

As these last elements leave, at this point a doctor or hospital staff may try to use electrical or other invasive measures to try and shock people back to life. This is extremely painful—painful beyond description for the individuals in this state of dissipation to suffer. It's so extremely painful that you mustn't think you're being good to the person who is dying when you impose this upon them because you don't want them to leave. Life and death are just processes of transformation that we're going through all the time, so it's best to accept the inevitable and let them leave in peace. When the body isn't even a fit vehicle for cultivation any longer, why cling to it? What are you really trying to accomplish?

Next, as the heat element begins to leave the body, the body will start to become cold. If you want to know the realm the person goes to after death, you can feel the body after it's dead, and the location of the last bit of remaining warmth will indicate the realm of the next incarnation. If the heat recedes from the body, going from the feet upward, this is indicative of rebirth in a fortunate realm, whereas when the heat leaves the body from the top of the head downward, the next incarnation will not be so fortunate. In terms of specific destinations, if the top of the head is the last region to remain warm, the individual has gone on to rebirth in the heavens, and his or her face will look beautiful or peaceful. If the forehead or brow is the last area to remain warm, and the face looks a little angry, strong, or stern, this person has gone on to be reborn in the realm of the *asuras*, or angry gods. If the heart is the last place that remains warm, the next stage of transformation will be among humans again.

The warmth of these regions is very easy to distinguish, but it's harder to distinguish the lingering warmth if it is present in the body's lower regions. If the stomach is the last place where the heat leaves, though this is not easy to distinguish, the individual will be reborn in the animal realm. If the knees are the last place to remain warm, he or she will become a *preta*, or hungry ghost, and if the feet are the last things to remain warm, the person will be reborn in the hells because of the weight of his or her evil deeds. These last three states are difficult to see and detect. People always tend to think that they'll be reborn as human because they forget that there are many realms of existence, and in terms of the larger cycle of life and repeated incarnations, the present period of being human is just one particular phenomenon. The important thing is that death means a new life, and a new life means death; people just change their form and continue progressing through the realms of cyclical existence, caught in the never-ending cycle of birth and death. There's no chance of ever escaping from this process unless you master the process of cultivation, which is one of the reasons that people choose to cultivate.

We mention this process to show you that the true essence of life is always here, but the outward form that carries life continually undergoes transformation. Hence we can say that life isn't purely materialistic, nor consciousness-only, but some union of the two aspects. When we say that we "live" or "die," it's just that a certain stage in this continuously changing process is finished. The essence which allows you to live or die never dies, but is eternal and changeless, giving rise to all these states in the manner of an illusion without real existence. So our rebirths and previous lives are just these different phases of continual ephemeral transformation, a cycle of never-ending impermanence and change, whereas the real one never changes. That's the one which "knows" and which we realize through Tao. We establish arbitrary separations on this continual sequence, but there isn't any such thing because it's just one continual process, and, in truth, there aren't even any inherent divisions. Coming to this world and being human is just one phase of this sequence, and even here we can see the phases of life as evidence of this continual process of change and transformation. What's important is that when you cultivate to a certain level, you'll be able to control this process of transformation and determine where you're going to go next. Or, you can jump out of it altogether. The Arhats try to finish with it forever, while the Buddhas and Enlightened Bodhisattvas strive to master it so that they can skillfully and effectively help others.

Now, at the very moment you die and stop breathing there's a moment of tremendous pressure that collapses, producing a fabulous feeling of freedom—like a bird who's been trapped for years and finally escapes out of his cage. This is the point where your spirit becomes free of the confines of the physical body. It's also a moment when you experience an extreme amount of sexual desire. The moment of death and the time of entry of spirit into the womb are the two times in life when your sexual desire rises to a maximum peak. That's why if you can't free yourself from sexual desire you'll never accomplish much as to your stage of cultivation, nor will you ever be able to control the rounds of birth and death.

The next step of the death process is that of entering a state of mental coma or unconsciousness. We can call this a state of no-thought, no-mind, or no-perception because its nature is quite similar to fainting. The time spent in this state, if we were to measure it according to human time, would be about thirty hours or so. Some people say it's about twenty hours, but the important point is that it's like a long sleep and then you "wake up" out of that state. After you wake up, you assume a different form than that of your previous physical body. Some people think you take the form of a spirit or ghost, but that's incorrect. Rather, you arise in the form of a "bardo body," which is also called an "intermediate body," or "yin-body" in the Tao school. This body is similar in form to the human body but it's composed of subtle chi. A closer approximation would be to say that it resembles our dream body that arises during sleep, which is also composed of chi, but the bardo body is more radiant and powerful than the dream body. Sometimes a relative or friend can receive a visitation from this bardo body, for the bardo body suffers fewer constraints of space and time than does our coarser physical form.

The way the bardo yoga works is the following. It's a natural characteristic of the state of sleep that when you're just about to wake up—on the border of sleep and wakefulness—you experience a very special moment of mind for a very brief instant: the clarity of the mind which we call "luminosity." Of course this is not a physical light but a state of mind, a type of clear, untangled awareness which we refer to as the "clear light." So after death, as you wake up out of this state of unconsciousness, just as you're about to assume the bardo body, you will also experience this clear light, and you must try to access it and remain in this state as the practice of bardo cultivation.

When you cultivate so as to reach a high level of samadhi, you will also experience the stage of clear light as well. At that point you will experience a profound peace and serenity and the "child light of mind." The best way we can describe the clear light is to say that the experience is very serene, comfortable, peaceful, empty, and clear; awareness is "bright" and endless. The experience is like coming upon an endless expanse of cloudless sky on a clear, crisp day in the cool, settled autumn. This clear light is the same state you momentarily experience when you are just about to wake up to assume the bardo body. If you can grasp that moment when you wake up in that state, then you can remain cultivating in that state and stay out of reincarnation for a very long time. Hence that particular state of clarity or purity is what we call "nirvana." Nirvana doesn't mean deletion, extinction, or annihilation, as some early translators supposed, but is a *visaya* (mental state or experiential realm) of supreme peace, clarity, and calm—descriptive terms that still don't do justice to this term. That's why we leave the term nirvana translated as is. While the transitory world of samsara is totally characterized by movement, including the opposite dualistic state of stillness we call emptiness, nirvana is nonmoving, formless, blissful, indescribable. Nirvana is the real nature of reality.

For forty-nine years Shakyamuni Buddha taught that all things are empty of self, are impure, involve suffering, and are impermanent. However, at the end of this life he taught the *Nirvana Sutra* where he said there is a true self of purity, bliss, and permanence. That's the original essence of life, which is blissful and pure. That's what you try to reach through cultivation because it's the answer to all your questions and longings. As human beings we can't recognize this original essence because we keep grasping onto things like pleasure and nonpleasure, or we become attached to our thoughts and sensations. Hence we cover over this experience although it's there all the time and has never left us. And since the state of motion will always change into nonmotion, and nonmotion back into motion again—because all states are impermanent—so thoughts and internal silence will never be the way to Tao. To reach nirvana you have to get rid of these two states, you have to detach from these two extremes and realize what's accessing these states—prajna-transcendental wisdom. Nirvana isn't in either existence or nonexistence. Between the two states it's easiest to perceive the true nature of nirvana but in everyday life we just don't realize it and thus we have to cultivate. And because we can't recognize this state of nirvana, we still continue going round and round the cycle of birth and death. Is there a god in charge of this process? No, there isn't. The only gatekeeper to the process is yourself. You're the one ultimately responsible for all your actions and behavior, including all the events which happen to you because of the karmic seeds you've sown; there's only your own karmic seeds, which constantly undergo a subtle perfuming process of transformation, that manifest when conditions are ripe in the world of interdependent arisings. This is the way this universe works; there is no outside force that gives you a personal fate, but only yourself. Thus, there's no controller of the process other than yourself, and only through cultivation can you master this.

In the bardo state, all your previous life experiences show up as in a movie preview, and you can see all the interconnections you've experienced in life, and all the good and bad you've done to others in a sort of macro life-review. If you've cultivated to a good extent, many of your past-life experiences can be seen as well. In the bardo state we may also see images of a god, a gatekeeper, or the "doors to heaven or hell," but these are all part of our shadow consciousness. These images are our own projections because of cultural conditionings; there is no outside controller over our destiny. Even though we seem to have no control over our destiny, we're actually the ones in charge who determine everything. There is no being in charge of this process other than ourselves, so the cultivation for mastering this ultimate process comes down to mastering our functions and behavior. We plant the seeds that create our future, and those seeds are never destroyed, they'll always bear fruit in the future. When the seeds finally sprout because conditions arise, our various experiences come into being. That's just the way this illusory realm of interdependent causation works. There's no creator being behind it, and it is itself an empty illusion without any lasting, holding, inherent true nature. Even what we think of as the self is just an egoless process of causes and conditions that undergo a sequence of transformation. But what is it that ceaselessly holds the key to awareness throughout this process? That's the *true one*, the never-changing one you strive to find. Finding it is called awakening, self-realization, or getting the Tao.

Now the bardo body you arise in after death has its own life and death. Using human time, we can say that every seven days it's born and then dies. If the strength of habit energy isn't enough to pull the bardo individual into the next incarnation when their bardo body dies, the individual will go unconscious and then awaken in another new bardo body. It's said that at most you can go through seven of these transformations. Therefore you might stay in the bardo for up to forty-nine days, waiting for all the right conditions to come together (it usually takes from two to thirty days), before you assume a new incarnation and the transference of consciousness is completed. But don't fixate upon these numbers, as the bardo stage description is just a metaphor for helping you understand what goes on after death. What's important is that during the transformation from the one bardo body to the next, upon awakening there's that flash of "base luminosity" or "ground awareness" we call the clear light, and if one can recognize that experience and rest in it, they have the chance of attaining enlightenment. That's the essence of the bardo state yoga. Otherwise, if you can't access the Tao at this point, you'll just fall into the next existence of the bardo state, or you'll experience the unconscious consciousness-transference into a human rebirth, or new life in another realm. The practice of training to perform a deliberate consciousness-transference is yet another cultivation technique found in the Tibetan tantras, such as the *Six Yogas of Naropa,* but it's rarely used.

The dream state that is somewhat hazy but sort of under our control is a state called the shadow consciousness that is a bit like the bardo state. The bardo body can eat, smell, and have sensations just like our dream state body, but these bardo experiences are clearer than in the dream state. Hence any proficiency that you can achieve in the sleep and dream yogas will bring great benefits at the time of death because they'll help you master the death bardo cultivation yoga. In other words, when you enter into the clear light of the moment of sleep and then pass into the dream state, the illusory dream body that arises is similar to the bardo body. The Tibet school also has a specific technology for generating an illusory body (similar to the bardo body) with which to cultivate the Tao, and this is similar to the yin and yang bodies of the Tao school, which are either invisible or visible to the naked eye.

If you practice meditating on the clear light of the waking state, the clear light of sleep and the clear light of death, all of which involve the fact that the vital energies dissolve and are drawn into the central channel, then you can possibly master the bardo yoga technique. Because of this requirement, the Tibet school says its mastery depends upon proficiency in kundalini yoga. In general, that's the basis of attaining the clear light of the path in the Tibetan "completion stage" yogas, but as to the clear light of sleep, during sleep you try to cultivate the state of presence, and blend your awareness with the clear light of sleep no matter how deep your sleep is. As to the bardo clear light, you have to recognize this state and then blend it with emptiness, but you'll only be able to recognize the state if you have prior yogic training and know these particular instructions.

Only two types of individuals don't go through the bardo state upon death. Those who are extremely virtuous can go directly to heaven and extremely evil people will go directly to the hells without passing through the bardo. The bardo body can also travel everywhere in the world except to two places: the realms of the bodhisattvas and inside a woman's womb. If a bardo body entered into the bodhisattva's experiential realm, it would be enlightened, and if it entered into the woman's womb, then that would be its next incarnation. Hence these two doors of experience are closed.

The question arises as to how can one take control to direct where their next cycle of life will be? The answer is: who is it that makes the karma? It's you! You're the one who makes your karma as you live your life and decide on what to think, say, and do. It's not the act of a god or someone else that directs you into a certain state or experience, nor is it a function of chemical reactions or random material events. It's all a function of your own mind. Does the bardo body have a material content? It's composed of a subtle form of chi, so sometimes people describe the bardo body as having a subtle substance or subtle energy. Its other aspect is that it's also a mental state that doesn't have any substance. This is a very deep and difficult subject to discuss, so this is as much as we can provide here on the bardo state, and bardo yoga.

13

Focusing the Vision on an Object

 Another type of cultivation technique involves focusing our vision on an external object in order to attain mental cessation. This method of focusing is cultivating concentration and the basic method behind this practice covers many hundreds of related techniques. If you understand this one particular method, however, then you will understand the basic principles behind them all.

First you relax the body and breathing while sitting in front of some object you've selected for your visual focus. Typically, your object of focus should remain at eye level about three to five feet in front of you. If you have high blood pressure you should undertake this practice while sitting, or you can assume a martial arts "horse-standing" posture so that your chi and blood descend to the soles of the feet. In cultivation, it's always a great accomplishment if you can open the chi channels running to the bottom of the feet.

The best type of object to be using in this meditation reflects a little light, like a crystal, and is joyful or auspicious in connotation. Another type of object is a picture of a Buddha in their Buddha land, which is something you might be able to see while visiting a museum, or within a book having such pictures. In this type of practice, the area to focus upon in these pictures is the curly lock of hair between the eyebrows of the Buddha (the third eye region). There are many reasons for choosing this spot as a particular focus (point of concentration), but we cannot go into them here.

As to the practice itself, you simply relax the body and become mentally absorbed in one point; you focus on the object you've selected while ignoring any other thoughts which might be running around in your head. Just keep focusing on the one point, making it smaller and smaller as the intensity of your concentration increases, and let those other thoughts be. When watching the object, don't try to mentally describe it through any internal mental dialogue. Rather, let it become the sole center of your attention so that it totally absorbs your concentration: your mind becomes fixed on that one point. In this manner, you can attain single-mindedness of concentration.

The color of the object is an important concern as it may affect the mood of some practitioners. For instance, the color red is related to joy and to blood, so a red object might tend to increase one's energy or create problems for those having high blood pressure. People with quick minds should practice using darker, more calming colors. In general, the color yellow is related to the stomach and balance, green is related to anger and the liver, and black is related to the kidneys and sorrow. No strict rules can be given for these correspondences, as the ultimate effect of any colors will depend upon the practitioner's personality, mentality, and physical condition. Thus the important point is to select an object with which one feels very comfortable. You'll see the results from personal practice and will know how to adjust yourself accordingly.

If you really succeed in cultivating your visual focus to attain mental cessation, you will reach the stage of being able to focus your concentration. This is indeed a type of samadhi, but it's the samadhi of ordinary people rather than the samadhi of deeper cultivation. Even sports professionals can at times attain some minor realm of samadhi focus such as this. So if you want to go beyond this type of samadhi to enter the deeper samadhi of cultivation, once you master the stage of focusing you should practice by changing the scenario.

This next step is to turn your focus within and to visualize your inner body. If you can concentrate to see within your own body, in time you will eventually see all your internal organs, the circulation of the blood, the energy meridians, and so on. In ancient times, people discovered acupuncture because they could see all these structures, and you'll also be able to locate obstructions within your body through this technique. This type of seeing from within will also enable you to cure all sorts of disease and live a longer life, so it's good to practice from this point of view alone. If the body is uncomfortable in some spot, you can just focus your internal vision on it and it will eventually get better. The mind and body are linked, so fixing the mind on a portion of your body will send life-giving chi to the same area, and if the obstructions to this chi flow are eliminated, you will be able to experience internal healing.

In the past, people who wanted to obtain the capacity to see in darkness or see for hundreds of miles would practice this focusing technique during the night, which is a means of cultivating the chi that supports the eye and eye-consciousness. When they successfully became absorbed in one object, even a darkened room would seem to become brighter and they could end up seeing for long distances, sometimes obtaining clairvoyance. Archery was thus an ancient means for developing samadhi because it involved practicing one-pointed focus on a distant object. An individual can also choose to gaze at the light of a small candle, the light emitted by a body of fire, the light reflected off the surface of a lake, or the natural light of the sky. The fundamental technique is the basis of a variety of different cultivation methods. Thus you can understand the words! The *Vijnanabhairava Tantra*, which summarizes for us a slightly different technique, says, "Oh, goddess, if after casting one's gaze on some object, one withdraws it slowly and eliminates the knowledge of that object along with the thought and impressions of it, he will abide in emptiness." The purpose of these techniques is always aimed at attaining the stillness, or emptiness, of samadhi.

14

Athletic "Peak Performance" and Chi Cultivation

The path of physical exercise, in conjunction with a focused coordination between the mind and breath, can indeed help athletes reach a type of mundane samadhi. This type of peak experience that athletes sometimes encounter goes by a variety of names: "flow," "the white spot" or "white moment," "the zone," "being centered," "living in real time," "riding the wave," or "being in the groove," and so forth. In this state, an athlete's performance seems supernormal because they experience a quiet mental realm of perfect serenity and calm wherein their conscious thought seems suspended, their concentration is heightened to an extreme, time appears as if it's standing still, and they feel as if they're fully alive, connected with all things, and fully living in the radiant present.

Unfortunately, this condition is not the state of spiritual samadhi referred to in cultivation. Rather, we can only say that it is a type of mundane samadhi, a type of kung-fu that occurs when the body is really healthy and the chi, hormones, and blood circulation become fully energized and coordinated. Although the experience seems quite profound and heightened when compared to everyday experience, it is actually just an ordinary state of peace and quiet that is still within the realm of the mundane. Hence it is not the samadhi of Tao and it is not a mark of progress on your cultivation toward the Tao.

As an example, suppose you become absorbed in some kind of sports activity requiring coordinated movement and deep concentration. If your blood, chi, and breath become coordinated through this activity so tht they unite into one, then it's possible to encounter this type of "peak experience" or state of "flow." But this state of concentration doesn't qualify as spiritual practice because it's lacking merit and prajna-wisdom. Unlike samadhi, athletes don't know how to repeat this experience and enter it at will, nor do they know how to integrate this state with their ordinary lives. Doing so requires that you go further to cultivate the genuine samadhi, such as the four dhyanas, which in turn requires that you cultivate merit and the prajna-wisdom of emptiness. Nevertheless, some athletes who parallel the path of cultivation in their training will gain some small shadow insight into these higher realms and will be able to improve their performance along the way.

People often point to the Sufi dervish dances, which entail whipping the body into a supersensible state through movement, as an example of a physical practice by which you can enter into samadhi. However, these also fall into this category of the mundane "flow" experience. For instance, if anyone were to keep spinning the body the turning itself will generate a state of joy and produce the sensation of forgetting the body and the self. Through this type of effort, we can say that the quiet aspect of life is moved, which in turn generates the feelings of joy and bliss. But this isn't samadhi. If you do such exercises to an appropriate level you might become healthier; going overboard, you might harm yourself. Hence we have the Taoist injunction to cultivate the body through movement and to cultivate the mind through stillness. This is simultaneous training of the body and mind. In this way you'll maintain both mental and physical health.

Practicing Tai Chi, Aikido, and the other martial arts, or even classical yoga also fall into the category of movement exercises that can at most lead to mundane samadhi. Despite what people may say, no physical practice can take you to Tao. Physical exercises are good for your health and help you perfect your concentration and regulate your chi, but physical movement alone, or even physical exercise combined with concentration, cannot possibly take you into genuine spiritual samadhi. They can only help you transform the body on a coarse level by softening your muscles, ligaments, fascia, and other body tissues. Nonetheless this is a very worthwhile goal because transforming the physical nature, even to a small degree, clears the way for further progress in your cultivation practice. Hence deep tissue massage, visceral manipulation, chiropractic adjustments, and so forth often achieve quite useful results for the cultivation path. But in this aspect we must always remember an ancient Chinese maxim: "To learn martial arts kung-fu without internal cultivation, one will regret this for life. To learn internal kung-fu for meditation without martial arts [or other physical practices] one will enjoy countless wonderful benefits."

Traditionally, there are four progressive steps one follows in order to cultivate the Tao through the initial road of physical practice. First, you (1) undertake martial arts practice, from which your muscles and tendons will become soft and supple; then (2) chi-gong practice, which focuses on breathing exercises such as anapana or pranayama; then (3) Tao-gong practices, which encompass the Taoist internal exercises that cultivate the body's chi channels. Finally, (4) you enter Zen style mind-only practice if you really wish to become enlightened. Today chi-gong practices are quite popular, but they're the lowest form of materialistic cultivation (left over from the Chinese Communist Cultural Revolution) that only deals with sensations of wind. If you don't reach the point in these practices where the breath naturally subsides in hsi and you end up cultivating the mind, they are only a coarse means to help engender health and longevity.

Anyway, this is the traditional four-step progress of entering the Tao beginning with the road of physical exercise. Most athletes on this course simply restrict themselves to the lower task of cultivating their chi. They start by learning how to centralize and coordinate their chi, then how to extend its influence to affect others and the environment, and only then do they learn how to get in touch with the source of their chi—which they can do when the breathing stops. However, this is still classified as mundane practice unless the practitioner can match this state with the internal practice of looking within. When martial artists or others can match the cessation of external breathing with internal contemplation, and thereby reach the state called hsi, shakti, or kundalini initiation, they then start on the genuine route to Tao. This is blending the route of mundane achievement into the route of transcendental achievements.

Thus physical exercise is only a means to help purify the physical body and prepare it for cultivation but it cannot take you into samadhi. For instance, hatha yoga by itself, without the supplementary activities of breath and mind coordination, will never produce dhyana. Nevertheless, it's true that to attain samadhi you need to first have a healthy body, which you can achieve by working on breathing exercises and internal practices such as those found in the schools of Taoism, yoga, and esoteric Buddhism. Those who think too much or who lack physical activity should particularly engage in some sort of physical exercise as part of their cultivation path. This is why the first Zen patriarch of China, Bodhidharma, introduced various stretching and kung-fu exercises to the monks at Shaolin temple. But the ultimate path of cultivation is not through the body, but through the wisdom of mind-only, as taught in Zen. The body is only a form, and if you seek the Tao through form, you are treading a mistaken path. But, if you try to awaken to the Tao by mind cultivation, this is the fastest and most direct route to enlightenment.

15

Ingesting Wai-dan
(Siddhi Medicine, or External Alchemy)

Many cultivation schools tell you to eat special herbs and medicines to restore the vitality of the body, to harmonize its internal organs, and to help correct any biochemical imbalances that stand in the way of cultivation progress. Their main effect is to purify the body—especially the digestive, endocrine, nervous, and other systems—and then bring it to an optimal state of health from which it is much easier to enter samadhi. After all, to slightly alter the formula mentioned in the Introduction, Health (Kung-fu) + Method (Practice) + Merit (Morality) = Cultivation. Thus, through the ages the various yogic, Taoist, and other esoteric schools have always taught students how to ingest special medicines to help transform the hormones, organs, and mai. External medicines, called *wai-dan* in Taoism and *rasayana* or *siddhi* medicines in Indian ayurveda, have been especially emphasized by these form-based schools because they concentrate on cultivating the physical body as a pathway to Tao. The Zen school, on the other hand, doesn't emphasize these matters since the body will naturally purify and heal itself as one cultivates samadhi directly. Nevertheless, that doesn't mean it objects to

正禪方。

春桑耳　夏桑子　秋桑葉　冬桑白皮

右參味等分擣篩以水一斗煮小豆一升令大熟以桑末
一升和煮微沸著鹽豉服之日三服飽服無妨三日外稍
去小豆身輕目明無眠睡十日覺遠智通初地禪服二十
日到二禪定百日得三禪定累一年得四禪定萬相皆見
壞欲界觀境界如視掌中得見佛性

Figure 7. Taoism, Buddhism, Tantra, and yoga all have various prescriptions for siddhi medicines that can help change the body, making it easier to enter into samadhi. This thousand-year-old Chinese recipe, based on the mulberry, is an example of such formulas. Naturally, no psychotropic substances or hallucinatory drugs are included in this category of helpful cultivation substances and mixtures. The wai-dan substances of cultivation are simple materials that aid in detoxifying and purifying the physical body.

the use of medicine; if you are sick, you should take the appropriate remedies to heal yourself.

Unfortunately, most specialized medicines used in cultivation schools cannot be safely ingested unless an individual has already reached some particular stage of kung-fu, such as the stage where they can survive by "eating air" alone. Many of these substances are poisonous; were ordinary individuals to eat these materials, they would surely die. Despite what others may say, we must also note that the genuine medicinal substances in cultivation are always minerals or herbs and are never made from other living beings. These substances work to help you purify the body's wind and water elements and to encourage transformations in the chi and mai; their modern counterparts can be found in vitamins, nutrients, and herbal supplements. Nevertheless, while external substances can be helpful in this process of physical transformation, the actual substances we rely upon in cultivation are the states of jing, chi, and shen we produce within.

In actual fact, no medicine or drug can take an individual into samadhi, which is a mental phenomenon, for they can only affect the physical nature. Nevertheless, the mind and body are interlinked, so maximizing the body's state of health (by cleansing the intestines with colonics, for example) will make it much easier to cultivate the mind. It's absolutely essential that you create a clean and healthy body if you want to succeed in cultivation, so the first phases of cultivation are aimed at purifying its impure nature and restoring its natural vitality. That's why true cultivators always watch their diets, because food is nothing other than our daily medicine. Our daily sickness is hunger, and food is the means by which we treat this illness.

On this note, because of cultivation or health purposes, our food should always be fresh, clean, and easy to digest. We shouldn't consume too much raw food, or eat food to excess (the stomach should always be a little bit empty after we eat), and periods of fasting can be very helpful in this process of internal purification. Too much food is actually poison. In general, people who have too much nutrition experience an excess of random thoughts and sexual desires, both of which make it much harder to succeed in cultivation.

Now a proper diet along with certain herbal supplements can help the body transform its mai so that one can reach samadhi more quickly. Because of the importance of jing and chi, or chi and mai, the air we breath and the internal balance of hormones within are extremely important factors for this alchemical process. In the effort to transform the body so that it's more fit for cultivation, we must not neglect vitamins and minerals (most of the esoteric substances that can change the physical nature involve minerals) that can help us become clear and alert. Even with a nutritional supplements program and healthy living, however, an individual must still meditate regularly and refrain from losing jing (seminal essence), since preservation of jing and its transmutation into chi is the basis of any sort of physical transformation achieved through cultivation. Without jing your chi will be insufficient, and without sufficient chi there will be no opening of the energy meridians and chakras for attaining samadhi and dhyana. If you don't cultivate your chi, you will never reach the initial stage of internal luminosity where you can see a light within the physical body, as well as all its internal organs and internal functions. This stage is mentioned in many cultivation schools, and in Buddhism it corresponds to breaking through the form skandha.

The reason ordinary people don't experience these various transformations is because their bodies are too dirty inside, contain too many obstructions, and because they lose their jing and chi through excessive sexual activity. Therefore, the secret principle behind siddhi medicines, or wai-dan, is that they help clean and purify the internal body, just as we would clean a dirty house. If the body becomes clean inside and an individual practices sexual restraint, the body will be able to naturally recover its original functions and readily enter into samadhi. When you are already sick, however, you must be very careful about the supplementary nutrients you take because some substances, such as ginseng, will drive illness chi further into the body to block internal healing and speed up the aging process. Most sick people who take these substances think they are healing themselves, whereas they are actually suppressing their illness without curing it by driving it deeper into the body. Often the popular rejuvenation tonics taken by so many people just add to health problems rather than heal them.

To believe that special substances will take you into samadhi is a great mistake, for there is no external substance in the entire world that can generate or bring about any stage of spiritual attainment. None! Thus, you should never use drugs or intoxicants in cultivation because they can cause you to lose control of your mind and enter the world of the solitary shadow consciousness, which is the yin side of the sixth mind. The feelings or visions that arise from intoxicants are not holy states, just body-generated phenomena, or realms verging on mental illness. One should ingest substances with the aim of trying to detoxify, clean, and purify the physical body only. This is the preparatory stage of working on the body's chi and mai, which corresponds to the "generation stage" yogas in the schools of esoteric Tantra, and the Mahayana stages of prayoga.

16

Sexual Cultivation

 The key to attaining samadhi is to practice discipline, accumulate merit, become healthy, and to practice some form of meditative concentration. Maintaining discipline includes the injunction that you shouldn't lose your jing, and when this stipulation is followed your jing will become full. The Tao school says, "when one's jing becomes full, there will be little sexual desire; when one's chi is full, there will be little desire to eat; and when one's shen is full, there will be little need to sleep." When one retains jing through sexual abstinence (which Christianity calls celibacy or chastity, and Hinduism refers to as brahmacarya), and cultivates the mind of emptiness, then jing can be transformed into chi during cultivation. Without this process of transformation, however, it is hard for an individual to scale the ranks of spiritual attainment. In other words, celibacy without transformation is useless.

Unfortunately, as many people cultivate their vitality builds, but because their chi isn't evenly balanced they succumb to sexual desire. Whether it is from physiological or psychological origins, they engage in sexual activity, lose jing and thus forfeit the chance of making any further cultivation progress. Because of this great problem, the Tao school recommends various methods of sexual intercourse wherein there is no loss of jing. In these methods of sexual congress, both partners engage in joyful sexual intercourse without desire and without ejaculation. The sexual partners strive to become satisfied through reaching a full body comfortableness, rather than orgasm, and in this manner intercourse can be prolonged for many hours. If done correctly, the Tao school says this is a way to balance your yin and yang natures, and it's simply a form of chi-mai practice.

The basic Taoist technique is joyful sexual exercise, without orgasm, during a peaceful mental state that is absent of sexual desire. Ordinary people who cannot free themselves from sexual lusts can try to employ this sort of practice, like using fire to fight fire, as a medicine to rid themselves of sexual desire. The principle behind this technique is that the physical body becomes comfortable because of sexual activity, which causes your chi to become full and equally distributed throughout, and in this state of comfortableness you might be able to see the Tao. Hence it's a method of cultivating the chi so as to enter samadhi.

Couples must be particularly careful to avoid exposing themselves to any cold wind during sexual activities, such as engaging in sexual intercourse while in front of the air conditioner or an open window, for the wind can easily enter the body during such times. Chinese medicine even suggests that you protect yourself from drafts for at least forty minutes after sexual activity. Uncomfortable feelings such as headaches or stupor the morning after any type of sexual relations indicate that you have performed sexual relations incorrectly or have failed to protect yourself as noted, and therefore suffer what Chinese medicine calls an external "wind invasion." This is the result of "incorrect sex," and you can even die from this type of exposure. For the Mahayana practitioner, sex may not necessarily be considered a breach of discipline, but incorrect sexual technique such as this, or its incorrect timing (such as during a woman's menstruation) are definite examples of a breach of discipline.

During cultivation sexual practice, the partners must protect their bodies and adjust their sexual activities so as to cultivate emptiness whenever they feel they are near orgasm or ejaculation. The Taoist school says, "Slow foreplay is important every time a man lies with a woman so that the two spirits will be in harmony. Only after the spirits are perfectly moved for a long time should the couple unite. The man should enter the woman when the penis is soft and pull it back out when it becomes firm and strong. He should penetrate only without ejaculating. He who can have intercourse many times in a single day without letting his essence leak will increase his lifespan and heal himself of all disease." Hence in its crudest form, Taoist sexual practice is a form of physical harmonization and nonejaculation yoga.

Taoism says that the real chi is born from the bottom of the feet, which is why Chuang Tzu said that "the real man breathes from his heels," and when this chi is activated and ascends upward to the sexual organs, the leaking of jing is sure to occur (through ejaculation or orgasm) unless the practitioner can remain empty prior to and during those moments. Therefore, alternately stopping and proceeding in an appropriate fashion, while cultivating emptiness and maintaining an absence of desire, two sexual partners will be able to peacefully prevent any loss of jing and yet both will become comfortable, full and satisfied. If you can reach a comfortable stage where your chi is full, wherein you can cultivate the emptiness of mind and body, you can enter into samadhi. These are the basic principles of the Tao school sexual practice, which may take some training to master. Sexual activities are particularly helpful to those who use their minds a lot, as this type of sexual exercise can help the chi descend to the feet.

The methods of Tibetan sexual tantra are very similar to the Tao school "left-hand door" sexual practices, yet are referred to as the karmamudra practices of "co-emergent emptiness and bliss." What's the purpose of these practices? To help you jump out of the Desire Realm through a method akin to hammering a nail upward from the bottom of a table to knock out the nail situated above. But to really understand the method of sexual tantra, you must already be familiar with the following sequence of successful cultivation practice:

After one year of practice, your chi will be transformed.

After two years of practice, your blood will be transformed.

After three years, your mai (chi channels) will be transformed.

After four years, your muscles (flesh) will be transformed.

After five years, your marrow will be transformed.

After six years, your sinews and tendons will be transformed.

After seven years, your bones will be transformed.

After eight years, your hair will be transformed.

After nine years of cultivation, your body's form (shape) will be transformed.

This sequential process summarizes how you cultivate the wind, water, fire, and earth elements of the body and is related to the Taoist stages of "laying the foundation" (one hundred days), "pregnancy" (ten months), "suckling the baby" (three years), and "facing the wall" (nine years). In view of these processes, it's only when you enter the thirteenth year of accomplished practice that you can just begin to make inroads into cultivating the space element of the body, which corresponds to the all-pervading chi that permeates the physical nature. This is the *vyana prana* of Hinduism that is spread throughout the entire body, helping to resist physical disintegration and circulate nutrients, fluid, and energy. So in terms of chi cultivation, you go into this practice, after laying a strong foundation of attainment, because you want to speed up the process of transformation and quickly bring the all-pervading wind (that is difficult to control) into the central channel. Otherwise, it would take thirteen years just to begin to be able to touch upon this aspect of cultivation.

To be qualified for and ultimately be successful in these practices, *you must already be proficient in breathing exercises, the skeleton meditation, cessation and contemplation, and must have already achieved some level of dhyana.* For instance, the sixth Dalai Lama of Tibet wanted to engage in this practice, but his advisors wouldn't let him. One day he gathered them together and urinated while standing on the wall of a monastery, but before his urine reached the ground he withdrew it back into his penis. When his advisors saw his mastery of chi to this level, they no longer objected to his qualifications for this type of practice.

Thus the particular techniques of Tantra are not taught publicly, mostly because people are not qualified for the practices, which properly belong to the Desire Realm heavens. However, one can readily recognize that the principles involve the dual union of joyful mental emptiness with the comfortable physical bliss generated through sexual intercourse, and this bliss occurs when the jing descends just as in kundalini yoga. The parallels between sexual bliss and the bliss required to succeed in the kundalini yoga is why high level practitioners often turn to this technique. However, during intercourse an ordinary pyschic heat develops, which isn't the tumo fire, but due to this heat the bodhicitta jing melts and descends. You mustn't mistakenly identify the bliss and joy of sexual cultivation with the crazy excitement of sexual lust we see in the movies, for the co-emergent joy and bliss you experience in sexual cultivation are the results of becoming satiated with chi from the stimulation of sexual activity. Even so, this type of joy and bliss cannot match the joys and blisses of the four dhyanas, which are a hundred thousand or even a million times more powerful than worldly sexual ecstasy.

To bring about the stages of joy and bliss in sexual cultivation is a means of cultivating the chi and mai and melting the subtle drops of bodhicitta (or bindus) that are referred to in the practices of kundalini cultivation. Hence in the very initial stages of correct practice, a practitioner's saliva will become sweet because the endocrine pituitary hormones are activated, which marks the initial stages of jing descending from above to produce bliss. Then you will reach a stage where it seems as if your chi expands, and through this chi you can touch the borders of your room or your locality where you reside. Why can you do this?

Because the sixth consciousness is everywhere, and so is the chi upon which it rides. Thus, when you cultivate your chi so that it "stretches between the sky and the earth," you can naturally become conscious of these realms.

Next you reach a stage of emptiness where your mind is joyful, open and free and it seems as if you don't possess a body any more; it seems as if you can't find your body. Abiding in this state of emptiness-bliss and progressing further, a cultivation practitioner must detach from any vestiges of sexual desire to forget body and mind completely and enter into the first dhyana. These are the basics of the correct practice. If you think you can learn sexual cultivation from the popular books claiming to teach this topic, you have to ask yourself, which book has ever described even these rudimentary principles? And even though the Tantric schools make such practices sound profound, to be perfectly accurate, we can only say that sexual practice is a technique that enables you to exercise the internal organs of the body!

Unfortunately, most people cannot succeed with sexual cultivation practices, whose highest stages of accomplishment reach only to the top of the Desire Realm, and just into the initial Form Realm heavens. Rather than being able to detach from the body and mind, most people practicing sexual yoga will end up dropping to sexual lust; they will become greedy for even more sexual activities and even prolong their period of practice to a detrimental extreme whereby they lose their chi. Hence, even though Shakyamuni had lots of highly qualified students, he chose never to teach these practices. Nagarjuna, who established the foundations of the esoteric school that evolved into tantra, never taught anything even resembling sexual cultivation either, and the great Tibetan reformer Tsongkhapa of the Yellow Sect forbade these practices entirely. Rather, Tsongkhapa permitted the sexual cultivation practices only during the bardo stage after death. Since the purpose of cultivation practices is to lead people upward rather than downward, and as these practices usually result in practitioners descending rather than ascending, so they are rarely discussed. Nonetheless, people can use these basic principles in their normal sexual relations to help further their cultivation progress, but they must never confuse sexual activities with cultivation.

Some people will even try to steal energy from their partner during sex, as taught in certain schools of yoga and Taoism, and this mentality of vampirism and stealing will definitely lead to rebirths in the lower realms. Many misguided individuals adopt such evil practices without realizing that once out of the body, all substances are poisons like feces, urine, phlegm, and pus. Furthermore, trying to suck energy from a partner can only lead to obstructions in the hind region of the brain and other physical problems; history shows individuals taking this route always die a painful death. Therefore a true cultivator who knows what he or she is doing does not try to take, or even circulate, energy from their partner during sexual intercourse. These are common, but mistaken notions. Sexual practice with a partner of the opposite sex is just a means to ignite bliss within your own body, and there is nothing you try to take, absorb, or circulate from your partner; to think so is to cultivate a mind of thievery and greed, as well as a mistaken emphasis on form once again.

In cultivation matters, one must learn to recognize whether sexual desire arises from the body or from the mind. Typically, the desire for sexual relations is a mental habit which arises in response to bodily conditions. In other words, its roots often come from physiological sensations. Thus when body-generated desire arises, one should refrain from allowing their thoughts to drift into sexual fantasy and must let any discomfort which arises pass like a cloud traversing a mountain top. If you bear this period in emptiness, then the extreme of yin will give birth to yang, and you will easily increase your cultivation achievements. As to psychologically generated sexual desire, it is best when you find yourself in such a condition to stop the flow of such thoughts by turning the mind to other topics. What methods you use to do so constitute your mastery of "skillful means," so almost anything will do if it works for you.

As possible alternatives, one can turn to mantra practice or try to increase the tumo fire when sexual desire arises, for you want the "downward flowing wind" to flow upward in cultivation rather than leak away. Overall, however, there are only two ways to really reduce sexual desire: to eat less (also refraining from stimulating or "heating" foods such as onions, garlic, pepper, spices, and so on) and to use breathing methods when sexual desire is strong, with the goal of transforming the energies and balancing the chi. To decrease sexual desires, it's extremely important to watch the diet and to occupy the mind with other thoughts if mental desires are aroused. The stipulation to watch the diet is why monks and nuns usually eat one meal a day around noontime, and consume just enough to sustain the body. But if you eat too little, that's wrong, too, because you have to be optimally healthy to succeed in spiritual cultivation.

Generally speaking, women have an easier time than men in getting over the hurdle of sexual desires in their cultivation but find it much harder than men to detach from the next higher hurdle of emotional and mental attachments. Men usually fail in cultivation because they cannot surmount the very first hurdle of overcoming sexual desires, but those who do develop the wisdom and willpower to triumph over this obstacle have usually cultivated the necessary skills, in the process, which are needed to surmount the higher difficulties of the path. This is why more men than women usually succeed in cultivation, even though the woman's body is better suited to the process, and yet it's still a fact that few men or women at all succeed in cultivation. But men fail primarily because of the inability to detach from the view of possessing a body and because of sexual desire.

As a caution, it is good to know that when you successfully cultivate the skeleton visualization, the visualization of some deity (as in the Tibetan school stage of the generation yogas), anapana, or other methods, a time will come when your chi will become loose and free, and resultingly, your sexual desires will become exceedingly strong. You may not realize that these states are directly connected, but your full body sexual desire will have arisen because you've progressed in your practice of cultivating the chi and mai. This extreme stage of sexual desire, however, through continued sexual restraint and the process of mentally detaching from the body, can actually be turned around and transformed into the first stage of cultivation bliss. It means that you're on the very border, the very edge of an initial great success, if you can calm yourself and turn this desire "inside out" so that it transforms into bliss. It's like being able to change the spin of atoms from a clockwise to counterclockwise rotation, and so someone with great wisdom can transform desire into bodily bliss.

You're very close to the first bliss of the first dhyana if you don't retrogress at this stage, if you can abandon (ignore) this sexual desire by letting the chi permeate the body evenly, and if you can detach from the body while continuing to cultivate one-pointedness. This is the time at which you really have to cultivate one-pointedness—using it like a match to light the fire of your prenatal chi. At this time, you must also abandon the view of having a body. Your sexual desire may seem extreme because you've cultivated all your body chi and all your cells are being activated, and you might even find it hard to sleep because your chi is starting to transform into shen. As Taoists say, "when the shen is full, you don't think of sleep." During these stages, you have to throw yourself into cultivation even more.

If your cultivation is proper at this uncomfortable stage, you can now ignite your prenatal chi and bring about the true kundalini warmth and its accompanying state of physical bliss. But unfortunately, most people never realize that this is possible when they actually reach this stage because they don't know how to identify it clearly: the physical sexual feelings can be compared to a room full of extremely excited gas molecules bouncing all over, ready to ignite. If you detach from the body at this point, continue to cultivate joy and one-pointedness, and use wisdom to turn this sexual desire inside out then you can triumphantly enter into the first dhyana. Cultivation schools rarely tell you that this is what you have to do with this particular stage of sexual desire, but this is what you must do and so we stress it again and again.

For instance, at this point you continue joyfully visualizing the clear radiance of your white shining skeleton, or a radiant Buddha, heavenly deity, or little tongues of flame (light) at various chakra locations. No matter how you feel, you plunge into one-pointed concentration and simultaneously let go of any feelings of possessing a body with a fixed perimeter (or at a lower stage, you can imagine the body is like an empty sack). You forget about having a body, and cultivate one-pointed concentration, mental joy, and emptiness. Then these physical sexual feelings, which occur because your jing is transforming to chi, can be transformed into a high state of physical bliss, and you can slide into the first dhyana.

Why did visualizing a deity or your internal white skeleton bring you to this state? Because when you visualize the three-dimensional body of a deity, even though it's an external image, you're actually transforming the chi and mai of your own three-dimensional body at the same time! If you cultivate your dazzling white skeleton, this is cultivating an internal image and your internal body at the same time. But as to the external image, the Hindu and Tibetan schools never tell you this, but the more clearly you can visualize an external Buddha or deity, the more you are actually cultivating the three-dimensional phenomenal form of your own inner chi body, so it's actually a means of smoothing and evening out your own inner body of chi and mai. When you've successfully visualized your internal dazzling white skeleton—which is a way to do this directly—or a deity, then you've completed this task and a full-body sexual desire will arise. Why does sexual desire arise? Because you've cultivated your jing to chi, your hormones (the bodhicitta, bindu, or subtle drops of the esoteric schools) are starting to descend, and all your cells have been energized with vital energy.

If you stay celibate and have enough wisdom to be able to transform matters, then you can get over this very first cultivation barrier, so at this stage some people go into retreat to avoid the distractions of the world and make this task easier. Now you know why you can't lose the internal chi you've cultivated at this stage, and why your jing and chi become particularly precious at this point. One of the purposes of celibacy, besides its reduction of worldly distractions, is to retain the most refined portions of jing and chi, which are responsible for the process of transformation. If the most precious and refined materials go missing because of sexual activities that involve leakage, it will take twice as long (or even longer) to accumulate them once again. And if you practice celibacy without transforming your jing to chi or chi to shen, at which point the internal luminosity arrives, then your celibacy will also amount to nothing.

This is a stage when all the mai in your body are opening and the chi is sufficiently free, and one simply needs a spark of some type to arrive at the stage of internal light where you're cultivating the form skandha of the physical nature. So when you reach the point where sexual desire becomes extreme, this is when you should double your efforts at cultivation, and continue with one-pointedness so that the friction of the chi in one area of concentration will ignite into the stage of internal physical luminosity (seeing a light within the body). Don't "leak" at this stage, because if you lose all your good jing and chi at this point, it'll take twice as long to regain this high quality material and enter into the same level of cultivation.

In reading this book you'll find many methods of one-pointedness you can use as a spark, but some high level practitioners will even use the visualized images of Buddha deities in sexual union at certain chakra locations (especially the brow, head, or heart chakras) to ignite the internal fire. However, when they do this they still refrain from dropping into sexual desire themselves, and only use the visualization as you would momentarily use a match to ignite a flame. The bliss factor is already there ready to ignite, so they try to cultivate a momentary extreme of joyfulness as an electric spark to strike the necessary flame, and then merge into the joy, bliss, and emptiness of the first dhyana. So the visualization of Buddhas and consorts in sexual embrace is a momentary illustration of skillful means. After you're done with a raft you don't carry it on your back, and likewise after the match has been struck you don't keep holding on to it, otherwise it'll burn you!

In bhakti yoga, this joyful match comes from the factor of extreme emotional reverence to a deity, and in the skeleton meditation you're

joyfully offering away your body and at the same time you're extremely joyful because you know this is satisfying past debts, like paying back
a loan for good. This has to be a full-body joy so that all your chi can
become smooth and evenly balanced throughout. Of course these are
only means to reach the first dhyana, which Hinduism calls *vitarka
samadhi*, so you have to detach from this coarse stage to progress further from here. As stated, only the particularly skillful and wise can use
the image of joyful sexual joining as the match that ignites their inner
chi circulation into a blazing fullness.

Even fewer can use the actual act of sexual intercourse as a cultivation technique, and we have to remember that this is the basis of sexual tantra. The whole process of turning around sexual desire can only
happen if you've reached the stage where you've cultivated your chi
and mai sufficently. Furthermore, if you have wisdom and kung-fu, the
process of transformation should only require ten or fifteen minutes.
So in the genuine schools of Tantra that no longer exist, a celibate
might use the practice of sexual intercourse just once at the beginning
of the cultivation path (in the "generation stage") or at certain places
in their "completion stage" practices for the final push into samadhi.
The purpose behind the practice would be for entering the Form
Realm samadhis, whereby they would finally be out of the realm of
sexual desire. These are the basic principles behind this sort of practice,
so you shouldn't get confused about the matter.

As previously stated, sexual cultivation is a very difficult path to
practice, and a difficult topic to discuss. You can use these techniques as
a tool for cultivation progress or you can drop into them and descend
into the lower realms. Most people *cannot* use this method of cultivation—even Shakyamuni's students weren't allowed to use it—but we
have to explain it today because the mistaken notions are so prevalent
and people commonly use the outward attractiveness of this path to
cheat others. Like food, sex is either a medicine that can be used skillfully with no unwholesome after effects, or a poison that can kill you.
Thus be extremely careful how you deal with this matter, as *it is the most
common reason that people fail in cultivation and never reach the first dhyana.*

Nonetheless, if you can understand the process as explained, you'll also be able to understand the actualities behind the other processes of the cultivation path, such as visualizing tiny flames in kundalini yoga as a means to ignite an internal luminosity. In cultivation, we often say that you must increase your stores of merit, but most of all your wisdom: you shouldn't go about cheating others, you shouldn't let others cheat you, but most of all you shouldn't cheat yourself. Then it's quite possible that you can scale the ranks of spiritual progress.

One-Pointed Visualizations

 Visualization methods are just another expedient technique we can use to focus the mind and attain mental quiet. By focusing the mind on a simple or complicated mental image, we can arrive at the single-mindedness of samadhi concentration. Due to this state, our chi and mai will transform, and then with continued practice we can eventually enter into an even deeper state of mental calm. The ranks of spiritual attainment common to the cultivation schools of the world all involve this single-mindedness or one-pointed concentration. When miscellaneous thoughts are abandoned and the mind is calmed through concentration, this is the samadhi stage of "stopping."

One means to attain this type of concentration is to internally visualize an image of some simple auspicious object (such as a Buddha or holy letter) which will not create any subconscious problems. When a practitioner can finally visualize this image so clearly and completely that the mind becomes concentrated to a point, they should then switch their focus from the mental image to contemplate emptiness. In other words, the practitioner concentrates until whatever they envision becomes radiantly sharp, or crystal clear (which is the sign of successful concentration), and then they must release this mental fabrication to enjoy the realm of mental quiet we call "emptiness." Within this emptiness, they must look around to realize that this emptiness they experience is still a thought construction. We can say this emptiness "floats" in the formless nature of the mind and when you recognize this formless mind rather than the emptiness or thoughts it gives birth to, this is prajna-wisdom.

Another alternative to the achievement of concentration is to keep reducing the size of your visualization to such a microscopic point that the furthest point of reduction naturally blends into an empty state of void. This takes an extreme amount of concentration and is similar to the idea of continually splitting a particle of dust in half until you arrive at atoms; keep splitting the atom in halves and you eventually arrive at emptiness. Of course, at that point of concentrated visualization a practitioner must really let go and forget everything, even emptiness itself, and this begins the practice of contemplating mind.

In general, one-pointed visualization practice is simply a technique for achieving cessation by tightly tying the sixth consciousness to a visualized mental image. After you attain the requisite concentration, you must abandon your visualization and use insight-contemplation to investigate the fundamental nature of the mind. So as in most of the methods we have examined, the point is to reach some stage of cessation or stopping, in which the mad rushing mind comes to a halt, and then to cultivate a wisdom awareness of this void. This emptiness is also a type of thought phenomenon, so if you can realize that this is also a thought and abandon this idea of emptiness, then you're really making progress in cultivation. This is really "turning within," since the thought of emptiness is still something without. After all, a mind of true purity has no thought of the purity of the mind.

An alternative route, followed in the school of Tibetan Buddhism, is not to visualize a simple object, but to tax the practitioner's concentration with a complicated object so persistently that they finally, under the strain, let go completely to attain emptiness. Thus the Tibetan school asks practitioners to visualize a complicated mandala, with hundreds of layers of detail, while simultaneously reciting mantras, performing mudras, ringing bells, imagining that they're a divine deity, and performing all sorts of other complicated instructions. In this practice, the individual assumes so many burdens upon their concentration that they eventually tire from the effort and relax from the strain by abandoning everything, which results in cessation. This is reaching discriminative emptiness through overloading thoughts, rather than by subtracting thoughts.

A similar example would be the case of imposing so many tasks on a computer that it finally slows to a halt, or loading a bridge with so much weight that it finally breaks. Naturally we're not talking about a mental breakdown, but a pathway for reaching emptiness by demanding that one's normal concentration expands to include limitless detail. Rather than reduce things to the simplicity of a microscopic point of concentration, one expands mental tasks to include the complexity of the infinite.

Many people pursue complicated visualization practices without realizing this key point—that they must construct from nothing, and then abandon, a highly complicated mental fabrication in order to achieve emptiness. Unfortunately, many people believe that the purpose of visualizations is to actually build up one's "imagination muscles" by holding onto a visualization rather than to attain the state free of any images. It's true that you want to arrive at the state of one-pointedness in concentration, which leads to cessation and samadhi, but you want to do this in a certain special way. Even when people perform visualization practice somewhat successfully, they usually attain some stage similar to the samadhi of neither thought nor no-thought, whereas the actual goal of visualization practice is to attain the samadhi of infinite consciousness. But this level of technical detail is something we can't enter into.

In short, *the actual measure of success in visualization practice is whether or not you can attain a state of spiritual samadhi rather than whether you can hold a stable image in the mind, which can just as easily correspond to mun-*

dane mental stabilization. One should attain the view of emptiness by abandoning the visualization and apply introspection (internal watching, or observation turned inward) to see who is doing the seeing. Originally our mind is empty, but in visualization practice we mentally construct an object of focus. The object is not special in itself, but just a provisional means for focusing our attention. It's just a transient phenomenon with no special importance other than providing a focus point (hopefully auspicious) for our attention. After you focus on this provisional construction in order to get rid of excessive mental chatter, you must then abandon your fixation and apply contemplation, which is the silent mental watching and nondiscriminative awareness that gives rise to prajna-wisdom. Visualization practices, like many other cultivation techniques, thus do not depart from the standard principles of cessation and contemplation practice.

You can reduce a visualized image to such a tiny point that only emptiness is left, or you can widen the visualization to such a large extent that the magnitude of the effort virtually overwhelms your mental chatter, producing cessation. This is similar to the method proposed by the Mexican sorcerer Don Juan, who suggested that the practitioner gorge the field of vision with an entire horizon in order to shut off mental chatter. In either case, you are not seeking to produce a state of emptiness characterized by blockage, which can happen here, but rather a state of empty but clear awareness. If the mind isn't empty and *free*, the cultivation practice is incorrect.

Yet another form of one-pointed visualization practice, which is popular in esoteric Buddhism, is to focus one's visualization efforts on a particular Tantric deity. In this practice, you form your deity visualization by moving your awareness from the top downward, and then from the feet upward, flowing through the visualized form so as to cultivate a rough image of the deity and its attributes. If you really practice well, which is usually done in sessions lasting three or more continuous hours, people who pass by your room will often see you in the image of your visualized deity. The Tibetans have many symbolic mandala and visualization ceremonies, but this is the real sort of true visualization practice of esoteric Buddhism, and properly performed it will quickly transform your chi and mai.

At the start of this type of practice, the image you're concentrating upon won't appear clearly but will fade every now and then. When that happens and the image becomes unclear, you must simply return to rejuvenate the visualization and continue meditating. Eventually the radiant presence of the visualization will increase, and you will attain the evenness of mental stability. The esoteric schools never tell you the secret importance of this practice, but its main effect is for cultivating your chi and mai; as the image becomes clear and stable, you're actually cultivating the areas of chi in your own body that match to the parts you are visualizing in your image.

In effect, everything we see is a visualization, everything about us is a mandala, everything will appear like a vivid dream if we can just attain mastery of our chi and mai, and then move onward from there. There's no difference between a visualized mental image or the real world of images about us, so everything we see can be used as mandala practice if we learn detachment and view the world as if it's a dream. In I-Ching studies, we would say everything is a hexagram just hanging there in space ready for our interpretation, and in esotericism we would say everything is a radiant mandala. Every state constitutes a vision of "radiant appearance," and so all phenomena should be viewed as if they are being seen in a vivid, lucid dream. After all, just as in a dream, there's nothing you can grab hold of in the regular world; even though it seems more dense than the dream state, it's just as unreliable. Thus every situation should become a moment of practice; this is how visualization practice enters the everyday world.

Visualizations are "adding cultivation practices" which cause you to add on more and more things until you can naturally let go and rest. They're often suited to people who are naturally busy-minded, tending to think too much. "Subtraction cultivation methods," on the other hand, aim at reducing your mental content until you reach emptiness through convergence of mental emptiness with true emptiness. Such techniques are suited for those who are naturally less prone to incessant mental chatter. On the other hand, those who don't use their thinking processes too much might consider practicing visualization techniques in order to train their mind and help it become more refined. This is how you must consider affairs in cultivation. If you can identify that you have a problem, you take the proper antidote to correct it, especially in regard to meditation techniques. But don't cling to techniques, as that's not the proper way either.

Visualization practices are sometimes hard for people to master if they lose sight of these various principles of practice we've discussed. However, you should try to see if you have any karmic affinity for this type of practice. The point is not whether you like a particular cultivation practice, but whether it is effective for you and produces results. The best cultivation practices for us are typically those we hate to undertake, for this dislike is often indicative of bad karma trying to intercede and prevent us from making spiritual cultivation progress.

18

Bhakti Yoga

 The method of bhakti yoga is often espoused in Hinduism, but it has also been widely championed in Christianity, Judaism, and Islam as well. It is the practice of constant remembrance and fervent devotion to a higher power, such as Jesus, Krishna, or Vishnu, while beseeching that power for the grace to unite with their being. To be really effective, it also contains a large element of visualization practice so that it can lead to positive transformations in your chi and mai, and hence it has similarities to the deity yoga visualization practices of Tibetan Tantra.

In essence, bhakti yoga is to practice a form of fervent worship in order to forget the self (cultivate a degree of selflessness), and to thereby enter into samadhi. It is similar to the generation stage yoga of deity visualization in the Tibetan school, whose purpose is to transform the body's chi and mai—its wind and water elements—before the initiation of kundalini. So in bhakti yoga, thinking of the Lord or some chosen deity *should also involve a measure of visualization practice that becomes a constant habit,* such as keeping their image constantly before you, or reducing a colorful image to a tiny size and locating it in the region of the third eye or heart chakra. That will lead to the necessary one-pointed concentration that is essential to the success of this form of practice, and the placement of the visualized image at various points in the body is important for other reasons previously explained. For instance, the *Shiva Samhita* suggests, "The one who always contemplates on the ajna chakra [the third eye] will destroy all the karmas of his past life without any opposition." This means that if you concentrate on this point, as we have already explained, you can eventually enter samadhi.

You can achieve samadhi through the bhakti yoga method, but you can only achieve a very low level of samadhi, since bhakti yoga depends on the emotions and doesn't take you past the lower stages of one-pointedness. Furthermore, this cultivation technique, because it is emotionally based, primarily deals with our jing and chi. This is what accounts for the state of ecstasy or bliss produced through this cultivation method. If a devoted practitioner wishes to transform this bliss and joy into the actual bliss and joy of the first dhyana, a bhakti practitioner must (like all other practitioners) remain celibate and refrain from losing their jing (seminal essence). The bhakti schools don't tell you this, but it's a cardinal requirement at the early stages of cultivating the chi and mai.

The bhakti method of cultivation often entails the use of prayer, mantra, singing, dancing, rituals, or some other form of remembering a deity's physical actions. Since you really have to be sincere in this cultivation practice, as well as recite mantras (or prayers) and perform certain physical actions, it is a method of cultivating mind, speech, and body together.

The traditional nine types of pure bhakti devotion—listening to stories about the Lord; singing and chanting about the Lord; remembering his qualities, name, and presence; serving Him; offering respectful worship, as in *puja* (ceremonial offering); offering prayers and prostrations; becoming His servant; considering Him as your best friend; and completely surrendering everything (all cares, concerns, and the self) unto Him—can become simply religious exercises rather than a means to spiritual attainment *if* the practitioners don't understand the cultivation principles behind what they're doing. When cultivation practitioners of any school or technique don't understand the principles of their practice, they're just being superstitious rather than following the path of cultivation. In any school of cultivation, this is something to avoid.

Now, bhakti yoga differs from "mindfulness of the Buddha" practice in that Buddha-mindfulness requires that you first know the theory of cultivation. The proper road of Buddha-mindfulness (which also stands for Krishna-mindfulness, Jesus-mindfulness, Vishnu-mindfulness, and so on) is quite refined in that you don't simply bathe yourself in an attitude of nondiscriminatory love for some divine being. Rather, Buddha-mindfulness asks for more from the individual in terms of understanding the theory and practice of cultivation, and in terms of mental practice and the refinement of one's actions. Hence the ultimate stage of achievement is also much higher.

In the technique of Buddha-mindfulness, you might recite the name of a Buddha (or deity), or internally visualize his image (such as the lock of hair between his eyebrows), or contemplate his visage while looking at his picture, or try to match yourself and become one with his mind (which is trying to achieve dhyana directly). Hence you can perform this practice with understanding, and rather than indulging in emotional excess you also remain in peaceful unison and conformity with society at large.

No matter what cultivation school you follow, if you don't possess the correct theory and view you can never reach the highest states of samadhi. Even if you do reach the samadhis corresponding to the lower heavens in the Desire Realm, without the correct view it's quite easy to mistakenly believe they are the very end of the path. After all, you've reached the heavenly realms and so you might mistakenly believe there aren't any realms higher. So possessing the correct theory and view means cultivating prajna-wisdom; without wisdom, the bhakti method in particular can easily turn into the road of religious superstition.

To see the correct results of cultivation practice, we need only take the great Zen masters as our role models, for they could equally serve in the role of politicians, generals, or kings in dealing with all the troublesome affairs of the world. Rather than becoming simpleminded to the world, or people who cling to the emotions, they became more effective as a result of their practice and unafraid to do what had to be done in order to set things right, teach others, and lead society. They were able to bring peace to society and had the wisdom to function in all sorts of situations.

19

Prayer

The general principle behind the approach to samadhi through prayer is that you become very sincere in your intent and focus your mental concentration through praying. To attain samadhi through prayer, you must get rid of all your random thoughts and have only the one objective of prayer in your mind.

When you become really focused and sincere, and reach the state where you can forget about yourself, Westerners say that you become "absorbed in God." Meister Eckhart tried to describe this state by saying, "God rests in those who rest in him," but Easterners prefer to simply call this state "the union of samadhi with prajna." Needless to say, samadhi is thus a possible outcome from the one-pointed focusing of prayer. Because samadhi can produce wondrous effects, sincere prayer to the extent of dhyana can result in wondrous effects as well.

As a cultivation technique, prayer can enable you to attain the achievements of the heavenly beings in the lower Desire Realm heavens, but it's hard to make higher progress unless you know the correct principles of cultivation and use more advanced cultivation practices. As a comparison with other cultivation techniques, it's typical to say

WILLIAM BODRI & LEE SHU-MEI

"amen" after praying, which is actually equivalent to the mantra OHM AH HUNG that many schools use for trying to open the central channel. Prayer also has a visualization aspect to it, even if subconscious, but this aspect is different from the visualizations espoused in esoteric Buddhism, Taoism, or Hindu bhakti.

In Christian prayer, there is no cross-legged sitting as in the Eastern cultivation schools, but there is still a type of formal sitting which we also find in Confucianism. While sitting in prayer, you concentrate on attaining union with God and regard even your own thoughts and emotions as a form of pollution standing in the way of this union. Thus to obtain this perfect union, you have to give everything away. If you can abandon your own mental thoughts and desires through cultivating an open honesty and sincerity to emptiness (which some people also call the "fullness of God") then you can reach a state where you totally forget about the self and enter samadhi. It's a state similar to that mentioned by Chuang Tzu, when he said, "Man and Heaven merge into one." So all the schools agree on this practice. Christianity also has the method of "vocal prayer," which is equivalent to mantra reciting, and many mystics spoke of the practice of "silent prayer," which is emptiness meditation itself.

In Christianity, there is also a method of repentance called confession. By performing confession, which is openly admitting to your bad thoughts and behavior, you hope to get rid of your guilt and the propensity to fall into bad ways again. This has some similarities to prayer, but the focus is on clearing away bad habits and karma. If this practice actually changes your habits, fine, but most people continue to perform the same evil acts rather than actually repenting—which means to refrain from performing any evil in the future. Furthermore, when we compare the act of confession to the practice of prayer, we find that it's not as powerful a cultivation technique because it only produces a short moment of mental clarity and peacefulness.

Most people pray thinking of the things of this world—money, lovers, fame, and fortune—whereas the best thing to pray for, in order to reach samadhi, is union with God. To attain some stage of attainment from this practice, it's helpful to pray for this goal while remembering the New Testament statement that God is light. Another possibility is to pray for union with God while remembering that God is everywhere, which can lead to the attainment of the infinite consciousness samadhi. But in all these cases, the principle behind prayer is still the principle of concentrated focus (mental absorption), sincerity (devoted effort), and emptiness (no-thought, no-ego, or selflessness). These principles for attaining the "blessed state" of samadhi are worded in different ways in different religions, but they remain invariable.

As to the Eastern esoteric schools, they also encourage people to pray for blessings, but the objectives here entail asking the Buddhas for help in attaining Tao. Hence a cultivation aspirant will pray to the Buddhas for help in finding an enlightened master who can teach them. They'll pray for help in making their body as soft and healthy as a baby's, so that the physical nature is sufficiently comfortable that it can be ignored, and present but a little obstacle to cultivation. They'll pray for help in opening their mai, whereby their body will become soft and smooth. They'll pray to reach the point where their chi circulates smoothly without obstruction, so that they can become calm and abandon any violent tendencies. They'll pray for help in mastering the tan-tien tumo fire so that they can reach the stage of calmness, bliss, and warmth (kundalini). Basically, they'll pray that the Buddhas help them transform the four elements of their body. This is essentially praying for the help to transform your physical nature as an adjunct to transforming your mental states and behavior.

In the school of esoteric Buddhism, people also ask the Buddhas for assistance in achieving the union of bliss and emptiness where there aren't any random thoughts anymore, and practitioners ask the Buddhas to help them change all their bad habits so that their mind can enter into the dharma fully. This is the idea of wanting to fully integrate with the dharma of Tao so that you aren't greedy for joy or bliss, and can integrate everything you've learned and accomplished in meditation with your outward behavior.

People also pray to the Buddhas to help them forget about self-love so that they can fully help others and quickly attain the seeds of wisdom. In general, with prayers and offerings, people make supplications to the Buddhas asking that their chi energies become joyous, and their energy channels subtle, so that they can attain the special experiences of bliss and emptiness that mark the various samadhi on the road to the Tao. If you sincerely pray to the Buddhas and ask for help in obtaining these objectives, it's possible to gain the assistance you need to succeed in cultivation. This external assistance is what Christianity refers to as "grace," but there is no such thing as grace by luck or from simply asking. In order to receive a helpful response, you must have cultivated the necessary merit. In other words, there is no grace without merit, just as there is no progress in cultivation without merit and hard work, as well.

20

Dream Yoga

Our ordinary mind of mental discrimination, which is technically termed the sixth consciousness, becomes easily entangled in everyday thoughts and attached to the mental realms that arise within. We already obscure our pristine fundamental nature with endless mental chatter, and being attached to this mental verbiage only further complicates the pollution. When sleeping, however, the incessant workings of the sixth consciousness are much lessened. Therefore, one particular cultivation technique is to make use of one's dream time for continued cultivation by concentrating on the region of the throat chakra before sleeping, as it is responsible for helping to produce the dream state.

A successful practitioner of this technique will eventually be able to realize they are dreaming during a dream, which is attaining the state of conscious presence during dreams. That's the first objective of this practice: to become aware while in the dream state that you're dreaming, and to be able to maintain this conscious awareness. Then you will be able to progress on to the next level of practice, which is to realize that though objects appear in the dream, they are empty of the nature of their appearance (a dream fire will not actually burn you, so it is actually empty of the true characteristics of fire). In other words, you try to experientially realize, on a very deep level, the empty appearance nature of phenomena. The third stage of practice is to bring mastery of this view into the everyday world, for it is a very profound state of samadhi.

Our world of wakeful appearances also appears in the nature of a dream, but people don't realize this fact and go about mentally clinging and attaching to things, trying to make them real when they won't stay. So we use the dream yoga techniques to try to bring about this realization, and carry this realization into the state of wakefulness. Like a dream, the conventional world is simply an insubstantial display with nothing you can grasp onto. It might appear to be fixed and solid, and function in a logical fashion according to the interdependent rules of cause and effect, but it has no fundamental reality to it even in its tiniest moment. It's simply one, shimmering, immaculate display absent of any true substance.

We can say that this worldly appearance corresponds to both emptiness and existence, and yet it corresponds to neither. Living beings and phenomena are all in a state of continuous transformation without a fixed self-nature, and though they're empty of any reality, they all function validly according to the laws of interdependent arising. Thus the world of dreams and the world of conventional wakefulness can both be described as real phenomena with a sort of functional validity to them, or false experiential realms as well. The big question is, what is it that gives rise to the awareness of these states? If we're not real and have no inherent identity, what is it that knows? Aha, that's the question you set out to answer. On the cultivation path, an awakening means to discover the nature of this true self.

Now during dream yoga practice, the dream yoga practitioner looks within to see what is doing the dreaming; they use this opportunity of conscious presence to cultivate wisdom and contemplate the true mind. In time, as a practitioner becomes more familiar with and more proficient at attaining the conscious dream state, they will eventually be able to cultivate prajna-wisdom and bring their awareness of the dream state into their normal waking life. In other words, an advanced practitioner who is acquainted with the dream state will master the detachment of emptiness and will be able to view everything in ordinary life as if it were a dream, and *this view is the correct view*. Everything will appear to flow like a moving picture, and will lack inherent identity even in the tiniest subdivisions of time. Thus there's no reason to get attached or to cling to phenomena because they're not real and won't stay. Everything that's born will flourish and then pass away according to the laws of cause and effect. In fact, it has to be this way. All appearances are empty of a true self-nature, yet manifest as illusions.

To recognize this at a deep experiential level is to see the true illusory nature of phenomena, and this view sometimes occurs accidentally when your energy channels become filled with chi to produce a sort of thick, "flowing" experiential realm of minor blissfulness. In the dream yoga practices you cultivate this state purposefully, rather than accidentally, and thus you can actively work with the state to discover the illusory nature of both dreams and wakefulness. Thus, it's a means that helps you learn how to walk the middle path that doesn't abide in the dualistic realms of emptiness or existence, for Tao doesn't fall into either of these extremes. These extremes are just projections of the fundamental mind, our original true nature.

Tao doesn't fall into the realm of existence or the stillness state of samadhi we call emptiness. Rather, it is beyond both these states of duality; it's the formless primordial knowingness that knows the state of samadhi but doesn't rest in it (the mental state rests in the samadhi of stillness) because this stillness is also a form of mental construction. It's the empty transcendental wisdom that can recognize when the body is in a state of blissful transformation but it doesn't abide in this realm either. Where is the true mind? It's formless and therefore it's everywhere, and you cultivate the samadhi and other attainments so that you can discover the true meaning behind these words. That's when you "see the Tao," "see the Truth," "recognize the clear light," or "see the path," and that's when you really begin genuine cultivation practice. All the spiritual exercises in existence are just a precursor to this awakening. After this awakening, then and only then can we properly say you are cultivating the Tao.

Now the dream state is also a state that helps us realize and transform our undesirable behaviors, because that's what we're responsible for within this shimmering realm of unreality. We may lack fixed reality, and yet living beings collect karma, experience the results and take rebirth according to their karma: so behavior is what we must master in this realm. Thus in everyday life, although we might normally be too serious or become easily angered when certain situations arise, we might not even realize these bad traits. During even an ordinary dream, however, an indication of these hidden personality traits will come out, giving us a chance to correct them, so that's another way that the cultivation practitioner makes use of this technique.

The goal of dream yoga is not really to train you to control your dreams—though that's one of its practices—but to develop the perception that everything is dreamlike in our ordinary view of reality, and to help us spot and then transform our behavioral faults. If we can change our behavior, then we won't get angry as easily, we won't get flustered when difficult situations arise, we won't be greedy or lustful, we won't remain as attached to our bodies or thoughts, and we can master the great virtue of fearlessness. In this way we can accumulate great merit and make even greater progress in our cultivation.

The conventional world is like a large dream play, but we can become great actors in this dream rather than small players when we master our actions and behavior. We can become really effective, and so relaxed that the body's vital energy channels and chi become full. As a result, we'll easily be able to reach a samadhi of mental detachment that we can carry around in wakefulness.

Thus, unlike many primitive tribes that also practice some form of dream cultivation, the purpose of dream yoga is not specifically to control the contents of one's dreams. The purpose is to become aware during one's dreams, to become aware of the illusory nature of dreams, and to introspect so as to investigate who is the ultimate dreamer. Becoming aware of the transitional phase between sleeping and waking, when the clear light of sleep arises, also constitutes a related form of cultivation practice. But when one can always see the world as dreamlike, this is the major stage of accomplishment. As the *Diamond Sutra* says,

All phenomena are like
A dream, an illusion, a bubble, and a shadow
Like a dew drop and flash of lightening.
Thus should you view them.

Now as a warning, one must never, upon reaching the state where the world appears dreamlike, become attached to the physical sensations that accompany this particular experiential realm, since the "thick," flowing characteristics of this blissful samadhi can be quite seductive. One must detach from all sensations while the mind rests in the clear, open, formless clarity of empty presence. The important point is to realize that *phenomena have a nature which is utterly different from their presence,* and thus to mentally detach from this realm of nonreality.

All phenomena are empty by nature, for if you slice their existence down to even the tiniest moment of time, you won't find a single item that is fixed and not being transformed. There's no fixed reality, there's no ultimate substance other than voidness, the absence of marks and stains. That's true formlessness because what's real has no shape. As to the phenomenal world, however, nothing ever stays, and so everything is always moving or transforming. Nothing remains fixed, so there is nothing you can point to as being real. There's only an ever-moving display that we call "appearance," but it doesn't have any true substance! That's the nature of of the universe about us. Hence, extending this concept further, there's not a single particle within living beings that we can call a final self. We're selfless. There's no final reliable thing that we can call a personal ego. Thus, all the actions we perform during our waking hours can be considered a type of dream, but unfortunately people don't know how to realize this true nature of phenomena.

So how do you go about cultivating the practice of dream yoga? One way is to cultivate samadhi during the waking state and then as you go to sleep you place the mind into the state of samadhi and continue your samadhi awareness into and during sleep. Another means is to master bringing the vital energies into the central channel during the waking state, as is done with kundalini yoga. Then at the time of sleep, you cultivate awareness of the realms of emptiness that occur during the stages of sleep; if you're successful at this, when dreams appear you will naturally recognize them as such.

Another means is to cultivate a strong resolution during the waking state to remain conscious during the dream state, but to succeed in this practice you must also meditate on the chakras of the body (especially the throat chakra) before going to sleep. When you meditate on your throat chakra before going to sleep, your dreams will tend to be more vivid and last longer. Once you're in the dream state and can maintain your conscious presence, then you engage in whatever spiritual practices are deemed important.

Today it's quite popular to study the dream state or to analyze dreams as a symbolic projection of reality. A real cultivator uses the indications of their dreams to realize their bad habits and thus effect changes in their behavior, such as overcoming fear. Changing one's bad habits is a pathway to Tao in itself, and hence dreams can be a useful indication on the path.

21

Mindfulness of Peace
and Mindfulness of Death

 In Buddhism, there are ten great roads of cultivation practice, the last of which is mindfulness of death—to drop everything, body and mind, as if one were no longer alive. However, the Zen masters say this should be the foremost practice of the ten. Swami Vivekananda suggested, "Let us make our bodies dead and cease to identify with them."[1] Meister Eckhart, the famous German mystic, said, "One must be dead to see God,"[2] and in the Western alchemical tradition, you must die to be reborn.

The reason most people can't get to samadhi is because they're always playing with their physical sensations; hence this practice technique is a way to bypass this problem. After all, if you imagine you're dead then you can freely ignore physical sensations and liberate yourself from the view of the body. Through this type of practice, you can then conquer your habit of grasping the physical nature. The body doesn't bother you and experiential realms don't bother you either. If

---

[1] *The Complete Works of Swami Vivekananda*, vol. III (Mayavati, Almora, Himalayas: Advaita Ashrama, 1922), p. 87.
[2] See *Meister Eckhart*, by Franz Pfeiffer, translated from the German published in Leipzig in 1857 by C. de B. Evans (London: John M. Watkins, 1924), p. 82.

WILLIAM BODRI & LEE SHU-MEI

you consider yourself as already dead, everything becomes indifferent
to you and you can remain at peace. Then you can enter into a profound samadhi, especially when you rest in the formlessness without
thoughts and abandon the view of possessing any body at all.

You can't rely on any of your sensations during cultivation
because they're inconstant and always changing; the body belongs to
the phenomenal realm of birth and death which is always in a process
of transformation, so the inconstant nature of sensations makes them
unreliable companions and unreliable focal points of the path. How
can you rely on the unreal to reach the real? Nevertheless, people
always make this mistake in concentration practice and spend useless
years focusing on the body and its physical sensations: hence we have
the method of death mindfulness where you throw everything away
to attain peace. So what if thoughts come and go, or sensations arise
and depart? Just ignore them, and be at peace!

If you practice imagining you are dead so as to be able to detach
from the body and mind, you'll be able to sufficiently relax and enter
samadhi. Perfect relaxation, or mindfulness of peace, is thus a related
meditation technique because, if you can really let go and abandon all
your concerns, you can naturally enter into a samadhi of deep calm. In
technical terms we would describe this as "contemplating the peaceful
nature of nirvana," and the nature of this contemplation includes resting both body and mind. In terms of the mental practice involved in
resting, you don't employ any mental energy in either rejecting or
accepting thought phenomena. You simply operate in open awareness
and watch them as they appear or disappear without becoming entangled or involved. Then the peace you desire will come about naturally. This is why the Zen school favors this practice.

Mindfulness of peace and mindfulness of death are basic techniques in cultivation. As for the mindfulness of death, we must remember that the high will turn into the low, things that accumulate will
eventually disperse, people who come together will eventually depart,
and life will be followed by death. Everything, every realm, is impermanent, and life is just another of the realms constantly undergoing

this never-ending, inconceivable process of transformation. Therefore, death isn't any process that should frighten us, for it's just the natural way: if there's a life there will be a death, and where there's a death there will be a new life. The state of living is a bardo period, the state immediately after death is a bardo period, the realm of rebirth is a bardo transitional period as well. They're all periods of transient intermission which go on and on and on. If none of them are final and this process goes on and on, which life is the real one? Which state has any inherent nature to it?

Life is forever, that's just how it is, and death is simply the transition phase between lives, a momentary period of transition. According to Taoism, life and death are like morning and night. Lao Tzu also suggested, if we can really forget the body (as in death), we can finally make great progress in our cultivation. It's actually the view of possessing a body that holds us back from this goal and prevents great cultivation achievement. So if you can go about your daily activities without giving energy to the idea of possessing any body of form, then you'll really master detachment and clinging, become free of the pulls of the senses and sexual desire, you'll eventually be relieved of any mental burdens or concerns and ultimately enter into samadhi. Then your cultivation practice will become exceptionally strong.

From an altogether different angle, we must remember that death can strike at any moment without warning or preparation. Everything is impermanent, so every phenomenon is engaged in the process of passing through the stages of birth, growth, maturation, and decay. It's as if every moment shouts "change, change, change; loss, loss, loss; death, death, death." But you have to consider that while the previous moment is dead, the future moment isn't here—wherever you go in every direction, there is only the present mind. That's what you cultivate, and when you truly cultivate, you find out that this present moment, this present mind is always empty. This tells us that cultivation is to awaken to the clear radiance of the present, and to detach from holding onto the past.

If you are a cultivator, you already know that you must learn detachment, learn to live in present time, and live a life that matters.

You mustn't waste any opportunities to do good things, accumulate merit, take responsibility for your actions, finish what has to be done, and cultivate to some stage of definite spiritual attainment, otherwise life isn't worthwhile. Cultivation assumes even greater importance when you have the opportunity of coming in contact with cultivation teachings, since the necessity of cultivation is always present, but you might not have this opportunity of contact in the future.

If you always remember that you can die at any moment, this can help you find your life's priorities and transform your living moments into a life that matters. The constant remembrance of death can act as a spur to your cultivation efforts and give power to your deeds, as seen in the example of the Japanese samurai. Hence mindfulness of death helps your cultivation practice become really powerful and pure. It helps you to start cultivation practice, to strive hard during your practice and put extra effort into your spiritual sadhana, and helps your practice reach a successful conclusion. If you work hard at your spiritual development, at the hour of death you can go with satisfaction because you'll know you have spent your life meaningfully. That's all you can ask for—a meaningful life.

Now, most people who practice mindfulness of death or peaceful resting lie on their backs or on their right side during practice, as this removes any physical strain on the heart and internal organs. The bardo practices of the Tibetan school are to be considered a different set of cultivation exercises from those that involve death-mindfulness or relaxation practice, so they shouldn't be confused with this technique. The bardo practices focus on realizing the clear light of death and they involve the phenomenal stages that occur when chi enters the sushumna central channel. This is quite a different practice than detaching from sensations and mental concerns as found in death and relaxation mindfulness. In these practices, you learn to detach from the view of having a body or mind, and thus you learn how to access an emptiness that leads to samadhi.

22

Meditating on the Water, Fire, Earth, Wind, and Space Elements

 In cultivation theory, the "five elements," or earth, wind, water, fire, and space essences, are responsible for building the physical, material world of phenomena. The most basic idea in cultivation, which people typically have a hard time expressing, is that the ordinary mind and the world of phenomena both come from the same source, and that neither will ever be destroyed. Consciousness will never be destroyed, and the essence of the material world will never be annihilated either. It will simply continue to be transformed.

On the one hand, we say that all beings and Buddha are of one body with empty true mind and that within this stainless fundamental nature there is no such thing as birth and death, or change and variation. On the other hand, we perceive the phenomenal world of transient events undergoing ceaseless transformation, forever subject to impermanence because of endless change. For not a single moment is anything still. Hence the world of mundane existence is false. It's empty of true self and thus existence because there's nothing within it that's fixed and unchanging.

The notion of cyclical existence just points to this phenomenal realm of ceaseless birth and death—the dreamlike world of continuing appearances without any true substance—but sentient beings become confused by this process and attach to this phenomenal side of fluctuation, thinking that it is what's real. They mistakenly think that the life we ride through these experiences is our true spiritual life. However, whether you are male or female, human or animal, or whether you're talking of the past, present, or future lives, these are all sibling components of the phenomenal realm undergoing the ceaseless phases of never-ending transformation. If you can find that original thing that doesn't change, however, but which allows everything material to change, then we say you achieve Tao. We also say Tao is empty or formless, since otherwise it would offer resistance to the phenomena that are always changing. Being formless and empty it lacks any phenomenal characteristics, so we also say it's stainless and "signless without marks."

Now, the highest secret in cultivation is that mind and body are really one: our original nature and this phenomenal aspect of false appearances really belong to one single whole, a one-without-a-second. The various phenomena we experience each have different functions and names, but they're actually one with our original mind, and thus equal to one another. Since the four great elements of the material world—earth, wind, water, and fire—are one with the fundamental nature, they actually have the same properties of true mind; they're neither born nor destroyed, neither pure nor impure, and neither increasing nor decreasing. Even using the highest concepts of cultivation science, this is very difficult to explain.

Modern physics is gradually awakening to this, however, for it has finally discovered that the energy of the shimmering cosmos is always conserved and never destroyed. It simply undergoes a process of ceaseless transformation, and thus it never increases or decreases, is neither pure nor impure, and has no beginning or end. After you smoke a cigarette and it becomes ashes, its material aspect is extinguished, but the original energy of the whole cigarette is never destroyed. So the material aspect of the fire, water, earth, and wind elements may change but their energy aspect is always conserved. What supports all these changes never dies, and is always there too. That's the thing we're looking for in cultivation—that one thing behind all these phenomenal realms.

The *Shurangama Sutra* and *Complete Enlightenment Sutra* say that these four elements have distinct properties, meaning that they each have their own independent domain that Buddha referred to by saying, "The four elements are distinct." However, this is just a reference to the phenomenal, material aspect of things. What actually enables the four elements to transform is emptiness; thus you can say that emptiness is the purity aspect, whereas material form is the impurity aspect of the fundamental nature. Then again, you can also say that forms and phenomena are perfectly clean and pure as well. Neither clean nor unclean, pure nor impure, neither increasing nor decreasing, neither real nor unreal—these are all possible explanations you could employ. But whether you cultivate form or the no-form aspect of emptiness, when you come to the ultimate final end there is only one Tao.

THE WATER ELEMENT

One way to cultivate toward Tao is to achieve the water visualization samadhi—a contemplation of the water element—and then to proceed to higher samadhi from there. In ancient times, people liked to cultivate by lakes, so they would live by the water and watch it. Even Confucius knew how to watch the water, for he said life is like a ceaseless flowing stream. Lao Tzu also taught people the philosophy of water, for he said that water nurtures the myriad things, is naturally pliant, and always flows to lower places where it collects, like the sea that holds everything. Therefore he taught people to imitate the nature of water, to be soft and yielding. Though soft, water is also the strongest element in the world because through gentleness it can wear away mountains. Softness, therefore, is stronger than iron or steel, so Lao Tzu taught us to influence other people through pliancy rather than through force. But this is an explanation of Mahayana water cultivation instead of the Hinayana water cultivation used for entering samadhi.

As to the Hinayana cultivation method, Lao Tzu also commented that people are reflected in still water rather than in flowing water. If you therefore reach a state of mental stillness without random thoughts, it's only then that you can see yourself clearly. Confucius also said that compassionate people have minds that are peaceful and grand as a mountain (the earth element), whereas wise people have minds as clear and still as water. Thus, not everyone is suited for the water visualization; those who can succeed at this method usually have a calm, still character as indicated by Confucius.

Now, to practice the water visualization, you must sit beside a clear body of clean water. Your eyelids should drop like curtains, but the eyes should also be able to see the nose naturally, without force, through the remaining slit. Old cultivation texts also say that "your nose should observe your heart," which means that you should be sitting in a straight line with your spine erect. After you assume this position, you start looking at the water without too much intent (no force) and you gradually become absorbed in the observation of the water (not the fish, rocks, or other objects inside).

Eventually your mind will become peaceful and quiet as you sit there visualizing calm and serene water. Progressing yet further, you'll reach a stage where you can forget about your body and mind so as to become unified with the water. When your mind becomes peaceful and clear and you can forget the mind, your body, your thoughts, the earth and sky, you'll be able to merge with the essence of the water to become one. That's the water visualization samadhi. Eventually you won't need to sit next to water to do this contemplation practice.

If you achieve this particular samadhi, to others it may seem as if your body disappears and transforms into water. Or, your body may become a bit swollen, which you can adjust through employing the skeleton visualization technique, or by imagining that water coming from the top of your head pours out and washes away all your internal obstructions and bad karma. These physical transformations are possible because the mind can indeed transform the material realm. But when the body appears as if it's transformed into water, this is not the highest stage of the water samadhi; it's only the stage of the "visualization achievement."

To go past this stage and attain Tao you must come back to focusing on the mind. Once you achieve the water visualization attainment, you must realize that everything is achieved through the mind, and that the mind and the body are one. Thus you must experientially prove through further meditation that the fundamental nature of water is, like anything else, empty. In other words, after achieving the water visualization attainment, you must turn to the wisdom cultivation of prajna. Then you can realize the emptiness nature of water, and that there is actually neither self nor water. This happens when you access your prajna-wisdom to attain the middle view in cultivation. The middle view is the correct view, of not falling into either the extreme of existence (mental busyness) or of nonexistence (the peaceful stillness, or emptiness we call samadhi). You even let go of samadhi so that there's no realm in which the mind dwells. This is called the "mind which doesn't abide."

All water is generated from the self-nature and therefore the fundamental nature of the water element is empty. When you reach the state of emptiness you've found the real fundamental nature of water. Our fundamental nature covers the entire dharma world, so a sage with high enough attainment can make water appear anywhere at will, or can easily change water into fire, wind, or earth, and all sorts of other transformations. But the extent to which you can understand and achieve this depends upon the degree of your cultivation—your karma, kung-fu, and your prajna-wisdom. We can say that water is a phenomenon while emptiness is its opposite, but whether we're speaking of existence or emptiness, Tao is all pervasive. All phenomena are but the true mind of Tao, and since mind and body (form) are linked, the mind can even affect matter. But this accomplishment is truly realized only at the higher stages of cultivation attainment.

THE FIRE ELEMENT

The fire visualization samadhi is attained via the same principles as the water visualization samadhi but is unique in that it is somewhat related to the kundalini phenomena. In the *Shurangama Sutra*, Buddha's student Ucchusma had very strong sexual desires that he realized were like a fire blazing in the mind. Like anger, if you can't control this fire it will eventually destroy you, just as the universe will eventually be destroyed by a great cosmic conflagration (fire catastrophe). Therefore, Ucchusma decided to cultivate the fire visualization technique, in conjunction with the skeleton method, to bring the fire element under control.

To cultivate the fire element visualization, you must first be able to imagine and hold in your mind an image of the fiery energy of the sun. You also need to bring into this visualization a remembrance of the light and heat given off by an ordinary fire. Anyone who has observed a burning candle flame can recognize that the hottest part of any fire belongs to its blue and white flames rather than to the yellow or red flames. The same holds true for stars, where the hottest stars are bluish-white and the older, cooler stars have turned yellow and red. This is useful to remember when we're doing the fire visualization and has implications for why we sometimes visualize the sushumna central channel as being blue.

Now some beginners for this practice start by visualizing a small flame or fire in the region of their tan-tien that gradually, in their imagination, grows bigger and bigger until the entire body burns like it's being cremated. As in kundalini cultivation, they can also imagine small tongues of flame at each of the major chakra locations and focus on these white-hot flames. Just as water can wash away impurities, in the fire visualization you imagine that all your internal obstructions and body impurities are burned away by a blazing fire. If you wish, you can also choose to visualize that everything is burned away until even the atoms are destroyed and only emptiness is left. Or, you can adopt an esoteric Buddhist technique and imagine that your body conjoins with the image of the sun, which radiates an irrepressible shining light that purifies your body and mind. The Tao school talks of transforming jing into chi and chi into shen, but here you imagine you are transforming your entire body into the brightly shining silvery light of a large round sun. This is a tremendous visualization for purifying the physical nature and entering samadhi.

Some individuals try to cultivate the fire element by attempting to absorb the light of the sun. In fact, there are a large number of such practices found in Taoism, yoga, and orthodox Hinduism. In Buddhism, the most popular techinique is imagining that you are sitting in the center of the sun, becoming unified with its being. You imagine your body and mind melt and merge with the sun, while remembering Buddha's saying that "The true nature of fire is emptiness. Because our fundamental nature is empty it can give birth to fire. Originally our fundamental nature is clear, calm, and peaceful, extending across the entire universe. The extent to which you can understand this depends upon your wisdom, practice and experience."

If you can attain the fire visualization samadhi, you can attain the ability to burn things at a thought or transform your body into a pillar of fire, as the Tibetan master Gampopa often demonstrated. However, if someone looks at you quite carefully during such a samadhi, they will still see the shadow of a person sitting there in the flames.

All of the four elements have a purity and impurity aspect; because of its purifying aspect, fire can thus be used to clean us, and each of the other elements can be used to purify the body as well. Thus each of the different elements can become a doorway to a stage of peacefulness and calm. The four elements all have an aspect of dirtiness as well as cleanliness which we can make use of to enter samadhi. If you can combine the fire visualization results with prajna, therefore, then you can achieve the real purity or cleanliness of emptiness.

THE EARTH ELEMENT

Lao Tzu said that "Man should harmonize with the Earth, Earth harmonizes with Heaven, Heaven harmonizes with Tao, and the Tao harmonizes with what is natural." Tao doesn't follow anything, for that's just its nature. "Nature" or "natural" means it's supposed to do this, that's why it's self-so. We have to become the same way in cultivation, and accord with our true nature.

All living beings survive and depend on this Earth, and when they die they return to it. The Earth gives us life, food, and happiness, and the way we show it our gratitude is to return to it our pollution. Human beings take away everything good, but return nothing good to Mother Earth at all. And yet Earth continues to give all things to every being without complaining. She just continues her compassionate giving and never stops protecting and providing life. If we can transform our mind so that it's as grand as the Earth, then this is the Mahayana way of earth cultivation.

The Hinayana method of earth cultivation is a different method entirely, and not many people have been able to successfully cultivate this practice in the past. To practice the earth visualization, you go into the mountains, or find a suitable cave or wall to face because you have to sit facing some solid earthen obstacle. When you find a suitable location, you assume the standard meditation posture, relax your body and mind, and then begin.

First, you let your eyes become still as you look at the earthen barrier, next you relax the eyes so they naturally recede a bit, then you visualize the earth element in front of you as becoming empty. That's all there is to the method. When you can finally achieve this to what we call a stage of attainment, which is accompanied by various "marks" or signs, you extend this emptiness to your body, and then to the entire world, and then the entire cosmos. If you can do it successfully then you'll obtain the "foot superpower," whereby you can walk through walls or mountains or be able to travel unimpeded underneath the ground; nothing will stop you. The Taoist equivalent of this is when the body becomes full of shen, and your body and shen become integrated into one.

The Bodhisattva Dharanimdhara attained the earth element samadhi through a slightly different method from the one described. He imagined that his body was made of atoms that he knew did not connect with one another. Since the air around him was also made of atoms that did not connect with one another, where did his body stop and his not-body begin? The elements of his body pervaded the universe—everything was his body—and contemplating this he was able to achieve samadhi. This is realizing the sameness of the earth element pervading existence, and one can use the same method for the water, fire, and wind elements as well.

THE WIND ELEMENT

Anapana or pranayama practices are the cultivation practices for the wind element. People think wind just refers to the nostril breathing of the lungs, but there are actually nine holes in the body (seven in the head and two below), and all of them are constantly breathing. Even the pores of our cells are breathing but human beings are usually only aware of their coarse nostril respiration. For most people, thoughts and breathing are separate, but in cultivating the wind element you try to reach the stage in which they combine into one. This is a cultivation method that Buddha taught to his son, Rahula, who succeeded using this technique.

As mentioned in the section on watching the breath, when your mind calms down both the mind that knows, and the object of your knowing become clear. Thus, to start cultivating the wind element, you should start observing your breath at every moment. If your breathing calms down to the point of cessation through this technique, and your mind becomes clear, then this is more powerful than thousands of other cultivation methods combined. But you must first start this process by observing the inhalation and exhalation of your breath, and particularly the point of cessation between them.

All the esoteric Buddhist methods rely on the cultivation of the wind element. The fire visualization, for instance, should be matched with the cultivation of the breath; when the wind element (breath) arises during the fire visualization, you imagine the fire getting bigger and increasing in size. In esoteric Buddhism, yoga, and kundalini cultivation, none of the teachings deviate from the practice of cultivating the wind element, which is the easiest element of the body to transform. Even mantra practice is often matched to the rhythm of the breath so that you can more easily enter samadhi; on exhalations the mantra stops so that the mind remains quiet.

The basic method of cultivating the wind element is to combine your mind with your breath during normal respiration. You first watch your inhalations and exhalations until your mind calms down. Or, you can count your breaths from one to ten, with the numbers corresponding to the out-breaths, until your breath calms down; the point is to practice not counting, but calming! The stage you eventually reach shouldn't be one of drowsiness or torpor, since if your mind is drowsy and unclear then you can't watch your mind and breath. Samadhi isn't a state of excitedness and it isn't a state of sleepiness, fogginess, or the unclarity we call torpor. True samadhi is always peaceful, clear, and calm.

The inherent idea behind this method is to focus on your breathing so that random thoughts will gradually decrease. In this way, focusing on the breathing is like using a rope to bind a wild monkey, preventing it from running around so that it doesn't get into trouble. After you do this roping, then you won't have many random thoughts anymore. That's the basics of this method; the other important points on anapana can be found in earlier sections.

A point to note is that the most difficult type of breathing to stop is brain breathing. When you reach the state of hsi, where you stop your outward breathing, you can start to detect the "breathing of the brain." When that finally disappears, your body becomes empty. At that time, however, there is still the "breathing of consciousness," for there are still thoughts coming and going by themselves—there is still the birth and death of thoughts. If you can stop this "breathing of the mind" by reaching the state where thoughts stop arising, then you'll be able to use the wind element to transform the material nature of the body. This is also somewhat related to the attainment of the Reward Body (*sambhogakaya*) in Buddhism.

THE SPACE ELEMENT

As to the practice of space cultivation, in Tibetan Buddhism there is a space visualization technique that even has its own particular mantra. In this cultivation practice, you use your mind (consciousness), or prajna-wisdom, to observe space. "Observing space" means cutting off thoughts since between each thought there is an empty space of silence. This gap is a lower Hinayana emptiness that has form, so we call it space, but to realize this phenomenon is still a commendable achievement since it marks the beginning of the higher Mahayana cultivation. However, you must certainly realize that it isn't yet the fundamental emptiness where space doesn't even exist anymore. It's still a semblance of emptiness that is grasped mentally. It's still a type of emptiness with form.

You need the right sort of environment to properly cultivate the practice of space visualization. It has to be done in isolation, preferably on a high mountaintop or on an open plain where there is a vast expanse of empty sky without obstructions. The method is to begin by using your eyes to view space, looking at an open, empty sky. Then you visualize that you and space become one, so that, whether your eyes are open or not, you are one with this endless expanse of space.

You first start by contemplating this in your mind, and then you extend this experiential realm to your whole body, and then you merge it with the entire universe. Then you are space, and space is you, and there is nothing in existence except space and only space. This will eventually lead to achieving the *infinite space samadhi*, one of the four formless samadhi absorptions that have abandoned the grosser characteristics of form. It's also called the infinite form samadhi because space is still a characteristic belonging to the realm of form!

Once you reach the infinite space samadhi, your job isn't finished because you must still move forward to attain the Mahayana emptiness by cultivating prajna. The Mahayana stage of attainment doesn't even include space and form, since prajna-wisdom is formless and cannot be described. The *Heart Sutra* says that all the dharma doors are empty, but infinite space still has a form while prajna doesn't. Thus the samadhi of infinite space may fool you into thinking you're enlightened, but it isn't enlightenment yet.

23

Mindfully Cultivating
Virtuous Behavior

When you cultivate the behavioral characteristics we typically call the "virtues"—charitable giving (karma yoga), discipline (commandment keeping), and patience—this practice is in itself a means of cultivating samadhi. The virtues recognized by all religions, when practiced correctly and to the full, can definitely lead to selflessness and non-ego. That's why they're recognized as "virtues" in the first place. But people also fail to realize another aspect to this: that practicing the selfless virtues is a way to realize detachment, emptiness and non-ego, and is thus a means to enter into samadhi. When great saints who had no formal meditation practice were able to exhibit all sorts of superpowers and miraculous abilities, it was because they had entered the road of Tao through this particular aspect.

So while everyone needs the merits of virtue, discipline, good works, ethics, and morality to ultimately succeed in their cultivation, mindfully cultivating the virtues is actually a cultivation path in itself. In fact, perfecting your behavior is actually the one and only pathway to Tao, and it's the never-ending path one follows after achieving Tao as well. This is why the various religions summarize matters through the words "love one another, cultivate harmony, do good and refrain from evil," for this summarizes the path in its entirety. The entire cultivation path revolves around cultivating the virtues but it's difficult to effect deep and lasting transformative changes in your behavior unless you also meditate and cultivate the realms of samadhi. Through virtue alone, you can reach Tao in three aeons of effort, but if you also apply yourself to meditation, you can achieve enlightenment in this very lifetime. Thus the two practices of good works and samadhi must always go together. Without virtue and merit, you cannot succeed on the path.

In cultivation we often talk about attaining samadhi and various experiential realms, but no matter how profound the states that come to meet us, they are ultimately transient realms that will never stay. Even if you could stay in a high-stage samadhi for 80,000 eons, in the end you'll have to leave that state because all experiential realms are impermanent and destined for departure. So in this never-ending cosmic cycle of ceaseless change and transformation, the only worthwhile task is to strive to master your behavior and perfect your inherent virtues; to do what's good and cut off what's evil, to let all unborn good arise and prevent all unborn evil from arising, and to help others in every way possible. The various samadhi are no more than a means in process that enable you to really accomplish these feats, so cultivation, in effect, is all about service to others.

Hence, the process of attaining the Way is the actual embodiment of the Way; the fruit of the path is the practice of the path, the purpose of the path, the basis of the path, the result of the path—it's all about disentangling your mental defilements and perfecting your outward behavior. In the Mahayana school, we say that the path to Tao consists of five stages: the stage of study and merit-accumulation, the second stage of preparatory practices, the third stage of seeing the path, the fourth stage of cultivating the path, and finally the last stage of realizing enlightenment. All the cultivation schools agree that the first step to enlightenment is accumulating merit and doing good deeds, as examplified in the stages of *yama* (discipline) and *niyama* (restraint) emphasized at the start of raja yoga practice. What people often don't realize is that all the chi, mai, chakra, samadhi, kundalini, and other meditative practices we've discussed constitute only the second stage of preparatory practices on the path. They're not the actual stage of cultivation practice, just a preliminary stage of preparation.

Even the various samadhi and dhyanas do not constitute the stage of cultivation, and there are all sorts of masters who have attained lots of samadhis and superpowers but still lack the merit and wisdom necessary to see the Tao! You're not yet at the stage of "cultivating the path to enlightenment" until you have seen the true path, until you've turned around within to see the Tao. So all these various exercises are only a form of play, a means of helping you transform your body, mind, and behavior to the point where you can finally see the path and then begin your real efforts at cultivation practice. The various samadhi are only realms of quiet: transient phenomenal realms of the mind. We say they're empty, but they're still phenomenal constructions. This may seem surprising, but it is so.

Buddhism also describes this spiritual process another way, with the concept of "purifying the skandhas." Purifying the skandha of form—the five great elements of earth, wind, fire, water, and space— you can finally see within and outside your body by an internal light. You then purify the skandha of sensation—all the ideas of pleasant and unpleasant feelings—after which you can finally generate a thought-born body. This is equivalent to the "illusory body" in Tantra, the yin or yang bodies of Taoism and the astral double of Western mysticism. The next skandha to purify is that of conception, so that you finally reach a mental realm of profound emptiness. All along you're cultivating the various dhyanas, but it takes a while to break through these barriers and really develop the true emptiness and clarity of samadhi.

When you finally cultivate through the skandha of conception, the mind seems like a bright mirror to which nothing can cling; you've freed yourself from many deep habitual tendencies, and impressions can come and go without sticking. This is the third stage of "seeing the Tao" on the Mahayana path and is equivalent to the stage of clear light in Tibetan esotericism and the stage of shen transforming to emptiness in Taoism. That's when you finally "see the path" and know how you should properly practice, but what's in front of you? What confronts you is the task of purifying the skandha of volition, which consists of all your deep-rooted mental habits, perverted mental entanglements, and bad behaviors. This is the stage of purifying the "afflicted mind" of ego, which is called the seventh consciousness. *So you basically cultivate all the samadhis and dhyanas, engage in all sorts of meditation methods and sadhanas just to reach this point when you can start working on truly purifying your physical and mental behaviors. That's what cultivation is all about—purifying your mind and behavior, and doing so for the benefit of all beings.*

The skandha of volition encompasses the five poisons of greediness, anger, pride, doubt, and ignorance. It embodies the five erroneous perspectives we hold onto of clinging to the body (or form) as the self, attaching to one-sided views, holding false views as true, clinging to our own personal views, and clinging to rules and codes of conduct rather than being spontaneous and reacting with skillful means in this giant universe. It also represents all sorts of other afflictive impulses that tend to impel us, such as belligerence, envy, resentment, deceit, hypocrisy, guile, shamelessness, avarice, and so on. All these things you have to change through the cultivation of wisdom, and the devoted effort of practice. With prajna-wisdom you can cut through many of them with one stroke and be free, but with others you must continually work hard at transforming their deep-seated, habitually rooted natures.

The skandha of volition also consists of good factors, so the stage of cultivating the Tao entails encouraging all the good you possess to arise as well. By just cutting off errors you receive the rewards of past merit, but without creating any new merit of your own the past rewards are soon extinguished and you'll have no ability to make the future brighter for yourself or others. Thus, what does the fourth stage of "cultivating the path" actually come down to? It comes down to mindfully cultivating our thoughts, speech, and behavior to let all the good virtues arise, and to purify all our bad seeds of behavior. *It means cultivating all our volitional impulses, such that every mind moment is virtuous through and through.* When you can purify this aggregate of factors, then you can reach the point of perceiving the clear base of consciousness embodied by the skandha of consciousness, and if you can cultivate this base of consciousness called the *alaya* storehouse, or eighth consciousness, then you'll finally be able to attain self-realization. But it all starts from the simple foundation of mindfully cultivating the virtues, which is the basis, practice, and fruit of the path.

There's no final samadhi you can rest in when you attain Tao; there's no final place you can go to and "call it quits," since the practice of perfecting the seeds of mental behavior is never ending. The universe is always in a state of transformation, and there's no phenomenal state you can reach that doesn't share in this subtle process of interdependent seeds sprouting forth. It's just that some states and mental realms in the cosmos look quieter and thus more exalted than others, but they're phenomenal realms nonetheless and always engaged in the process of subtle transformation. They may seem like they're states of nonmovement, but it's just that the movement is very deep and subtle, or we can say it's so fast, like the flashings of a strobe light, that we can't notice it at all! Thus the never-ending task in this shimmering universal pot of ceaseless transformation is *the process of transforming any and all bad seeds into good ones, and encouraging the good ones to shine brighter and extend farther.* With eternity in front of you, with the fact that both the mind and the phenomenal realm will never be destroyed (just transformed), this is the only task worthwhile. Of course you can become an arhat and just take a long vacation from everything for a while, but a bodhisattva sees things for how they really are and jumps into this mess to help relieve the sufferings of others. You not only cultivate the seeds of your own thoughts and behavior but you also try to transform outside phenomena for the better. However, knowing how to do this requires wisdom, and the power to do so depends upon your accumulation of merit. With great wisdom, great merit, and great proficiency in skillful means, only then can you do great things and save the world. Who cares that the ignorant don't understand you—you set about anyway on accomplishing your own vows of compassion. The ignorant cannot possibly understand your miraculous engagement of skillful means. That's the fate of any man of Tao.

The cultivation path, in its truest sense, is thus the path of *perfecting your functioning connection to this grand scheme of interdependent arisings*, and the various samadhi are just a means of helping you realize this attainment. That's all there is! People think that the path is attaining the samadhi and dhyana, or transforming jing to chi and chi to shen, or opening up the chakras and mai, attaining astral bodies that can travel the universe and psychic abilities and so on, but this isn't the real process of cultivation. These are just the adjunct stages of transformational change that happen along the way; they are just the scenery of the process. So there are an awful lot of supportive teachings that go into these various factors to help explain the cultivation path, but the attainment of virtue is the true end goal and crux of the process. The cultivation path is perfecting your behavior—in body, speech, and mind—and using your merits and attainments for the benefit of others. That's the bodhisattva ideal, which is also the Christian ideal of the savior who takes on the sins of the world in order to help others.

From a more mundane standpoint, doing good deeds and working for the welfare of others is known as the cultivation path of karma yoga, its foremost practice being charity. In learning how to transform situations to the benefit of others, you have to learn how to exercise skillful means, and one such means is the practice of charity. So charity is basically a process of skillful transformation that turns a situation of inauspiciousness into a situation of auspiciousness for others. Practicing charity is the basis of accumulating merit, so you should always practice charity if you want to ultimately succeed in self-realization.

In practicing charitable giving, you can offer your life, material possessions, fearlessness, and cultivation teachings to others, but the goal is always one of benefiting others and transforming their situation in a positive way; helping others without imposing your own afflictions upon them, taking their sufferings and troubles onto yourself. This is the true practice of the bodhisattva; in changing a small situation for the better, you're changing the universe as a whole.

In the practice of giving, you're actually cultivating mental detachment, and hence charity is a way to open the mind to emptiness. In addition, by satisfying another's needs and putting their desires to rest, you will earn the merit of a peaceful mind in turn, which is itself a type of samadhi achievement. However, the highest type of charity involves cultivating samadhi directly, for it means constantly giving away one's thoughts to attain selfless emptiness, clarity, and wisdom. This is why we say that the highest prayer is to give everything over to God, for this type of charity can result in the samadhi of freedom from thoughts.

In this light, the virtue of "fasting" should be seen as refraining from discursive thought, the virtue of "renunciation" should be seen as giving up thought possessions, and "being selfless" should be seen as reaching toward the state of non-ego through abandoning the concept of a self. In all these cases, the religious virtues are actually models of cultivation practice, as well as the natural results of cultivation efforts. Mindfully cultivating the virtues, or excellences of behavior, thus becomes a method of cultivating samadhi.

As another example, patience under provocation is considered a virtue because it also involves mastering the emptiness of mind. In this light, practicing patience doesn't mean using forceful effort to restrain yourself in order to "peacefully" tolerate a situation. If this were true, then wearing a straitjacket or tethering yourself to a stake would both equally qualify as instances of patience. Rather, *patience means detaching from the fundamental volitional impulses that impel you to act*; you are practicing patience when you abide in a calm state of open, empty awareness while these impulses surge without your succumbing to their influence.

Fire that never touches you doesn't burn, so when you detach from impulses that would normally stir you, this is practicing true patience. Hence, patience under provocation is also a method for mastering mental detachment. It's a form of watching one's thoughts without becoming involved or attached, and we already know that this form of practice will lead to the stillness of cessation. Athletes who master a form of inner patience required by their sport make fine candidates for cultivation because often they can easily learn this skill. And when you can extend this expertise to view life as if it were a dream, patience is even more easily mastered. Through the practice of patience, you can definitely arrive at samadhi.

Following strict discipline, which in Buddhism is called *Vinayapitaka,* is also a method for cultivating samadhi. Cultivating discipline doesn't mean holding the mind and body in strict forms that correspond to rigid regulations and rules of conduct, nor does it mean becoming solemnly strict in one's personality and behavior. In fact, you must remember that if a person is overly strict and rigid, he or she will never let the joy arise that leads into the bliss of the first dhyana. The strict person's bones will be hard and his or her body won't be supple. Practicing discipline actually means to constantly shine awareness on your thoughts and motivations to see that no breach of discipline ever arises. In the meantime, however, you always keep your body loose and relaxed and you should be smiling in harmony with your environment—otherwise you're being tied up by forms again.

Eventually, the virtue of maintaining discipline in this manner will converge into cessation and contemplation practice from which you can enter into samadhi. We must remember that the mind is fundamentally empty, so there are no rules of discipline to be found in it at all, but when you slip out of its stainless state, this is the greatest breach of discipline. So the state of samadhi is actually the highest practice of discipline in existence, whereas following external rules of conduct is just mastering the outward appearance of transient form, which is no true discipline at all.

For those who are trying to master the virtues but are inhibited by their own bad habits and behavioral tendencies, there are various meditations you can undertake to help in the effort. For instance, a person who is dominated by hatred can meditate on love. A person dominated by desire can meditate on ugliness and the uncleanness of the physical body. Someone dominated by pride can meditate on the interdependence of phenomena to realize that we are just an agglomeration of various component factors. In this way they'll realize there is no such thing as ego and therefore nothing to be proud of. Someone who is unclear or confused can meditate on the Buddhist concept of dependent-arising and someone who thinks too much can meditate on the inhalations and exhalations of the breath.

There are always antidotes for counteracting an unsteady mind or nonvirtuous behavior, and to meditate on these antidotes is a form of cultivation. We have already mentioned the precept that there are 84,000 afflictions of mind during the moment of a single breath, and so there are 84,000 different dharma doors available for pacifying each of these afflictions. The one you choose is up to your own wisdom because it's like cooking rice over a fire: you're the only one who can adjust the heat to the situation and know which method to use. Applying the appropriate remedy to your situation may look foolish or unusual to others, but the proper usage is the actual practice of "skillful means." How often this is misunderstood!

Thus all the true religious virtues are forms of cultivation practice for mastering afflictions and attaining samadhi. The world's religions call samadhi the state of perfect selflessness, non-ego, God's love, or emptiness and serenity; yet however it is worded, it is samadhi nonetheless. This is how you should view the cultivation of religious virtues: in their truest sense, they are the path to Tao. They are the method of the path and the result of the path, the beginning of the path and the purpose of the path.

How did Confucius describe the path to enlightenment? As the process of revealing our bright virtue (the fundamental nature), loving the people by working for the benefit of others, and resting in the highest perfection (of samadhi). He said that to bring peace to the world and society at large you have to start with perfecting yourself, and in perfecting your behavior, there are seven steps to this process. The first two steps are knowing how to stop the mind and stopping (reaching cessation) so that you can reach the third step of attaining samadhi. From samadhi you can arrive at stillness, from stillness comes peacefulness and comfort (because all your chi and mai have opened), from there you can attain prajna-wisdom and, finally, the self-realization of enlightenment. Confucius often described the process in terms of the perfection of outward behavior, but it's ultimately the same process of mental cultivation we've been discussing because the mind is at the root.

Hence whether one practices Buddhism, Taoism, Hinduism, Islam, Christianity, Taoism, Confucianism, or some other religion, if one practices giving but still clings to the giver, giving, or object, it isn't true giving. Why? Because such giving doesn't embody mental detachment or emptiness. If you seem patient on the outside but are internally straining to restrain yourself, this isn't true patience either. If you perfectly follow religious rules and regulations that make your body rigid and destroy your joyful demeanor, you shouldn't think you're following the path of discipline or religious conduct at all: you're just able to manipulate your outside form like an acrobat, who can simply perform certain movements beyond the normal range. This is how the virtues should be seen.

It's not the outward form, but the internal form and inner meaning of these practices that can lead to samadhi attainments. To mindfully cultivate the virtues, you must cultivate the mind. That's what it's all about. This is an extremely advanced concept and is difficult to relate, so even the Zen masters rarely speak of it. In the Tibetan school, the idea that basis, path, and result are one and the same is considered the highest type of teaching, but few people ever reach this realm of understanding. People all sit in meditation and say they're cultivating the path, but this isn't cultivating the path. That's nonsense talk! But what we can say is that in aligning oneself with the behavior of the path, one actually achieves the path, and this is correct. Thus, expressing the Tao through the virtuous perfections is not just the end result of the path, but the very way to attain Tao, practice Tao, reveal Tao, and exhibit Tao.

Don't be misled by all the talk on samadhi, chi, mai, psychic abilities, kundalini, and chakras: the true cultivation path is the practice of doing good and cutting off evil, of perfecting and purifying your behavior and becoming skillfully able to extend this into the world of phenomena. So we call it the path of mindfully cultivating the virtues, and this has the same rank, if not higher, as the other methods for attaining samadhi.

24

Concentrating on a Hua-tou, or Meditation Saying

 The Zen school was originally brought to China by the Indian monk Bodhidharma, who described Zen as:

The special transmission outside the scriptural teachings,
Which doesn't rely on words or letters,
Which directly points to the true essence of mind,
Thus enabling people to see their true nature and
*   become Buddhas.*

The Zen masters in China initially employed no fixed format or teaching method. Rather, they just used whatever circumstances were at hand to help students awaken by directly pointing to the true essence of being. This method of dispensing teaching according to the situation was called expedient means, or skillful means, and this spontaneous teaching response to situations is the basis of all true Zen teaching. Thus, if you say that Zen teaching has a fixed or unresponsive form, it's not true Zen.

In time the wisdom of Zen students declined so that few could reach samadhi anymore through this direct method. People could discuss all sorts of principles on the theory of self-realization, and they could engage in witty Zen repartee, but the more they talked and studied, the further and further they got away from true Zen. Some people even mistook sitting in silent meditation as Zen, and this error has even come down to us today. As a response to this decline, the practice of investigating meditation sayings, known as koans or hua-tou, was devised to help all these people awaken. Since Zen is the method of no-method, when Zen started to use the method of the hua-tou because the caliber of its students had declined, it was no longer Zen. People may object to this, but it's the truth; and what we call Zen practice today is not real Zen.

Hua-tou refers to the mind before it is stirred by thought, so using a hua-tou is an attempt to get to that empty state of mind. When you use a hua-tou, you focus all your thoughts on a particular question or saying and let them get all tangled up in the matter. We call this "developing an intense questioning mood," or feeling of doubt, which is so strong that your concentration penetrates into the deepest layers of consciousness. This is using the discriminative aspect of the sixth consciousness, or thinking mind, to get rid of random thoughts and reach cessation.

In hua-tou practice, you become so absorbed and so concentrated on dealing with a question that you tie up the omnipresent activities of discrimination and attention and end up focusing your intent to an extreme. When your intent becomes solid and stable, you naturally attain the cessation of samadhi, or mental halting. In other words, concentration reaches an extreme of one-pointedness and then you can abandon your random thoughts and realize some level of mental clarity and stillness.

The purpose of hua-tou practice is to look into (investigate) a meditation saying until you reach the point where your discursive thought comes to a halt. This breakthrough is called *satori* in Japanese, but this is not yet a stage of true realization. Rather, it is just a minor period of mental cessation that corresponds to a temporary calming of the sixth consciousness. However, it does establish a temporary quieting of your busy consciousness; thus you can look into this quiet and start contemplating the mind. The hua-tou can bring about the state of cessation, but if you don't exercise transcendental wisdom to see who's experienced the stopping, then you're wasting your time.

Hence "contemplating the mind" is similar in meaning to the contemplation practices of the Tien-tai school, for while the hua-tou may help you break through to some minor degree of emptiness, you must still rely on prajna-wisdom to investigate the nature of this clearing. Hua-tou practice does not mean you should gaze on a saying or watch over your thoughts as a mother stands watching over her children. Rather, the purpose of concentrating on a hua-tou is to mass your concentration to such an extent that this concentration becomes extremely one-pointed, thus settling your ordinary mentation. People nowadays think that hua-tou or Zen koans are a high cultivation technique, but they are actually a low-level practice that was developed in response to the fact that Zen students weren't so bright anymore. And because it's a method, from a fundamental viewpoint it's no longer Zen.

Fundamentally, there are two types of hua-tou. Those of the first type have a logical meaning, such as, "Who is the one that's thinking?" or "Where is your mind ultimately coming from?" Though this first type of hua-tou has a meaning, the hua-tou doesn't involve finding a rational solution to the question. "Working on the hua-tou" means investigating what it's asking in order to turn one's concentration inward.

As a result of "concentrated concentration," it's indeed possible to break through to an experiential realm of mental quiet. You're not supposed to take the hua-tou as some school question deserving a logical solution. Rather, you have to develop such a deep questioning mood over your hua-tou that you experience some form of mental breakthrough. That's the important thing: the mental state produced. This mental state is the "answer," and it's basically a calming of consciousness.

The second type of hua-tou have no logical meaning at all, such as, "What is Buddha? A dry piece of shit." With this type of hua-tou, the mind gets totally tangled up trying to decipher a situation that doesn't seem to have any logical solution. Hence you end up wrapping yourself around the meditation searching for a reason, like a string of wire pulled so tightly around an egg that it breaks. But after the egg breaks, after the sixth consciousness clears, you still must use contemplation to look into the emptiness produced. So working on a hua-tou or koan can produce a bit of cessation, but silently sitting on this emptiness is useless. Silent sitting, without prajna-wisdom contemplation, is the ground of "dry Zen" attainment, which leads nowhere. One must still use insight to investigate within, which means examining the characteristics of the mental state that is produced. This is the only way to give birth to prajna and higher stages of attainment.

25

Jnana Yoga, or Abhidharma Analysis

 One of the more difficult means for attaining samadhi is to arrive at an intellectual comprehension of emptiness that directly leads to cessation. Another means is to create an intellectual realization that is so startling, like the TNT explosions used to blow out burning oil wells, that the sixth mind is momentarily cleared and actually tastes the experience of emptiness. When you arrive at the realm of cessation through a route of careful logical reasoning that defeats one's internal clinging, this is the method of jnana yoga.

In this method, people study a system of logic—such as Buddhist abhidharma analysis—that comprehensively and convincingly proves to the individual that there is no such thing as the fixed ego entity or individual self. Letting go of the concept of the ego, one can then enter into cessation. As you accept the logical reasoning behind the state of emptiness and no-self, your mind will naturally detach from clinging and resolve into the state of emptiness. Hence, your sixth consciousness will slowly come to a halt.

Another possible outcome is that you're abruptly shocked into this realization, just as a loud sound can momentarily quiet the mind.

Another possibility is that the mental concentration required to understand the logical train of thought causes all your random mentation to come to a halt because you reach a state of extreme one-pointedness from study.

Either way, you can definitely reach a state where your mental wanderings come to a halt if you study a suitable system of cultivation logic. For instance, if you really concentrate on a train of cultivation logic—to the same extent required for investigating a hua-tou or performing a mandala visualization—this concentration can cause you to suddenly jump out of your mundane mind-set to experience some larger or smaller degree of emptiness. Consider this: if you divide the smallest parts of an atom into smaller parts still, and then smaller still, until they are reduced to emptiness, what are you left with? Now follow this train of logic in your imagination, and then imagine that state of extinction!

Another question is to consider the matter from the opposite end: from this initial state of emptiness, how much emptiness must be massed together to make form? In pondering this question, did your mind freeze for a moment? Thus for some individuals we have another alternative in useful cultivation techniques. However, the more orthodox and profound method of attaining samadhi through jnana yoga can only succeed if concentration is applied, in a nonsuperficial fashion, to a specially designed system of cultivation logic. Then it is indeed possible to arrive at an experiential realm of mental cessation. But to succeed in this route, you must also follow the practices of accumulating merit, sexual discipline, and regular meditation practice as well. Some individuals would like to think that there is a purely intellectual path to Tao, but cessation isn't going to happen unless your jing transforms into chi, and your chi settles and transforms into shen. The cultivation path of the mind always involves physical transformations, so they have to occur on this path as well.

Nevertheless, this discriminative approach to the experience of emptiness was promulgated in the early eras of Buddhism through the study of abhidharma analysis. It was also popular in various Vedic schools of thought, for the Indian culture originated many forms of philosophy and intellectual analysis. The popular method of *neti, neti* ("not this, not this") is one such approach found in Vedanta. You intellectually realize that "I am not the body, I am not the thoughts, I am not the experiential realms that arise" from moment to moment and detach from these phenomena to realize samadhi.

Even Confucianism has its own form of analysis leading to emptiness, for people were told to devote themselves to learning and "investigate things" to their roots, which actually means to investigate phenomena until you discover their inherent emptiness. So it is indeed possible to follow an investigative road of logic to reach an experience of non-ego and samadhi. Following the reasonings of Nagarjuna in his *Treatise on the Middle Way,* is one example. Nagarjuna wrote that phenomena are neither existent nor non-existent, so what are they? As he stated,

All the various objects of experience
Are like the moon reflected in water—
Neither really true nor really false.
Those appreciating this do not lose the way.

As Nagarjuna suggested, you cannot think of phenomena as being real, and they aren't false either. Rather, they should be viewed as if they were an illusion or dream. Why? Because everything you see in the conventional world is always in a state of continual transformation, so all objects lack a final self-nature or objective existence; they are empty of fixed reality. Empty of what they appear to be, they lack reality. But for the moment in which they appear, they do seem to exist.

Thus, the conventional workings of the phenomenal world do indeed proceed according to the interdependent laws of cause and effect. Hence you can't possibly deny this conventional validity and talk about falsity, emptiness, nonexistence or the extreme of nihilism. On the other hand, phenomena are not really real, either. The best we can say is that they're like a dream: they seem to exist, but there's nothing you can grab onto, nothing you can ever fix for even the tiniest moment. In fact, things only exist because of their dependence on everything else, so they lack a self-so nature. This is the absence of reality, and yet this wonderful, shimmering, never-ending tapestry of appearances functions according to mutual interdependence and karma, and thus you can't say it's unreal either. So, the best way to cultivate is to reach the stage at which you can always see the world as if it were a dream, illusion, or magician's display. What you should be concentrating on throughout this dream is that one thing that knows you are angry, or unclear, or happy, and so on. *That one thing that is aware of this illusive display is the important thing, not the transient phenomena passing by.*

Nagarjuna also wrote,

Phenomena are not born from themselves,
nor are they born from others,
nor are they born together with others,
nor are they born without cause.
Thus they are said to be unborn.

If you ever come upon a set of logic like this that seems like a paradox, and it makes your mental state come to a halt when you study what it's really saying, then you should seize upon this moment to look within at the nature of the mind. This is also the method of jnana yoga. So Nagarjuna's writings are not only designed to explain the transcendental in a logical fashion, but to help us silence our internal mental dialogue and bring about an experience of this state. Thus, studying his writings is a way to reach cessation, the common principle of cessation found in countless meditation techniques.

There are other suitable topics to study that can also lead you to realizing emptiness, such as dependent origination, the nature of perception, five skandhas analysis, and so on. When you study such a topic deeply, you can break your false beliefs about the unity of the self, the self as causal agent, and the self as the enjoyer of experience. And if you can attain an experience of selflessness, or non-ego (emptiness), this is none other than samadhi.

In other words, when you study mental events to a very fine detail, and through this means understand the causes and conditions that support the operation of ordinary self-oriented experience, you can break away from the view of a self and attain samadhi. For instance, in meditating on the element of discrimination you'll find that all perceptual experiences are made up of empty mind moments, and the deeper this realization goes, the more it will remove your attachment to the idea of a self. This is the Hinayana cultivation of emptiness.

In thus pursuing these roads of analysis to analyze the world and mental phenomena, one can ultimately reach a point where the sixth consciousness comes to a halt and discrimination is held in abeyance because there's nothing left to discriminate. This is the point at which one can contemplate the mean between existence and emptiness. Investigating matters in this way, and contemplating the state produced, one can make inroads to samadhi, which has been the purpose of this book.

1

The Nine Basic Samadhi Inherent in All the World's Religious Schools

 The nine basic samadhi, which are attainable through the proper efforts of spiritual cultivation as described in this book, are inherent in all the world's genuine cultivation traditions. Because they are common to all schools, they are often termed the "common stages" because they are nondenominational in nature. In fact, these various realms of concentration are common to all the sentient beings in the universe.

Unfortunately, most people have trouble realizing this fact, for they get lost beneath the curtains of religious dogma and spend useless efforts arguing over whether one spiritual path or tradition is vastly superior to another, usually defending their own (that they were born into). However, it doesn't matter what tradition you follow as long as you strive to climb the ranks of samadhi. If you fail to even make this effort, then it's not worth our comments. In fact, even the world's cultivation methods are not holy in themselves, but are just expedient means created for helping individuals change their behavior and attain Tao. They are no more than this—they are simply skillful means. It's said there are over 84,000 afflictions of the mind, and so you can use 84,000 different dharma doors to solve these afflictions when they arise. After you've dissolved the afflictions of the mind, you can let go of your method like the raft that is left at the water's edge when its purpose has been fulfilled.

Now, since the nine samadhi are nondenominational in nature, you also simply use them because they produce the effects intended: religion doesn't even enter into the picture. And since the nine samadhi are themselves naturally occurring states of mind that manifest as the mind becomes purer through "resting," no one can argue that the samadhi are unnatural, evil, or artificial creations. Their sequence of manifestation and their individual characteristics can even be described as quite natural, or even scientific in nature. Hence the principles revealed within this text for attaining the samadhi are not just empty philosophical thought and theories, but actually produce the results described.

It is beyond the scope of this introductory text to discuss the nature of the nine samadhi in detail. However, it's useful to at least know their names and general rudimentary characteristics, which run as follows:

1. The *first dhyana* is characterized by one-pointed concentration, physical bliss, and mental joy. Taoists say that in this stage your thoughts stop because you've reached an initial degree of mental cessation. This dhyana corresponds to initial entry into the Form Realm heavens, has three levels, and is sometimes called the Joyous Ground of Separating from Production. In his *Yoga-Sutra*, Patanjali calls this *vitarka-samadhi*. If you attain this samadhi, you've greatly freed yourself from the lust for food and sexual relations.

2. The *second dhyana* is characterized by one-pointed concentration, inner clarity (purity), and a much higher stage of physical bliss and mental joy. In this stage, we say that your chi stops and in terms of the physical body, your external respiration has certainly ceased by this stage. This samadhi corresponds to accomplishment in the Form Realm heavens, has three levels, and is sometimes called the Joyous Ground of Producing Samadhi. Patanjali calls this the stage of *vicara-samadhi*.

3. The *third dhyana* is characterized by one-pointed concentration, equanimity, mindfulness, and an even higher stage of physical bliss. Taoists say that in this absorption, your pulse can stop. The dhyana has three levels and is sometimes called the Wonderful Blissful Ground of Separating from Joy. This is the stage of *ananda-samadhi*, mentioned in the classical yoga schools. Naturally, its main characteristic is physical bliss, as *ananda* means bliss.

4. The *fourth dhyana* is characterized by one-pointed concentration, completely pure equanimity, and neutrality. In this stage, one's mind is extremely clear, which can be described as a great emptiness due to the absence of thoughts. It corresponds to the top of the Form Realm heavens, has nine levels, and is sometimes referred to as the Pure Ground of Renouncing Thought. This is the *asmita-samadhi* of classical yoga.

5. The *samadhi of infinite (boundless) space* is also known as the samadhi of infinite form, and corresponds to initial entry into the Formless Realm heavens.

6. The *samadhi of infinite (boundless) consciousness,* a samadhi of the Formless Realm, can be described as an experiential state of consciousness-only.

7. The *samadhi of nothingness,* another Formless Realm samadhi, is hard to describe. The best we can say is that nothing is taken to mind, and so we use the word "nothingness" for lack of better words. In this stage of samadhi you view even consciousness as gross and so you abide in a state where there are no such discriminations at all.

8. The *samadhi of neither thought nor no-thought* (without thought and without no-thought, or neither perception nor non-perception) corresponds to the very top of the Formless Realm heavens and so is also called the *Peak of Cyclic Existence.*

9. The *Arhat's nirvana* (with remainder), because of its requisite stage of prajna-wisdom attainment, is a samadhi found only in Buddhism.

After these nine samadhi comes the stage of enlightenment or self-realization, which we call Tao. This is the stage of the bodhisattvas and buddhas who work in the world helping others; their bodies function in the world of form but their minds transcend all mundane reality. We're currently preparing an extensive book that deals with these nine samadhi, the stages of the cultivation path as measured by various other schools having their own specific terminology, and how these stages match-up between the different schools and their teachings. For instance, Buddhism describes cultivation attainment in several alternative schemes: the nine samadhi, breaking through the five skandhas, the eight consciousnesses, and in terms of transforming the great elements. Taoism describes the path in terms of physical characteristics such as transformations of jing, chi, and shen, and in terms of various kung-fu accomplishments. Classical yoga and Hinduism have the various samadhi and other measures, Tibetan Tantra has the opening of the central channel and the stages of co-emergent emptiness and bliss, Western alchemy has its own stages of physical transformation, Confucianism has the steps of cultivating one's "inherent bright virtue," and so on.

All these stages sound different when you glance at the terminology of different schools, but they are just different ways of describing the same process of attainment, different means of cutting the same piece of cake. For a preliminary understanding of these stages and how they relate to one another across schools, refer to the following volumes.

Arya, Pandit Usharbudh. *Yoga-Sutras of Patanjali with the Exposition of Vyasa.* Vol. 1. Samadhi-pada. Honesdale, PA: The Himalayan International Institute of Yoga Science and Philosophy, 1986.

Gyatso, Geshe Kelsang. *Tantric Grounds and Paths.* London: Tharpa Publications, 1994.

Lodoe, Yangchen Gawai. *Paths and Ground of Guhyasamaja According to Arya Nagarjuna.* Dharamsala, India: LTWA, 1995.

Nan, Huai-Chin. *To Realize Enlightenment: Practice of the Cultivation Path.* York Beach, ME: Samuel Weiser, 1994.

————. *Working toward Enlightenment: The Cultivation of Practice.* York Beach, ME: Samuel Weiser, 1993.

Rinpoche, Lati, and Denma Locho Rinpoche. *Meditative States in Tibetan Buddhism.* Boston: Wisdom Publications, 1997.

Wen, Kuan Chu, and Huai-Chin Nan. *Tao and Longevity: Mind-Body Transformation.* York Beach, ME: Samuel Weiser, 1984.

2

Shakyamuni's Ten Great Roads of Cultivation Practice

Shakyamuni Buddha lived in ancient India at a time when there were literally hundreds of different cultivation schools, spiritual teachings, and sadhana practice techniques for attaining samadhi. After mastering all these various schools and methods, Shakyamuni relied on his personal insight, study, and experience to divide the most useful and genuine practices into ten major divisions, all of which are quite advantageous to study. The full list of Hinayana sadhana categories are:

1. Mindfulness of Buddha practices, which involve deeply concentrating upon and identifying with a divine form (such as Buddha, Jesus, Krishna, and so on), so that one attains the state of samadhi. To chant Amitofo's name with devotion is one such technique. Hindu bhakti yoga or the remembrance of Christ are similar methods.

2. Mindfulness of dharma practices that, like Hindu jnana yoga, involve arriving at the experience of emptiness (true selflessness), and attaining samadhi through an understanding of dharma principles. Dharma mindfulness is attained by logical analysis and discriminative understanding. To study the Consciousness-only school of Buddhist philosophy is one type of dharma practice.

3. Mindfulness of sangha practices that, like the guru yoga of the Tibetan school, involve following the instructions of an enlightened teacher (or individual with cultivation attainments) for attaining self-realization. These practices mean depending upon the guidance of the enlightened, no matter what their cultivation school or tradition, to attain samadhi.

4. Precept mindfulness or discipline mindfulness practices, which involve constantly shining attention on one's mind and motivations until they become pure, whereby one attains samadhi. The Vinaya-pita-ka sect of Buddhism, whose members constantly reflect on both their internal and external behavior, is one which practices mindfulness of discipline.

5. Mindfulness of generosity practices, as in the karma yoga of Hinduism and charitable giving practices of Christianity (the "Way of Martha"), which entail making constant offerings of charity to others. The meaning of charity includes constantly giving away all one's thoughts and discriminative attachments so as to attain the emptiness of samadhi. In the process, practitioners accumulate the merit necessary for entering into samadhi and finally achieve the stage of selflessness themselves.

6. Mindfulness of heaven practices, as illustrated by the cultivation practices of the Christian mystics and Moslems, which entail trying to purify defilements in order to spiritually ascend to higher realms. One reminds oneself that the heavenly beings (such as angels and devas) are born into such exalted states because of their virtues. One therefore tries to ascend to a heavenly plane through spiritual purification, and to continue advancing from there until one is entirely free of the realms of Desire, Form, and Formlessness.

7. Mindfulness of the breath practices, which are practiced in the Hindu, Yoga, Tibetan, Taoist, Sufi, Buddhist, and countless other cultivation schools. Breathing practices, called "anapana" or "pranayama," entail calming respiration until both breathing and thoughts dissolve into one. This finally results in samadhi when the breath reaches a state of extinction. Kundalini yoga is actually a special type of breathing mindfulness. In fact, most of the esoteric Buddhist teachings are essentially based on breathing practices.

8. Mindfulness of peace, or resting practices, which entail really letting go of everything by resting all your connections until you rest yourself, so to speak, into the stage of samadhi. This is a means of contemplating the peaceful attributes of nirvana. If you can drop happiness, pain, and everything else, then you can really relax so as to even drop your dropping and experience true emptiness. Some drunken kung-fu martial arts practices are similar to resting-relaxation.

9. Mindfulness of the body, which involves detaching from the physical body and its sensations, including abandoning one's craving for form. Meditation on the impurity or repulsiveness of the body, and the skeleton method visualization, are two such body-mindfulness techniques. The Confucian school's reverence for the body, since it comes from our parents, is an opposite type of body mindfulness practice.

10. Mindfulness of death, which involves mentally dropping absolutely everything, and so detaching from phenomenal afflictions that you enter into the experience of samadhi. To deeply investigate where you come from before you are born, and where you'll go to after your death, is also a way to eventually jump out of birth and death. Tibetan bardo practices are also a form of this category of practice. Reminding yourself that you may die at any moment is a way to make every moment count in cultivation. One's death is absolutely certain, and when it comes you must relinquish everything.

3

Further Recommended Reading

 People commonly ask us for a short list of books they can read in order to understand the road of cultivation and learn a variety of spiritual techniques. Typically, the wisest practitioners are not only interested in techniques but in why they work. This is because in cultivation you must mix practice with theory for attainment, like mixing flour and water to obtain dough. Only when you know the theory and principles of cultivation can you be sure your path is correct; only when you practice can you discover the true meaning of the cultivation principles and recognize what they really mean.

Thus, the following list of titles will provide a firm foundation for anyone who wishes to tread the cultivation path, for together they will introduce various aspects of the path and illuminate the correct principles of the cultivation trail. Lacking access to a spiritual master, these can help you gain the theoretical basis of the path, to learn the do's and don't's of true cultivation practice.

Blofeld, John, trans. *Zen Teaching of Instantaneous Awakening*. London: Buddhist Publishing Group, 1995.

Chang, C. C., ed. *A Treasury of Mahayana Sutras*. Delhi: Motilal Banarsidass Publishers, 1991.

Chu, Wen Kuan, and Huai-Chin Nan. *Tao and Longevity: Mind-Body Transformation*. York Beach, ME: Samuel Weiser, 1984.

Cleary, Thomas. *Minding Mind: A Course in Basic Meditation*. Boston: Shambhala Publications, 1995.

Cozort, Daniel. *Highest Yoga Tantra*. Ithaca, NY: Snow Lion Publications, 1986.

Dowman, Keith. *Sky Dancer: The Secret Life and Songs of the Lady Yeshe Tsogyel*. London: Arkana, 1989.

Lhalungpa, Lobsang P., trans. *The Life of Milarepa*. London: Arkana, 1992.

Lysebeth, Andre van. *Pranayama: The Yoga of Breathing*. London: Unwin Paperbacks, 1985.

Mullin, Glen, trans. *Tsong Khapa's Six Yogas of Naropa*. Ithaca, NY: Snow Lion Publications, 1996.

Nan, Huai-Chin. *To Realize Enlightenment: Practice of the Cultivation Path*. York Beach, ME: Samuel Weiser, 1994.

———. *Working toward Enlightenment: The Cultivation of Practice*. York Beach, ME: Samuel Weiser, 1993.

Ni, Maoshing, trans. *The Yellow Emperor's Classic of Medicine*. Boston: Shambhala Publications, 1995.

Price, A. F., and Wong Mou-lam, trans. *The Diamond Sutra & The Sutra of Hui-Neng*. Boston: Shambhala Publications, 1990.

Rieker, Hans-Ulrich. *The Yoga of Light*. London: Unwin Paperbacks, 1971.

Rinpoche, Lati, and Denma Locho Rinpoche. *Meditative States in Tibetan Buddhism*. Boston: Wisdom Publications, 1997.

Saraswati, Swami Satyananda. *A Systematic Course in the Ancient Tantric Techniques of Yoga and Kriya*. Monghyr, India: Bihar School of Yoga, 1981.

Wile, Douglas. *Art of the Bedchamber: The Chinese Sexual Yoga Classics Including Women's Solo Meditation Texts.* New York: SUNY Press, 1992.

Yu, Lu K'uan. *Ch'an and Zen Teachings: First, Second and Third Series.* London: Rider, 1962; York Beach, ME: Samuel Weiser, 1993.

————. *The Transmission of the Mind Outside the Teaching.* London: Rider, 1974.

4

Postscript and References for the Twenty-Five Doors to Meditation

 It's impossible to fully discuss all the important points for each of the cultivation techniques we've introduced. Thus we've added this section to further clarify a few of the simpler points and to introduce additional reading for the inquiring practitioner. This book has been meant as an introductory text, and also as a manual for teachers who wish to give lectures or provide instructions on each individual technique and need material from which to start. We hope that this extra information will help supply the background needed to make this possible.

1. UNION WITH CHILD LIGHT TO REALIZE MOTHER LIGHT

This particular technique we've related for "seeing light" can be used anywhere in the universe, for there is no place in existence where there is a perfect absence of light. Any instances of darkness are just situations of dimmer light. Since there's no place you can go without encountering light, this is a good method to teach those who are lonely or easily frightened, for when they realize that light is everywhere and always about them, they'll never feel alone anymore. Hence you could even practice this technique in the darkest hells. That's because the light of awareness is always shining, only the phenomenal realms change. Wherever you go, the mind never moves, so rather than say you "go somewhere," we can say that the scenery changes around you and that the clear light of awareness always functions without moving. When you cultivate to recognize this clear light, that's trying to recognize the "ground state of luminosity" that accompanies being. In cultivation, we say that you try to cultivate the child clear light of the path and blend it with the mother clear light of perfect illumination, which is the stage of complete enlightenment, or nirvana.

One of Buddha's students, Mahakashyapa, resides sealed within a cliffside cave on Chicken Foot Mountain (in China's Yunnan province) while cultivating this particular practice. Hence he is often called the "eater of light" or "drinker of light." After Shakyamuni, Mahakashyapa was the first Zen master of India and passed the role of succession to Buddha's cousin Ananda, after whom it passed through the India Zen masters until the Indian sage Bodhidharma came to China. Since that time, the heart of Zen cultivation has always remained in China.

Now, in this technique of seeing the light we've introduced, you must remember to use your eyes without putting any strain on your eyeballs. If your eyes feel irritated when you relax them, it is because the chi is trying to pass through and repair them. So reestablishing any sense of eye strain to terminate this uncomfortable feeling is actually impeding an internal healing process as well as inhibiting the microcosmic chi circulation in the head.

In this practice, you should forget all your sensations and the fact that you have any body at all. Thus you should ignore any special sensations that arise during practice. This includes sensations within your eyes or skull, and you shouldn't cling to the thoughts in your head either, for all of these are just sensations of vital energy and consciousness that will pass. The method of seeing the light entails going empty by dropping everything, and you don't try to visualize anything either: you just realize the light and merge with it. This method of combining with the light is so powerful because, in Taoist terminology, it is one of the few methods that enables you to directly "transform chi into shen" (whereas most methods involve transforming jing into chi). Since our chi transforms into shen, we can realize samadhi quite quickly. In Christian mysticism, they symbolize this through the analogy of "air transforming into sunlight."

The real chi (or prana) of cultivation arises during the pause between our inhalations and exhalations, when respiration momentarily ceases. Sitting there with your eyes closed, combining with the light that has no boundaries and extends everywhere, the more you relax, the more you can realize shen and allow the real chi to arise between your respirations. If you continue practicing in this manner, a loose and relaxed body will fill with chi and you will naturally, gently extend the amount of time that your breathing ceases after an exhalation. Finally the state of hsi will arise, the body will become warm, and mental entanglements will die down.

You should maintain your effortless awareness without being frightened when you reach this point of cessation. If you can maintain your awareness of all-expansive light during this state, you will be combining your chi with shen, in effect enabling your chi to transform into shen at a fantastic rate. But this only happens at the point between the inhalations and exhalations of the breath, which is why you must relax to the point where your breath ceases during this practice.

A technique similar to this one is taught in Tibetan Buddhism, but Tibetan monks must typically wait twenty to thirty years before they're taught this technique. There are also various Taoist light practices, of a much coarser nature, which involve absorbing the essences of the sun, moon, or stars. These methods are different in nature from what we've taught here. Furthermore, they're popular with wilderness animals that cultivate, but they can only be undertaken at special periods of the year in certain remote and unobstructed locations. Some of these Taoist light practices are described in Eva Wong, *The Shambhala Guide to Taoism* (Boston: Shambhala Publications, 1997).

2. ZEN, THE METHOD OF NO-METHOD

There are many books on Zen that have been written for the modern reader. Many of these books incorrectly posit Zen as some psychological game, however, and totally overlook the fact that Zen training also produces the nine samadhi and the various stages of kung-fu found in the esoteric schools. Many of these Western texts on Zen have done a great service by introducing Zen to the West and helping to make it popular, but they have been written largely by students who did not have the benefit of genuine teachers from whom to learn and, relying on their own intuition, did not understand Zen correctly. For instance, from a quick and superficial impression of Zen classics, many Westerners get an idea of the Zen realm of spontaneous action, informality and humor, and think Zen is just like this. In bypassing the work on the five skandhas and nine samadhi, which is the heart of Zen, how could they possibly present the material correctly?

In regard to Zen, Master Huang-po said:

Mind is the Buddha and unmindfulness is the Tao. Just refrain from stirring your thinking process and from having the mind dwell on what is and is not, long and short, the self and others, or subject and object. Mind is fundamentally the Buddha, and Buddha is intrinsically mind. Mind is like empty space, hence it is also said that the Buddha's Truth body is like empty space. So there is no need to seek for anything elsewhere, as all longing and desire results in suffering. Even if you practice the six perfections (paramita) and myriad lines of bodhisattva conduct for countless eons, as many as the sand grains in the Ganges, to realize the Tao, it will not be the ultimate one. Why? Because the Tao you thus reach will be causally produced and when the good karma of its causes comes to an end, it will return to its original condition of nonexistence.

Hence it is said, "The Reward body and Transformation body are not the real buddha, nor are they preachers of the dharma." What you must ultimately do is just recognize the self-mind, which is free from selfness and otherness, for this is fundamentally Buddha.

. . . You must simply learn unmindfulness and you will wipe out all causality. If you refrain from giving rise to discriminatory thoughts, then you will eliminate all concepts of the self and other, desire, anger, like, gain, loss, and so on. Then you'll recover your true self-nature which is fundamentally pure and clean. This is the practice of samadhi, wisdom and buddhahood. If you do not understand this, although you may widen your intellectual knowledge, practice various difficult austerities, live on wild fruit and nuts, or cover your body with leaves and grass, you will fail to realize your true nature. These practices are just the heterodoxy practiced by heavenly demons and heretics, and by the ghosts and spirits of the lands and waters. What possible advantage can you expect to gain from such practices?

So Zen is not just some means to attain a minor psychological realization, as we find in pop psychology, nor is it the foundational philosophy for some sort of natural living, which is another popular misconception. If you're talking about Zen and you don't recognize the existence of the four dhyanas and four formless samadhi, or the Buddhist skandhas of form, sensation, conception, volition, and consciousness, then it isn't Zen. Because of the prevalence of these incorrect notions, the best Zen works that appear nowadays seem to be translations of ancient texts. Among the very best are:

Blofeld, John, trans. *Zen Teaching of Instantaneous Awakening*. London: Buddhist Publishing Group, 1995.

Chung-Yuan, Chang, trans. *Original Teachings of Ch'an Buddhism*. New York: Pantheon, 1969.

Cleary, J. C., trans. *Zen Dawn: Early Texts from Tun Huang*. Boston: Shambhala Publications, 1986.

Cleary, Thomas, trans. *The Five Houses of Zen*. Boston: Shambhala Publications, 1997.

———. *Minding Mind: A Course in Basic Meditation*. Boston: Shambhala Publications, 1995.

———. *The Original Face: An Anthology of Rinzai Zen*. New York: Grove Press, 1978.

Pine, Red, trans. *The Zen Teaching of Bodhidharma*. New York: North Point Press, 1987.

Yu, Lu K'uan. *Ch'an and Zen Teachings: First, Second and Third Series*. London: Rider, 1962; York Beach, ME: Samuel Weiser, 1993.

———. *The Transmission of the Mind Outside the Teaching*. London: Rider, 1974.

Contemporary Zen works of note include:

Nan, Huai-Chin. *To Realize Enlightenment: Practice of the Cultivation Path*. York Beach, ME: Samuel Weiser, 1994.

———. *The Story of Chinese Zen*. Boston: Charles E. Tuttle Co., 1995.

———. *Working toward Enlightenment: The Cultivation of Practice*. York Beach, ME: Samuel Weiser, 1993.

Wu, John C. H. *The Golden Age of Zen*. New York: Image Books, 1996.

Zen is very similar to Tibetan Mahamudra. Related books on Mahamudra that can assist you in your cultivation include:

Berzin, Alexander, trans. *The Mahamudra Eliminating the Darkness of Ignorance*. Delhi, India: Library of Tibetan Works and Archives, 1989.

Gyatso, Geshe Kelsang. *Clear Light of Bliss: Mahamudra in Vajrayana Buddhism*. London: Wisdom Publications, 1992.

Kongtrul, Jamgon. *Cloudless Sky: The Mahamudra Path of the Tibetan Buddhist Kagyu School*. Boston: Shambhala Publications, 1992.

Namgyal, Takpo Tashi. *Mahamudra: The Quintessence of Mind and Meditation*. Boston: Shambhala Publications, 1986.

Rangdrol, Tsele Natsok. *Lamp of Mahamudra*. Boston: Shambhala
Publications, 1989.

Related works on Dzogchen include:

Norbu, Namkhai. *Dzogchen: The Self-Perfected State*. London: Arkana,
1989.
Norbu, Namkhai, and Kennard Lipman, trans. *Primordial Experience*.
Boston: Shambhala Publications, 1987.
Rabjam, Longchen. *The Practice of Dzogchen*. Ithaca, NY: Snow Lion
Publications, 1996.

Unfortunately, two of the best Zen works of all time—the Chinese
classic *Finger Pointing at the Moon* and *The Source Mirror Record* by Zen
master Yongming—have not yet been translated by anyone into
English. Rather than see another book of koan translations, these are
two of the texts, in addition to Chih-i's *The Great Cessation and
Contemplation*, that would make an extremely profound impact on
modern culture and a great contribution to the path of cultivation.

3. KUAN-YIN'S METHOD OF LISTENING TO SOUND

The story of Han-shan, who used this technique, can be found in Lu
K'uan Yu, *Practical Buddhism* (London: Rider & Company, 1971).

For translations of the *Shurangama Sutra*, which contains Kuan-
Yin's method as well as a variety of other pertinent cultivation mater-
ial, please see Lu K'uan Yu, trans. *The Surangama Sutra* (Delhi: B. I.
Publications, 1966), and *The Shurangama Sutra*, vols. 1–8, Hsuan Hua
and The Buddhist Text Translation Society, trans. (Talmage, CA:
Dharma Realm Buddhist Association, 1977-1996).

This is one of the most important reference works for cultivation, and we hope that several alternative translations of this sutra can
eventually be produced in English. Of particular note are the details

it contains on the fifty great errors of cultivation practice that will confront individuals as they break through the various experiential realms and master the various samadhi. A forthcoming book, to be entitled *Measuring Meditation*, will contain a translation of this particular chapter.

Because of its great value to cultivators, it has been prophesied that the *Shurangama Sutra* will be the first of the Buddhist sutras to be destroyed so before that time, we urge that it be studied by true cultivators. The Zen school doesn't rely on words and phrases, yet bases itself upon the teachings in this text. That's an accurate indication of its degree of importance.

4. WATCHING THOUGHTS: CESSATION AND CONTEMPLATION PRACTICE

People who practice watching thoughts to achieve cessation and contemplation are advised to study a number of other cultivation techniques so that they do not fall into the trap of silent sitting. The popular texts on Theravada (Hinayana) shamatha-vipashyana practice champion this cultivation technique, yet are usually quite dry in tone because the authors concentrate on emptiness only, which encourages dry wisdom Zen.

To become enlightened, one must also know of the joyful side of existence, and must be sufficiently loose, relaxed, free, and joyful to have the blisses and joys of the four dhyanas arise. If one prevents joy and bliss from arising in the body and mind, they absolutely cannot enter into the four dhyanas. Most people don't know this, even the monks and nuns who cultivate, and so you'll see them all strict and serious without smiles on their faces when meditating. Thus, practicing cessation-contemplation doesn't mean you should adopt a solemn and strict demeanor. *You have to be open, free and relaxed during this practice, while detaching from everything.* So while you shouldn't force a smile during practice, you should let it happen and let an inner sense of joy arise that will help transform the physical body.

For further information on this particular technique, a variety of useful texts are now available, some of which include:

Chih-i. *Stopping and Seeing: A Comprehensive Course in Buddhist Meditation.* Thomas Cleary, trans. Boston: Shambhala, 1997.

Khantipalo, Bhikku. *Calm and Insight.* London: Curzon Press, 1987.

Lodro, Gedun. *Walking through Walls: A Presentation of Tibetan Meditation.* Ithaca, NY: Snow Lion Publications, 1992.

Thrangu, Khenchen. *The Practice of Tranquility and Insight.* Boston: Shambhala Publications, 1993.

Wallace, B. Alan. *The Bridge of Quiescence.* Peru, IL: Open Court Publishing, 1998.

Wayman, Alex, trans. *Calming the Mind and Discerning the Real: Buddhist Meditation and the Middle View From the* Lam rim chen mo *of Tsong-kha-pa.* New York: Columbia University Press, 1978.

Yu, Lu K'uan. *The Secrets of Chinese Meditation.* York Beach, ME: Samuel Weiser, 1964.

In time more and more books will continue to appear on this method, which seems to be more commonly known through its Sanskrit name, *shamatha-vipashyana*, than through its English equivalents. In Chinese, it is known as *chih-guan*, and is the basis of the Tien-tai school's "six miraculous dharma doors." Most stopping and contemplation exercises will help you reach a state of inner stillness, but not many people can detach from this realm to attain the joy and bliss of the first dhyana, or the higher dhyanas and formless absorptions.

The problem lies in the fact that people don't realize that the state of quiet is also a phenomenon that appears in the mind. In other words, it floats in the mind's awareness, which is empty, invisible, formless, and without substance. This is the thing that sees the emptiness, so you have to detach from the boundaries of emptiness to realize the clear bright nature of the mind. You can do this because emptiness is just a phenomenon that the mind knows; when your chi becomes full, you'll be able to realize the meaning of these words and detach from both thoughts and emptiness to cultivate the Tao. Then you're truly on the cultivation path. At this point your mai will all open, your natural vitality will return and wash away your internal illnesses, all sorts of psychic abilities and kung-fu will arise—and this will all occur through an entirely natural process. That's real cultivation! What occurs will transpire in a *predictable, orderly, scientific sequence* that is only appended due to your innate abilities and karmic seeds of past attainment.

5. DAZZLING WHITE SKELETON CONTEMPLATION

The white skeleton visualization practice is usually done in solitary retreat so that the practitioner is distanced from the distractions of the world. If you practice the skeleton visualization method correctly without leaking your jing, you can get rid of sexual desire because your chi will accumulate and give rise to the mental joy and physical bliss found in the lower dhyanas of detachment.

Older people don't have as much jing anymore, which is why they often look so solemn, strict, and unhappy, so they must first recover their jing and restore their vitality if they wish to succeed in cultivation. This will happen if they cultivate a state of stillness, which will help to cure all the illnesses of their body, and afterwards they can experience the bliss of cultivation as they recover their jing. The skeleton visualization, since it involves the internals of one's own body, is one of the quickest ways to recover lost vitality *if you don't let it leak when it returns*, causing sexual desire to arise through this practice.

It's important to remember that after you succeed in visualizing your skeleton through this particular practice, you must then *abandon the vision of a being a skeleton or possessing a body of any type whatsoever*; you joyfully and blissfully offer away your flesh and organs and then abandon any idea of possessing any body. Thus only emptiness will remain and your mental state can converge into that of samadhi. People who practice esoteric cultivation techniques by visualizing the chakras and mai can sometimes catch glimpses of their internal esoteric structures because they achieve an inner light that naturally arises as the refined chi accumulates within. However, they tend to forget that the esoteric body they see is also an illusory body that should be abandoned in the same manner.

Because of this tendency to cling to a body, even the Tibetan esoteric teachings on the chakra, mai, and generating an illusory body more often than not produce mental obstacles for practitioners. In cultivation, every step of the way involves abandoning the ideas of form and possessing an inherent self, and the steps of cultivation certainly get away from playing with bodily sensations. But when the chi starts to arise and accumulate, many people will fall into the temptations of lust and sexual desire, so it's only in abandoning the view of the body and detaching from sensations that you can be successful at these practices.

A related powerful cultivation technique for developing detachment from form is to contemplate the uncleanness or impurity of the body. You do this by observing that your own body, and everyone else's, is unclean. Thus this realization helps you to destroy sexual desire. In this particular practice of body-mindfulness, you also meditate on what happens to your body after you die, including all the ugly stages of decay. First you visualize your body swelling up and turning green all over. Next, you imagine its flesh breaking open so that blood and other filth flow out. Then you imagine that pus forms, and that the body starts to rot. Then, worms and maggots come to feast on the putrid flesh while the flesh begins to fall off in clumps and scatter. In the next stage, only the bare bones are left. In the final stage, you visualize that the remaining skeleton is burned by fire, so that only its ashes remain. These ashes then drift away until only emptiness is left. This technique is similar to the skeleton visualization, and can be combined with elements of the fire visualization technique as well.

Many monks have succeeded using this technique, for contemplating the uncleanness of the body helps conquer sexual desire, which is the greatest initial barrier for cultivators. However, all the various elements of this visualization help counteract other attachments as well: the swollen corpse helps those who lust after the beauty of form;

the discolored corpse helps those who lust after beauty of the skin and complexion; the festering corpse with a stench helps those who lust after perfumes and a sweet-smelling body; the fissured corpse showing body cavities helps those who lust after a firm body, the mangled corpse helps those who lust for a full body (such as full breasts); the dismembered corpse helps those who lust after graceful movements; the cut and dismembered corpse helps those who lust after perfection of body joints; the bleeding corpse helps those who lust for the beauty of adornments; and the worm-infested corpse helps those who attach to the idea of "I" and "mine."

Another cultivation technique somewhat related to the white skeleton visualization is the Chod ("cutting off") practice, founded by the enlightened female guru Machig Lapdron, which initially belonged to the Kagyupa sect of Tibetan Buddhism. In these practices, one practices the perfections of generosity and detachment by mentally offering one's body to demons as a feast. The purpose of the practice is to cut off our tendency to cling to the body (and the other aggregates). After one visualizes his or her body being cut up and devoured by demons, there is nothing left behind to which attachment can arise. If one can give up all the aggregates—of form, sensation, conception, volition, and consciousness—then only the state of emptiness will be left, from which it's easy to enter samadhi.

In the Chod practice, a practitioner first visualizes that their consciousness leaves the body through the top of the head. Then it forms into a wrathful deity that takes a crescent-shaped hooked knife and cuts off the top of the practitioner's head. This skull cup is then placed on a tripod of three skulls and rests over a burning flame. The rest of the body is then cut up piece by piece, and placed into the skull cap, which has greatly expanded in size. Then the whole cadaver is imagined to be transformed from the blood, flesh, bones, and entrails into the purest nectar, which is fed to every conceivable kind of being, thus satisfying their hungers, wishes, and desires.

After everyone has had their fill, the practitioner reminds himself or herself that the giver, offering, and recipients are all empty, and seeks to remain in that mental state of emptiness. The practice ends with prayers for the liberation of all beings. Thus the purpose and particulars of this practice are somewhat similar to the skeleton visualization method, but the white skeleton contemplation is superior in terms of changing the physical body and in enabling one to achieve samadhi because of the subsequent energy flows.

6. WATCHING THE BREATH

See Nan Huai-Chin's *Working Toward Enlightenment* and *To Realize Enlightenment* for a detailed working explanation of this method. A variety of Tao school breathing exercises can also be found in:

Huang, Jane. *The Primordial Breath*. Vol. 2. Rancho Palos Verdes, CA: Original Books, 1990.

Huang, Jane, and Michael Wurmbrand. *The Primordial Breath*. Vol. 1. Rancho Palos Verdes, CA: Original Books, 1987.

Yu, Lu K'uan. *The Secrets of Chinese Meditation*. York Beach, ME: Samuel Weiser, 1964.

Wong, Eva. *The Shambhala Guide to Taoism*. Boston: Shambhala Publications, 1997.

A variety of yoga pranayama techniques, with particular attention to Andre van Lysebeth's and Swami Saraswati's work, can be found in:

Hewitt, James. *The Complete Yoga Book: The Yoga of Breathing, Posture, and Meditation*. London: Rider, 1983.

Iyengar, B. K. S. *Light on Pranayama*. London: Unwin Paperbacks, 1988.

Lysebeth, Andre van. *Pranayama: The Yoga of Breathing*. London: Unwin Paperbacks, 1985.

Rama, Swami, Rudolph Ballantine, and Alan Hymes. *Science of Breath*. Honesdale, PA: Himalayan Institute, 1979.

Saraswati, Swami Muktibodhananda. *Swara Yoga*. Bihar, India: Bihar School of Yoga, 1984.

Saraswati, Swami Niranjanananda. *Prana, Pranayama, Prana Vidya*. Bihar, India: Bihar School of Yoga, 1994.

Sivapriyananda, Swami. *Secret Power of Tantric Breathing*. New Delhi: Abhinav Publications, 1996.

These books include the eight classical practices of pranayama: *sahita-kumbhaka, surya-bheda-kumbhaka, ujjayi-kumbhaka, shitali-kumbhaka, bhastrika-kumbhaka, bhramari-kumbhaka, murccha-kumbhaka,* and *kevali-kumbhaka.* These practices are important for purifying the physical body, but they cannot actually be regarded as "spiritual cultivation." Rather, as Patanjali said, "it's the cessation between the in-breath and out-breath [which] is pranayama," hence that's the important goal of breathing practices. It's not that you practice retaining the breath, but that you naturally reach a point of breath cessation, which is more easily attained if you first work to clean the mai through various other breathing practices.

Nonetheless, the eight classical methods of pranayama and other forms of breath practice can help you purify the body, open the mai, and cultivate the chi, although the real chi is not the external breath of oxygen that runs in and out through the body. Rather, the real chi arises during the point of rest between the inhalations and exhalations. If you can reach that point of stopping, and remain in that state, and have the mind and the breath combine into one, then you're on the correct path of cultivation. Be clear about this: don't forget this point!

That point of cessation is the stage of hsi that entails the initiation of the shakti, kundalini, or source of life. It's a stage that has tremendous force to transform the physical body, making it easier for you to enter samadhi. Some teachers suggest that you should count your breath rather than do these practices, but the counting of breaths is worthless in itself—the important matter is getting to that point of cessation. If counting your breath can help you calm the breath so that it arrives at that point, then it's worthwhile. Otherwise, it's just useless a exercise in counting and another means of busying your mind. Don't forget this principle.

When your breath finally does die down and stop, your thoughts will die down, the mind will become still, and then you can use your awareness to look around and see that this state is still a false construction but that the awareness that knows it and surrounds it is everywhere—formless, empty, without substance. This is using the discrimination of your prajna-wisdom to fathom the true nature of the mind. *This is the proper entry route into cultivation.* So don't get fooled or sidetracked by all the various breathing techniques in existence. This is their goal, which permits entry into the first dhyana. After you attain the first dhyana, you'll already have reached the point of respiratory cessation and you'll be perfectly clear about the significance of these practices. At that point you'll also switch your practice method and techniques, for like a raft that is used to cross a river, you leave it at the shore once its purpose is over.

7. THE ZHUNTI MANTRA

The story of Yuan Huang, and how he changed his fortune using the Zhunti mantra in conjunction with a ledger of merit and demerit, can be found in Cynthia J. Brokaw, *The Ledgers of Merit and Demerit,* (Princeton, NJ: Princeton University Press, 1991). Benjamin Franklin was able to transform his personality through a similar ledger based technique.

An abbreviated list of instructions for performing an intensive Zhunti sadhana are as follows:

Step 1: Sitting in a lotus posture, repeat the mantra OHM LAM twenty-one times, every seventh time adding a SVAHA (SO-HA).

Step 2: Repeat the mantra OHM CHAN twenty-one times, every seventh time adding a SVAHA as before. When done, seal the forehead, left shoulder, right shoulder, heart, and then throat with a touch of your closed fist. With each seal, say HUM. After the last touch, disperse the vajra seal mudra by opening the fist over the top of the head.

Step 3: Recite OHM MANI PADME HUM 108 times while visualizing Kuan-Yin bodhisattva in his four-armed form.

Step 4: Leave off any grasping of the self, the body, and the ego and imagine that everything becomes emptiness. Try to merge with emptiness so that you become immeasurable and formless. Imagine that all that exists is only emptiness, which is completely ungraspable.

Step 5: Within this emptiness, visualize a great wind arising that fills the entire universe. The friction of the wind makes it transform into a great universal fire. After a while, the heat of the fire produces an agglomeration of universal water and then the water cools to produce a diamond crystal earth. Visualize that from this crystal ground arises an eight-petalled lotus flower, and imagine that you are sitting in the center of this lotus with your head emitting a brilliantly shining light.

Step 6: Invite the original teacher, Vairocana Buddha, to appear, and imagine that he instantly manifests in a golden body. Make offerings to him, and then imagine that Vairocana enters your body through the top of your head so that the two of you become one.

Step 7: Visualize the buddha Manjushri manifesting in front of you and offer him all sorts of precious things. Imagine that he, too, enters into your body from the top of your head, so that now there are three bodies in one; together they have become one without any differentiation.

Step 8: Visualize a round mirror in front of you, in which an eighteen-armed Zhunti Buddha, seated in lotus posture, appears. When he appears, recite OHM HA-LI DEE-GA three times to see if he is a true or false manifestation. If he is genuine his visage will become clearer, but if he is false he will disappear. Then imagine that Zhunti Buddha merges with your body through the third eye located between your eyebrows. Imagine that you and Zhunti Buddha become one, non-dual, and non-distinct.

Step 9: Next visualize you become a transparent, crystal-like body that is completely pure and undefiled and that you are sitting on a red, eight-petalled lotus flower. A full moon then manifests above your head and is inscribed with the Sanskrit letters for the Zhunti mantra OHM ZHURLI ZHULI ZHUNTI SOHA. Begin reciting the

Zhunti mantra; as you recite it, the letters turn clockwise while shining brightly.

Step 10: When you are done reciting the Zhunti mantra several hundred times (the amount is up to the length of your mantra session), raise your hands above your head and release them; then return them to the sitting mudra position. Then imagine that all the letters in the moon disappear, except the letter for OHM. The moon becomes smaller and smaller until it becomes just a point of light which comes up to the top of the head, and then disappears into the void. Then there is no body, no emptiness, nothing at all. Remain in that state of meditation.

The OHM BRIN at the end of the Zhunti mantra was added by the wisdom buddha Manjushri in order to help practitioners achieve even quicker success in their practice.

As mentioned previously, you have to realize that the components of the Zhunti sadhana visualization are designed to mirror the stages of the path of cultivation in general, which also mirrors the process of material creation. In terms of the material or phenomenal aspect of the universe, you can say that everything started with emptiness or space. From this vast emptiness arose a type of movement akin to the functioning of wind. So from the stillness of yin the movement of yang was born. From the wind element the fire element evolved because of friction, and primordial chi became hot like fire. As it cooled it congealed to form the water element, meaning that it could flow like a stream of water. When it settled further, it became immovable like rock, which is the earth element, and yet the earth element has all the other elements within it. So the earth element can give birth to life, such as the flower on which Zhunti Buddha sits.

As to cultivation, from the stillness of mental cessation, your prenatal chi will begin to arise. This is emptiness giving birth to the wind element. Then the warmth element will arise; you chant or cultivate correctly, and the body will get warm. The stage of warming is the stage of kundalini, and with this heat the hormones at the top of the head (known as bindus, subtle drops, or jing in Taoism) will melt and descend to manifest bodily bliss. This is the bliss of the four dhyanas. From this stage you can then cultivate the entire body (the earth element), and then a new body will be formed (the earth element will give birth to life).

All this can happen if you cultivate the Zhunti mantra correctly, or the Vairocana mantra, which is especially aimed at transforming the body's elements. But the Zhunti is a special mantra in that it can help open up the heart chakra that lets you see the Tao and achieve enlightenment. That's why Zhunti Buddha is always visualized at either the brow chakra (third eye) or in the heart chakra. If you concentrate on a point within the body, the chi will concentrate in that point, and concentrated chi will bring about friction and an internal light. So cultivating in this manner, you can quickly change the body and bring about a stage of samadhi—and the Zhunti mantra is a particularly powerful method for doing so.

8. THE VAIROCANA MANTRA

In addition to the Vairocana mantra, other popular cultivation mantras include OHM MANI PADME HUM and OHM AH HUM. Hinduism has a number of other mantras as well, including invocations to the deities of the nine "planets" of the solar system, and mantras addressed to other celestial beings as well. However, these mantras typically address lower heavenly devas who have little power in helping people achieve ultimate self-realization. This is because they address celestial inhabitants who are also stuck in the Realm of Desire, rather than addressing fully enlightened buddhas for help. So while such mantras work on a coarse level, and can help us untangle the problems we encounter in our ordinary affairs—and while they can bring some assistance to our cultivation efforts—they can provide little of the assistance necessary for us to reach the great goal of liberation. Only the fully enlightened buddhas can provide such assistance.

9. THE AMITOFO MANTRA

In addition to the Amitofo mantra, there are many other mantras in the world which make use of the AH sound. This includes the mantras of AMEN, ALLELUIA, JEHOVAH, ALLAH, BRAHMA and so on. Thus the AH sound is extremely important. In fact, it is usually the first sound a being makes when it comes into the world.

Some practitioners recite the Amitofo mantra in conjunction with the three Amitabha Pure Land sutras or the *Lotus Sutra*, and many stories of the power behind sutra recitation can be found in *Miraculous Tales of the Lotus Sutra from Ancient Japan* (trans. by Yoshiko K. Dykstra, KUFS, 1983). Everyone has a different idea as to which translation of these sutras is the most elegant and wonderful, therefore the reader must choose. No matter which religion or creed you belong to, these are among the most beautiful pieces of spiritual literature available, which at the same time teach you how to cultivate.

Gomez, Luis O., trans. *The Land of Bliss: The Paradise of the Buddha of Measureless Light.* Honolulu: University of Hawaii Press, 1996.

Hisao, Inagaki, and Harold Stewart, trans. *The Three Pure Land Sutras.* Berkeley, CA: Numata Center for Buddhist Translation and Research, 1995.

Kato, Bunno, Yoshiro Tamura, and Kojiro Miyasaka, trans. *The Threefold Lotus Sutra.* Tokyo: Kosei Publishing Co., 1988.

Niwano, Nikkyo. *A Guide to the Threefold Lotus Sutra.* Tokyo: Kosei Publishing Co., 1988.

Soothill, W. E., trans. *The Lotus of the Wonderful Law.* London: Curzon Press, 1987.

Tsugunari, Kubo, and Yuhama Akira, trans. *The Lotus Sutra.* Berkeley, CA: Numata Center for Buddhist Translation and Research, 1993.

Watson, Burton, trans. *The Lotus Sutra.* New York: Columbia University Press, 1993.

Sutra recitation is itself a means of attaining samadhi, but in order for this method to be effective, the sutra must not simply be a holy text, but a text based on prajna-transcendental wisdom (and the translation must be excellent to reflect that as well). Thus we have the *Diamond Sutra* and other wisdom sutras, all of which are wonderful reading.

Buddhist Text Translation Society, trans. *Sutra of the Past Vows of Earth Store Bodhisattva.* New York: Institute for the Advanced Studies of World Religions, 1974.

Conze, Edward, trans. *The Large Sutra on Perfect Wisdom.* Berkeley, CA: University of California Press, 1975.

———. *Perfect Wisdom: The Short Prajnaparamita Texts.* London: Buddhist Publishing Group, 1993.

Hanh, Thich Nhat. *The Diamond That Cuts through Illusion: Commentaries on the Prajnaparamita Diamond Sutra.* Berkeley, CA: Parallax Press, 1992.

Hixon, Lex. *Mother of the Buddhas: Meditation on the Prajnaparamita Sutra.* Wheaton, IL: Quest Books, 1993.

Price, A. F., and Wong Mou-lam, trans. *The Diamond Sutra & The Sutra of Hui-Neng.* Boston: Shambhala Publications, 1990.

Thurman, Robert, trans. *The Holy Teaching of Vimalakirti.* Delhi: Motilal Banarsidass, 1991.

Yu, Lu K'uan, trans. *The Vimalakirti Nirdesa Sutra.* Boston: Shambhala Publications, 1972.

However, if there was just one sutra that a Westerner should read in order to gain an idea of the nature of Buddhism, the choice would have to be the *Great Jewel Heap Sutra.* Unfortunately, only part of this sutra has been translated in English, but it can be found in *A Treasury of Mahayana Sutras,* edited by C. C. Chang (Delhi: Motilal Banarsidass Publishers, 1991).

As to mantra practice itself, there are a number of titles on japa from India, but many deal with the lower mantras for obtaining luck and material possessions rather than for enlightenment. Any good book on Vedic astrology will contain mantras for the planetary devas used in astrological "remedial measures." A variety of mantra cassette tapes are also readily available from India, China, and Tibet. As to good references on Hindu japa practice, one can reference:

Alper, Harvey. *Understanding Mantra*. Albany, NY: SUNY Press, 1989.
Arya, Pandit Usharbudh. *Mantra and Meditation*. Honesdale, PA: The Himalayan Institute of Yoga Science and Philosophy, 1981.
Sivananda, Swami. *Japa Yoga*. Sivanandanagar, India: Divine Life Society, 1994.

10. NINE-STEP BOTTLED WIND PRACTICE

For more information on this particular practice, please see Glen Mullin, trans., *Tsong Khapa's Six Yogas of Naropa* (Ithaca, NY: Snow Lion Publications, 1996), and Sonam Chokyi Gyaltsan, *Tibetan Buddhist Meditation: A Systematic Analysis* (Hong Kong: Hong Kong Vajrayana Esoteric Society, 1985).

The importance of cleaning the body's chi channels (*nadi*) through this type of technique cannot be overstated. If you ever wish to succeed in the skeleton visualization, kundalini, or sexual yoga practices, as a cultivator *you must train in breath retention exercises that help open up the mai, clean the body, and thus prepare you for entering the state of respiratory cessation* when it occurs naturally through your other efforts.

To master breath retention exercises to the point where they have a positive effect on purifying the mai, you must eventually train to hold your breath for a minimum of several minutes. As the *Hatha Yoga Pradipika* states, you'll suffer in all sorts of ways as you first try to master this practice, so don't give up hope, and don't force it:

At the first stage perspiration will break out,
At the second stage the body will tremble,
At the third stage the chi will reach the center of the head
    by way of the central channel.
This is the way pranayama should be practiced.

So be gentle with yourself in this practice, yet consistent and persistent. Keep pushing for progress, but don't overextend yourself and "try to conquer Rome in a day." As Buddha said, you can't be too tight and you can't be too lax, and you mustn't hurt your physical body because you need it in cultivation. So use your wisdom to adjust your practice, as you would use it in adjusting the gas stove for cooking a meal, and don't hurt yourself through this practice.

To learn of the other methods of classical yoga pranayama forced breath retention, please see our previously referenced titles:

Hewitt, James. *The Complete Yoga Book: The Yoga of Breathing, Posture, and Meditation.* London: Rider, 1983.

Iyengar, B. K. S. *Light on Pranayama.* London: Unwin Paperbacks, 1988.

Lysebeth, Andre van. *Pranayama: The Yoga of Breathing.* London: Unwin Paperbacks, 1985.

Rama, Swami, Rudolph Ballantine, and Alan Hymes. *Science of Breath.* Honesdale, PA: Himalayan Institute, 1979.

Saraswati, Swami Muktibodhananda. *Swara Yoga.* Bihar, India: Bihar School of Yoga, 1984.

Saraswati, Swami Niranjanananda. *Prana, Pranayama, Prana Vidya.* Bihar, India: Bihar School of Yoga, 1994.

Saraswati, Swami Satyananda. *A Systematic Course in the Ancient Tantric Techniques of Yoga and Kriya.* Bihar, India: Bihar School of Yoga, 1981.

———. *Asana, Pranayama, Mudra, Bandha.* Bihar, India: Bihar School of Yoga, 1989.

In the coming years, more and more fine books on pranayama will be printed in English, but you must remember that these are only preparatory practices for the process of cultivation; they are not the true heart of cultivation in themselves. Furthermore, if you become too immersed in the technical details of pranayama, you'll get lost in a minor technique and bypass the meaning and purpose of the path. Hence if we had to choose one and only one pranayama practice to recommend to others, we would choose the nine-bottled wind practice, as it covers all the other methods within. In addition, we would encourage people to study the Chinese Tien-tai philosophy of using the breath as an entry into enlightenment, which we've revealed in the chapter on watching the breath.

This combination of practices from different schools is the proper, nonsectarian approach to attainment that is totally based on scientific principles. In the path of cultivation, your practice should be like running a factory for efficiency and maximum profits. Hence you should forget about dogma and particular religious backgrounds (do they not all lead to the same source?) but pick the best practices from among the world's schools in order to make progress. As a popular saying runs, "The stone of another mountain can be used to polish the jade."

Thus cultivation practices are nondenominational, cultivation principles are nondenominational scientific principles, the stages of kung-fu are predictable, scientific events, and the eight samadhi are nondenominational stages shared by all the cultivation schools and realms of beings. There is no such thing as sectarianship in the true path of cultivation; there is only friendship and the nondenominational desire to help others.

11. KUNDALINI YOGA FOR OPENING THE CENTRAL CHANNEL

There are scores of books on kundalini available today, with many new ones arriving from India now that "masters" have realized there is a market for this material, but most of these texts are useless. It seems that you can more readily sell a book if you put the word "kundalini" on the cover, and the problem has arisen in that almost everyone can talk about kundalini without ever having tasted the experience or even intellectually understanding what it actually entails.

This is a sorry state of affairs, and the overemphasis on kundalini as a goal in itself is ridiculous, since it's just the warming stage of cultivation. The real stage of cultivation lies beyond and has to do with transforming the mind and its knots and entanglements of bad behavior. But this overemphasis on a specific technology or phenomenon of the path is the problem that results when people take the external signs or marks of the path and try to make these results the central purpose of the path. In these cases, which are characteristics of the form-based cultivation paths, confusion always results.

Nevertheless, to really start researching the matter, the best references on kundalini we can find to date include:

Chang, Garma C. C., trans. *Teachings of Tibetan Yoga*. New York: Carol Publishing Group, 1993.

Cozort, Daniel. *Highest Yoga Tantra*. Ithaca, NY: Snow Lion Publications, 1986.

Dhargyey, Geshe Ngawang. *Kalacakra Tantra*. Delhi: Library of Tibetan Works and Archives, 1994.

Evans-Wentz, W. Y. *Tibetan Yoga and Secret Doctrines*. Oxford: Oxford University Press, 1967.

Gyatso, Geshe Kelsang. *Tantric Grounds and Paths*. London: Tharpa Publications, 1994.

Mullin, Glen, trans. *Readings on the Six Yogas of Naropa*. Ithaca, NY: Snow Lion Publicaitons, 1997.

———. *Tsong Khapa's Six Yogas of Naropa*. Ithaca, NY: Snow Lion Publications, 1996.

Nan, Huai-Chin. *Tao and Longevity: Mind-Body Transformation*. Wen Kuan Chu, trans. York Beach, ME: Samuel Weiser, 1984.

Rieker, Hans-Ulrich. *The Yoga of Light*. London: Unwin Paperbacks, 1971.

Saraswati, Swami Muktibodhananda. *Hatha Yoga Pradipika*. Monghyr, India: Bihar School of Yoga, 1993.

———. *Swara Yoga*. Bihar, India: Bihar School of Yoga, 1984.

Saraswati, Swami Satyananda. *A Systematic Course in the Ancient Tantric Techniques of Yoga and Kriya*. Monghyr, India: Bihar School of Yoga, 1981.

Silburn, Lillian. *Kundalini: Energy of the Depths*. Albany, NY: SUNY Press, 1988.

Tsong Khapa's *Six Yogas* is a particularly helpful text in decipher-ing many esoteric techniques, and any texts of the "Six Yogas of Naropa" specifically enter into the topic of kundalini cultivation, which is the technology of cultivating the tumo heat. The various Tibetan tantric methods, which can be confusing, can be understood by using this text in conjunction with Daniel Cozort's *Highest Yoga Tantra* and Kelsang Gyatso's *Tantric Grounds and Paths.*

As a warning about the practice of kundalini yoga, we must point out that it is not the only way to practice, *but just a convenient way to practice* among the many methods commonly available. An extraordi-narily large number of people who devote themselves to this sort of practice typically go astray because they become intoxicated with the desire for superpowers and experiential realms, or "secret supernatural teachings of miracles and marvels" which poison the true path to cul-tivation. The path of cultivation has to do with behavior; the samadhi and dhyanas are only a means to help you see your behavior and trans-form it. When you believe that kundalini cultivation is the path, you've already missed the path by a million miles!

There is a strong tendency for people to seek or come into con-tact with methods of cultivation that seem mysterious, and to turn to them with dizzying enthusiasm. Kundalini yoga is one such method that has suffered this fate. Hence many people succumb to the false notion that only Tibetan esoteric Buddhism, or kundalini cultivation, are the correct way to become enlightened in this lifetime. As to the other cultivation methods, they mistakenly feel they're not even worth trying. We can only say in response, "When the causal ground is not genuine, the results obtained are twisted."

12. BARDO PRACTICES

To practice the bardo yogas dealing with death, you have to become familiar with the bardo teachings well before your actual demise and, furthermore, you must also become familiar with the experience of emptiness. Otherwise, if you are not familiar with the bodiless state, then fear will grip you upon death and you won't be able to practice the bardo teachings. It's a little like flying in an airplane; the first time you might be very scared, but if you fly a lot and become accustomed to the practice, then it's old hat. Hence, if you familiarize yourself with the bardo teachings and practice to attain the state of emptiness before dying, you won't be frightened upon dying but will be able to put the teachings into practice.

For more information on the bardo yogas, please see:

Gyaltsen, Shardza Tashi. *Heart Drops of Dharmakaya*. Ithaca, NY: Snow Lion Publications, New York, 1993.

Mullin, Glen, trans. *Tsong Khapa's Six Yogas of Naropa*. Ithaca, NY: Snow Lion Publications, 1996.

Rangdrol, Tsele Natsok. *The Mirror of Mindfulness: The Cycle of the Four Bardos*. Boston: Shambhala Publications, 1989.

Rinpoche, Sogyal. *The Tibetan Book of Living and Dying*. San Francisco: HarperSanFrancisco, 1992.

Thurman, Robert, trans. *The Tibetan Book of the Dead*. New York: Bantam, 1994.

These books also explain the various stages of the death process, such as when the wind, water, earth, and fire elements of the physical body begin the process of dissolution, and when the various consciousnesses also begin to disintegrate. For virtuous people, death almost always starts in the feet and works upward, as illustrated in the story of how Socrates died after drinking the hemlock.

The actual stages of the death process can be found in the following texts, which are extremely useful for understanding these matters as well as a whole variety of Tibetan cultivation methods in general. Together with *Tsong Khapa's Six Yogas of Naropa* they provide a very complete introduction to the basics of esoteric Buddhist cultivation, which revolves around cultivating the body's wind element.

Dhargyey, Geshe Ngawang. *Kalacakra Tantra*. Delhi: Library of Tibetan Works and Archives, 1994.

Gyatso, Geshe Kelsang. *Clear Light of Bliss*. London: Wisdom Publications, 1982.

Rinpoche, Lati. *Meditative States in Tibetan Buddhism*. London: Wisdom Publications, 1983.

For more information on interpreting other bardo cultivation practices that focus on the center, such as the bardo intercessory periods between two thoughts, or the period between waking and sleeping, the period between two sensations, between two breaths, between two steps, or between any two experiences whatsoever, one can reference the many works now available on Kashmir Shaivism. As an example, the *Slokastaka* says, "If you maintain your awareness at that point that is found between waking and sleeping, you will be focused on that supreme felicity that is the supreme bliss of God consciousness." Suitable works mentioning the "practice of centering" found in Kashmir Shaivism, which is the bardo of intercessory periods, include:

Hughes, John. *Self-Realization in Kashmir Shaivism: The Oral Teachings of Swami Lakshmankjoo*. Albany, NY: SUNY Press, 1994.

Jee, Swami Lakshman. *Kashmir Shaivism: The Secret Supreme*. Albany, NY: SUNY Press, 1988.

Mishra, Kamalakar. *Kashmir Saivism: The Central Philosophy of Tantrism*. Portland, OR: Rudra Press, 1993.

Singh, Jaideva, trans. *The Yoga of Delight, Wonder, and Astonishment*. Albany, NY: SUNY Press, 1991.

But these aren't the only important works, because the school of Kashmir Shaivism is rich with its own methods and detailed process of cultivation. In fact, the *Vijnana-Bhairava* of the school describes 112 methods for concentrating the mind alone, and many of its suggestions can be used as a supplement to this text. Just as each cultivation school often has a definitive scholar and enlightened master you should reference—such as the great Hindu sage Shankara of Vedanta, or master

Tsongkhapa of the Tibetan school—one can study Kashmir Shaivism by reading the works of the sage Abhinavagupta, who detailed many cultivation methods.

For instance, there's meditation on the central channel, the sound of a musical instrument, the flow of the breath, the universe in its vast entirety, and meditation on the void. There's even meditation on sexual pleasure or the memory of sexual pleasure, as long as it doesn't lead to distraction, and you already know the warnings behind this. As we've often stated, once you know the basic method and principles, the ten thousand variations on a theme all become clear. What you use, and what path you choose is all up to your wisdom and use of expedient (skillful) methods. In cultivation, no one can "cook the rice" for you, since it's your own internal body and mind. You must learn for yourself how to balance things to achieve harmony.

13. FOCUSING THE VISION ON AN OBJECT

For a detailed discussion on this particular methodology, please see *Tao and Longevity: Mind-Body Transformation*. As stated there, you can extend the principles of this form of practice to meditation, or contemplation, which involves viewing natural lights such as the sun, moon, and stars.

In all these cases, you must remember that the body must be loose and free of restrictions, the breathing must be encouraged to calm down, and the mind must not veer off to play with thoughts; there should be only one object of focus. Even if you're doing one-pointed focus exercises, you must still reach the point where the breath recedes into cessation, otherwise you won't be able to enter into samadhi; you'll just develop the ability for mundane one-pointedness. If you understand these principles, and the principles of watching the breath and thoughts, then you can use this technique to enter a stage of one-pointed concentration.

In all the practices of cultivation, one can't emphasize these principles enough. If you know the principles, then eventually your practice will match the theory; you'll really grasp the meaning of these principles only after you achieve them, but you don't have to produce them forcefully since they'll happen naturally. Cultivation theory only charts them out for you, making it easier for you to recognize your progress and stage on the path.

Since focusing the vision on an object to attain samadhi is a practice common to most cultivation schools, one might also reference the following books:

Aranya, Swami Hariharananda. *Yoga Philosophy of Patanjali*. Albany, NY: SUNY Press, 1983.

Iyengar, B. K. S. *Light on the Yoga Sutras of Patanjali*. London: The Aquarian Press, 1993.

Prabhavananda, Swami, and Christopher Isherwood, trans. *How to Know God: The Yoga Aphorisms of Patanjali*. New York: Penguin, 1969.

Rieker, Hans-Ulrich. *The Yoga of Light*. London: Unwin Paperbacks, 1971.

Another route, which is related to one-pointed visualization practice, would be to research the methods within the *Visuddhi-magga (Path of Purification)* written by the Buddhist monk Buddhaghosha. In this Pali text, which was used as a training manual for monks on the Hinayana path, Buddhaghosha mentioned forty-two props that can be used as a focus for one-pointed concentration practice. These forty-two objects of focus include:

- ten kasinas (such as the marks of the five elements and special colors),
- ten loathesome objects (such as the stages of decaying corpses),
- ten ideas (such as the Buddhist dharma, sangha, and the great roads of practice),
- the four universal states of infinite friendship, compassion, joy, and equanimity,
- the four formless samadhi absorptions,
- the four qualities which material elements possess (extension, movement, heat, and cohesion).

Those who succeed in attaining the realm of samadhi concentration either by focusing on these objects or using them as focusing props for internal mental concentration often develop superpowers and psychic abilities. Before they succeed in achieving these various specialized samadhi, they often perceive a special "mark" or sign indicating the success of the samadhi in question. Most of this is explained in Bhadantacariya Buddhaghosha, *The Path of Purification (Visuddhimagga)*, trans. by Bhikkhu Nanamoli (Sri Lanka: Buddhist Publication Society, 1991).

14. ATHLETIC "PEAK PERFORMANCE" AND CHI CULTIVATION

There are a tremendous number of books now available on exercises for changing the physical body. We therefore mention only four that are indicative of the genre:

Iyengar, B. K. S. *Light on Yoga*. London: Unwin Paperbacks, 1988.
Kelder, Peter. *Tibetan Secrets of Youth and Vitality*. London: The Aquarian Press, 1985.
Liao, Waysun. *T'ai Chi Classics*. Boston: Shambhala Publications, 1990.
Saraswati, Swami Satyananda. *A Systematic Course in the Ancient Tantric Techniques of Yoga and Kriya*. Monghyr, India: Bihar School of Yoga, 1981.

The number of good books on yoga, Aikido, Tai Chi, and other soft martial arts (which end up helping the body because they concentrate on chi) is overwhelming and increasing every day, but in terms of changing the physical structure, one should also take note of the following fields:

- Chiropractic adjustment
- Deep tissue massage (Rolfing, Hellerwork, and so on)
- NMT (neuromuscular therapy)
- Lymph drainage

- Colonics
- Acupuncture
- Internal organ balancing
- Visceral manipulation
- The Taoist five organ sounds
- Cranial sacral work

And so on. All these methods can help change the physical nature and lighten the burden it imposes on the road of cultivation. Although they cannot lead you into samadhi, they are all encouraged as helping to adjust the physical nature to a more harmonious state. In cultivation, it is also important to understand medicine and anatomy, and such books are recommended as well.

In general, we can consider physical exercises as a means of purifying or cleansing the physical body to make it easier for the individual to succeed in cultivation. The skeleton visualization method, fasting, pranayama, and the ingestion of certain herbal medicines or dietary supplements have the same aim of helping to transform the physical nature and to clear it of obstructions that stand in the way of spiritual progress.

For instance, if the body is unhealthy or biochemically unbalanced, it is difficult to maintain a stable emotional state, or to act in a proper manner when the body is pulling you in another direction. Thus exercises should be seen as a way to tune and clean the physical body. In this light, the shat kriyas purification techniques of Hatha yoga and the related methods of the Chinese Tao school become very important. Some simple references include:

Berk, William. *Chinese Healing Arts*. Burbank, CA: Unique Publications, 1986.
Chia, Mantak. *Chi Self-Massage*. New York: Healing Tao Books, 1986.
Hewitt, James. *The Complete Yoga Book: The Yoga of Breathing, Posture, and Meditation*. London: Rider, 1983.
Iyengar, B. K. S. *Light on Yoga*. London: Unwin Paperbacks, 1988.

Kriyananda, Goswami. *The Spiritual Science of Kriya Yoga*. Chicago: The Temple of Kriya Yoga, 1992.

Saraswati, Swami Satyananda. *Asana, Pranayama, Mudra, Bandha*. Monghyr, India: Bihar School of Yoga, 1989.

In addition to sports performance, there are all sorts of other mundane samadhi, such as the jada samadhi practices, reached through mudra and pranayama practice, that allow a yogi to be buried under ground for weeks at a time without harm. Since these types of samadhi don't help destroy the passions, lead to spiritual wisdom, or help you escape from the cycle of birth and death to reach liberation, they are basically states of physical control rather than spiritual attainment. The state of trance doesn't qualify as samadhi either, for during a trance you are not clear and aware or in control of your mind.

15. INGESTING WAI-DAN (SIDDHI MEDICINE, OR EXTERNAL ALCHEMY)

In cultivation, there are schools of both internal and external alchemy. India calls its school of external alchemy *Siddhi medicine*, or *rasayana*, and its goal is to banish sickness, rejuvenate youth, bolster immunity, and enable the individual to live an endless life. There's even a yogic branch of medicine called *kaya kalpa* that is aimed at physical immortality. The Tao school calls its brand of internal alchemy *wai-dan*, which means "external elixirs" or medicines, and this school shares the same general goals and purposes.

These schools both use external substances such as mercury, gold, arsenic, sulfur, pearls, and special herbs to help kill germs (the three "worms") and transform the body. But substances cannot transform the body unless it is already internally balanced and clean, so a large variety of cultivation exercises and medicines are designed to *first help clean the practitioner's body*. In modern lingo, their primary purpose is one of internal cleansing and detoxification, especially as regards the digestive system and mai.

You can say the purpose of this is to rid the body of poisons, to restore the body's natural acid-alkaline, biochemical, and homeostatic balances, or to make it possible to deliver more oxygen to the cells, but the purpose is to remove obstructions within the body that deliver nutrients or carry away wastes, and to remove the accumulations of waste deposits. So the modern practices of liver detoxification using glutathione and N-acetylcysteine, or of arterial cleansing through chelation therapy using EDTA, or of colonic therapy to clean the colon, and of herbal remedies to counter parasites or Candida albicans, or of vitamin supplements and antioxidants, can all be classified as wai-dan.

We also have various Hatha yoga exercises for cleaning the internal body, and practices for "balancing the doshas," such as drinking the middle portion of one's urine upon arising in the morning (urine therapy). If you try to take medicinal substances when the body is internally unpurified (because the processes of elimination are hampered), its organs are unbalanced, and its pH is in disequilibrium, then adding pure medicines to a dirty body can be compared to throwing springwater into a cesspool.

For any sort of rejuvenation to occur during cultivation, you must rid the body of the poisons it has accumulated over the years. This is one reason why it is easier for younger people to cultivate than older people, another reason being their greater vitality. And yet the offsetting factor is that youth often allow their vitality to leak. But the important point is that the initial stages of cultivation, and all the sensations and physical reactions that result, are entirely the effects of a process of purification—purification of the chi, mai, and jing.

No one ever says this clearly, but this is the basis behind the initial stages of kung-fu. They're all a process of purification and refinement, in short, a form of mental and physical detoxification. The mind rides on chi, and initially our chi is too coarse and impure to allow us to see the Tao, so we have to go through a long process of preparatory practices to purify and refine the chi and master the mind, to be able to see the path and cultivate toward realization. Otherwise, our bodies and minds are just too impure. That's why the ordinary person doesn't get anywhere in cultivation practice. The entire purpose of the "illusory body" of Tibetan Tantra, the "thought-generated body" of Buddhism, which arises as you break through the skandha of sensation, the "yin and yang body" of Taoism, and so on, is to use this esoteric structure, which naturally arises during the course of cultivation, as a means to see the Tao, to realize emptiness and prajna-wisdom. They aren't real bodies in themselves, and they're no more important than our coarse bodies of form, but their purity enables some further progress and insight on the path of attainment. But don't get trapped into thinking that you need these forms for cultivation, or that only purified form enables you to see the Tao. What lets you realize the Tao is formless prajna-wisdom.

All the substances you can take to help heal and transform the physical body, such as ionic trace mineral preparations, which are especially helpful, are a wonderful assist to the cultivation path. But you mustn't get the idea that they are the path, or that any of the kung-fu that you can produce from your cultivation is the path either. As a famous Taoist said in regard to ingesting external substances to purify the body:

> As to the five special minerals and eight precious stones, yes they're good, but I know that the dharma is emptiness. If I want to become an immortal [spiritual sage], why should I use external herbs?—There's much better ways. I can actually produce this wonderful medicinal life essence [ambrosia] in my own body.

Hence he was referring to the process of transforming jing to chi, chi to shen and shen into emptiness, which is the basis of the school of internal alchemy.

Internal alchemy, rather than external alchemy, is a process of directly cultivating the internal substances of the body that produce our esoteric kung-fu, but you mustn't think that you have to force these essences into undergoing certain transformations, as the process of transmutation must be a totally natural, unforced process. It's a natural occurrence, that's why it's Tao.

We might even be feeding you poison in telling you all these "secret" principles and making clear how all these form teachings interrelate, as the history of cultivation shows that too much form school knowledge leads to wasting time in intellectualization rather than in spiritual practice, thus cutting off the cultivation path. This has been the case in Taoism, Tibetan esotericism, and Indian yoga, and now the New Age schools are following the same misguided route. But our modern era is one of science, so all these principles must now be clearly known. If they don't become known, and people don't realize that cultivation has a scientific basis, it will go the way of religion and slowly die off. Hence our discussion is meeting the needs of the times, and in several hundred years the needs will change once again.

All the forms of cultivation teachings arise in response to the needs of the time. The method and process and kung-fu of cultivation is the same, but the methods of description, the points of emphasis, and of course the phraseology and practices of transmission change to suit each era. Today the needs of modern people require that cultivation be discussed in the format of a science, and the cross-cultural nature of the path must also be brought out. In the short space provided, this is what we've tried to do in this book.

Unfortunately, just as in China's Sung dynasty, the New Age schools have seized on portions of the cultivation path and made a mess out of things. In addition, people don't recognize that the different spiritual traditions each contain part of the total picture but may be lacking important elements of the path. Hence people will look in the Bible for chakras; if they aren't there, well, forget about the path! Or people will grab onto certain practices like fads, going from crystals to dreams to channeling to chakras, and say this is cultivation.

When people try to become a little more scientific, lacking the fundamental basics they end up championing various misguided efforts such as chi-gong, which tries to forcefully guide your chi through the body's energy meridians in order to open up the chakras. If you cultivate emptiness, this will all happen naturally but with forced meditations this won't happen at all! However, chi-gong practice will indeed produce sensations of the wind element that will trick you into believing you've made some progress on the path. So lacking a knowledge of principles, people fall into their own self-delusions.

Such are examples of the mistakes in cultivation, especially those that occur in the cultivation schools based on manipulations of form. Science is another form-based school, and we can't say it's free of mistakes or superstition either. Science says one thing today and people flock to it in belief; five years later science reverses its opinion, and then people run off in the other direction. If you don't understand the principles of cultivation theory and practice, it's not cultivation. Instead, sadhana practice then falls into the realm of superstition.

On the path of cultivation, there is the belief that arises through ignorance and the belief that comes from wisdom, and the process of attainment in cultivation is always based on attainments in wisdom. In the traditional cultivation schools of Confucianism or Buddhism, if a practitioner didn't know something, he would feel ashamed; this is the same standard of behavior that should be adopted by a true cultivation practitioner today. In fact, there are five areas of understanding that a cultivation adept should try to master: (1) the inner understanding of the cultivation path and attainment, which comes from the process of cultivation and awakening to the path; (2) the understanding of the process of causation, which means mastering logic, philosophy, and the human and natural sciences; (3) the understanding of linguistics and literature, which is understanding "sound"; (4) the understanding of practical techniques, which is the world of technology; and (5) the understanding of medicines, which means becoming expert at medicines, nutrition, anatomy-physiology, and healing.

Hence in terms of wai-dan, there are many books available for learning about Chinese herbal medicine and rejuvenation tonics. Just a short list includes:

Kaptchuk, Ted. *The Web That Has No Weaver.* Congdon & Weed, New York, 1983.

Liu, Yanchi. *The Essential Book of Traditional Chinese Medicine,* vol. 1. New York: Columbia University Press, 1995.

Lu, Henry. *Legendary Chinese Healing Herbs.* Selangor Darul Ehsan, Malaysia: Pelanduk Publications, 1992.

Ni, Maoshing, trans. *The Yellow Emperor's Classic of Medicine.* Boston: Shambhala Publications, 1995.

Reid, Daniel. *Guarding the Three Treasures.* New York: Simon & Schuster, 1993.

———. *The Tao of Health, Sex and Longevity.* New York: Positive Paperbacks, 1991.

Every cultivator is encouraged to learn something about Chinese medicine, Indian ayurveda, herbs, and modern nutritional theories (vitamin-mineral supplements), and forms of structural alignment or body manipulation. These disciplines often can help you correct physical problems that appear in conjunction with cultivation kung-fu, whereas Western medicine would certainly fail in properly diagnosing and dealing with such situations, especially as it does not understand the physical changes experienced by cultivation practitioners. To learn something of the Indian *ayurvedic* (holistic medical) principles as they apply to siddhi medicines, one can reference:

Dash, Vaidya Bhagwan. *Alchemy and Metallic Medicines in Ayurveda.* Delhi: Concept Publishing, 1996.

Jaggi, O. P. *Yogic and Tantric Medicine.* Delhi: Atmas Ram and Sons, 1973.

Mahdihassan, S. *Indian Alchemy or Rasayana.* Delhi: Motilal Banarsidass Publications, 1991.

Murthy, T. S. Anantha. *Maharaj.* Lower Lake, CA: The Dawn Horse Press, 1972.

Velan, A. S. *Siddhar's Science of Longevity and Kalpa Medicine of India.* Madras, India: Sakthi Nilayam, 1963.

White, David Gordon. *The Alchemical Body.* Chicago: University of Chicago Press, 1996.

Zvelebil, Kamil V. *The Siddha Quest for Immortality*. Oxford, England: Mandrake, 1996.

To learn something of the sequences and substances of internal alchemy, please see:

Bertschinger, Richard. *The Secret of Everlasting Life*. Shaftesbury, England: Element Books, 1994.

Cleary, Thomas, trans. *Practical Taoism*. Boston: Shambhala Publications, 1996.

———. *The Inner Teachings of Taoism*. Boston: Shambhala Publications, 1986.

———. *The Secret of the Golden Flower*. New York: HarperCollins, 1991.

———. *Understanding Reality: A Taoist Alchemical Classic*. Honolulu: University of Hawaii Press, 1987.

———. *Vitality, Energy, Spirit: A Taoist Sourcebook*. Boston: Shambhala Publications, 1991.

Hwang, Shi Fu, and Cheney Crow, trans. *Tranquil Sitting*. St. Paul, MN: Dragon Door Publications, 1995.

Nan, Huai-Chin. *Tao and Longevity: Mind-Body Transformation*. Wen Kuan Chu, trans. York Beach, ME: Samuel Weiser, 1984.

Olson, Stuart Alve, trans. *The Jade Emperor's Mind Seal Classic*. St. Paul, MN: Dragon Door Publications, 1992.

Wong, Eva. *The Shambhala Guide to Taoism*. Boston: Shambhala Publications, 1997.

Wong, Eva, trans. *Cultivating Stillness*. Boston: Shambhala Publications, 1992.

———. *Harmonizing Yin and Yang* [*The Dragon-Tiger Classic*]. Boston: Shambhala Publications, 1997.

Yu, Lu K'uan. *Taoist Yoga: Alchemy and Immortality*. London: Rider, 1970; York Beach, ME: Samuel Weiser, 1970.

As stated, the basic principle behind wai-dan (external alchemy) is to clean the internal physical body and remove the obstructions which block the flow of chi. If this is done, the body will reach a state of optimum health and equilibrium that, because of its perfection, will more easily allow the transformation of jing into chi and chi into shen. When the body is healthy, you can more easily forget your physical nature and because of this detachment, more easily enter samadhi, whereas if you're sick you're always in pain, discomfort and distraction. If the body becomes purified and the organs function in biochemical equilibrium, it is easy to enter the bliss of the first dhyana, and if the body is really clean it is easy for the chi to reach the soles of the feet, after which one can extend life indefinitely.

Thus all the means of "transforming" and "perfecting" the physical body, whether through exercise or medicine, *have the one goal of purifying, cleaning, and internally balancing the physical body so that it becomes a better vehicle for cultivation.* The lower goal is health for health's sake, which is prizing form at the expense of the transcendental. After all, health disappears when you die, and from the moment of birth you are constantly dying, but the results of cultivation go on and on.

Ascetic practices, which cause harm to the body and inhibit the arising of bliss, therefore represent an obstruction on the path and are the antithesis of cultivation. As the *Pingala Upanishad* of Hinduism states, "Though men should perform difficult tapas, such as standing on one leg for a period of one thousand years, it will not, in the very least, be equal to one tiny part of dhyana meditation." And yet people will still take this route that harms the physical body, and think it to be cultivation. This is just ignorance, which is a lack of wisdom. However, the practices of internally purifying the physical body through exercise, such as found in the balance of Hatha yoga, can be very helpful in conjunction with wai-dan. Balance is a major principle of the path.

Because various wai-dan formulas can be quite helpful to beginning meditators at the initial stages of cleaning the physical body and transforming the chi and mai, the authors greatly welcome any information on siddhi medicines that readers might volunteer, from whatever school, which we hope to make available at a later date. The results of cultivation must be matched with science, and since such substances are already in a form that science can test, they offer a useful means to help science verify the claims of the lower stages of the path.

The gradual convergence of the schools of herbology, nutrition, and pharmacology, with an emphasis on scientific longevity and physical well-being, makes this task of collecting information on wai-dan medicines an important priority at this time in history. It's one of our priorities to interject a spiritual aspect, and cultivation understanding of these matters into these modern trends, otherwise the continual progress of science will lead us further and further away from true spirituality and true cultivation achievements. Then the paths of religious and cultivation practice will become totally extinct. Hence an effort must be made to bring scientific understanding into the higher path of cultivation, which actually includes science as one of its subsets. Otherwise the path and practice of cultivation itself may suffer extinction. Don't underestimate this because it is a very real possibility; this is a very serious matter. Hence we greatly welcome your contributions, information, sources and findings on various external medicines that help change the body and better prepare it for entry into samadhi.

16. SEXUAL CULTIVATION

Today there are lots of books on the topic of sexual tantra, and we could easily list several dozen that say they're teaching this topic. But you're not going to find any of the genuine sexual cultivation teachings in these books, or even in the *Kama Sutra, Perfumed Garden, Koka Shastra, Sutra of the Plain Girl* or in the tantric teachings taught publicly today, whether you study with one or even a hundred masters who claim a secret lineage or authority in these matters from some other empowerment. And you must particularly beware of "masters" from economically deprived or backward regions with a guru-worshipping culture, who come to more economically advanced (richer) countries and teach these topics in a "secret transmission." The process of cultivation involves becoming responsible for yourself and increasing your level of wisdom, but if you're lacking in wisdom no one can save you.

Hence none of the popular texts you can encounter can claim they actually contain the genuine principles of sexual cultivation. Of course you can find some interesting or even useful information on the *asanas* (positions) of sexual union for medical purposes in healing disease, and for producing a balanced flow of energies between the bodies in an embrace, but this information constitutes sexual yoga rather than sexual cultivation. Most of these textbooks are works on sexual positions and nonejaculation yoga that fruitlessly attempt to spiritualize lust. A cardinal tenet in sexual cultivation is that there be an absence of sexual desire, and the purpose is to rid you of sexual desire so that you can jump out of the Desire Realm heavens and into the first dhyana. Which book has ever dealt with such matters?

To be qualified for practicing sexual cultivation, *you must have tremendous merit, must already have achieved samadhi, must have progressed past the generation stage yogas of purifying your chi and mai, and you must be proficient at both the skeleton visualization and vase breathing practices.* It's even said that you must possess the merit of a king, or the merit of a queen, and even then you have the problem of finding a karmically related, qualified partner. So who on this world is qualified for these Desire Heaven practices? In the four classes of Tibetan Tantra, practitioners are supposed to cultivate bliss through looking, laughing, embracing, or holding hands, but people don't realize that these are the methods of sexual pleasure experienced in the Desire Realm heavens that rank higher than this world. Hence most of the tantric practices were meant for the inhabitants of heavenly levels with a higher degree of merit than we typically find in a human birth.

Nonetheless, information on these methods is starting to spread widely, so it's become necessary to at least point out some of the mistaken ways and false notions that people have succumbed to in their pursuit of "sexual cultivation." Without going into all the other necessary qualifications for this practice, we can assume a need for proficiency in samadhi and the fact that you've come in contact with these teachings as some partial indication of the requisite merit. But lacking great merit and the prerequisite of the samadhi corresponding to higher realms, don't even think about sexual cultivation. Lacking the pre-requisites, the practice becomes one of sexual yoga only: this is a fact.

In general, most people aren't even qualified to hear about sexual cultivation teachings, let alone practice them. That's why Shakyamuni Buddha, even with all his highly gifted students *who were so qualified that they were able to achieve enlightenment during his lifetime,* refused to teach these practices. The great Tibetan master Tsongkhapa, in viewing all the harm they had caused, also said that monks should not practice these techniques either, and the Ming dynasty Emperors of China out-lawed the esoteric school because of the abuses that arose from prac-ticing these techniques. Yet all individuals are attracted to the idea of sex, and hence everyone rushes to hear about these teachings when they couldn't care less about any of the other dharma doors to samad-hi. This is the way of the world.

People don't realize that it takes several lives of merit to be born with beautiful features and a pleasant-looking body, but several times this number of virtuous lives are required to accumulate enough merit to be born with the sexual organs suited for attainment with this technique. And this is not referring to the ability to master the vam-pirish practices of *vajroli mudra,* whose practitioners are destined for the hells because individuals try to suck the sexual energies from their partners. If people cannot understand even these basic issues, and lack even these basic qualifications, what makes them think they are qual-ified to practice the true sexual cultivation, or capable of learning it from a book?

Nevertheless, people can use the path of sexual yoga to try and make progress in their cultivation, but without the foundation we've indicated, people are just kidding themselves if they say they are using sex as a means of cultivation. You have to be clear on this notion. Anyone who wants to succeed in sexual cultivation must already have mastered some stage of samadhi, of opening the central channel, and must have mastered pranayama, cessation and contemplation, and the skeleton visualization technique. Those are the preliminary instructions for sexual yoga practice.

Now, if sexual cultivation partners fulfill these requirements and are successful with their practice, the partners will experience their bodies permeated with bliss during the sexual act, their minds will be joyful and calm (free of sexual desire), and they will be able to realize the *inherent clear brightness of the mind*. The Tibetan school has an overlooked teaching that points out that you might possibly see the Tao in a state of extreme anger, sadness, drunkenness, or joy (including during sexual intercourse)—though you shouldn't cultivate these states—and this point must be related here. However, the stage of attainment possible through sexual cultivation is only the first dhyana, which is just above the Desire Realm heavens; it isn't the true clear light.

There are no books which explain these details, but to understand sexual yoga (but not the true sexual cultivation), any couple would indeed benefit from the material found inside the following books, which are among the best of the genre (especially Douglas Wile's translations):

Chang, Jolan. *The Tao of Love and Sex: The Ancient Chinese Way to Ecstasy.* New York: Penguin, 1977.

Chang, Dr. Stephen T. *The Tao of Sexology: The Book of Infinite Wisdom.* San Francisco: Tao Publishing, 1986.

Wile, Douglas. *Art of the Bedchamber: The Chinese Sexual Yoga Classics Including Women's Solo Meditation Texts.* Albany, NY: SUNY Press, 1992.

The enlightened Padmasambhava said, "The basis for realizing enlightenment is a human body. Male or female, there is no great difference. But if she develops the mind bent on enlightenment, the woman's body is better." This is due to the fact that a woman's body appears yin on the outside but is of the yang nature internally. Since women's minds are symbolized by yin, they often report trouble in getting along with each other, whereas men's minds are yang and their bodies are yin.

This accounts for the mental and physical attractions between the sexes, as well as why men find it easier to cooperate with each other, and why there are more disciplinary rules for nuns than for monks in the world's many spiritual schools. But this is a very difficult subject to enter into here. All we can point out is that different methods of cultivation practice are recommended for men and women due to their different physical and mental conditions, and there will be different corresponding effects and signs of cultivation progress as well.

This principle of differences in practice and results also holds for individuals of different age groups. All these factors must be taken into account—sex, age, temperament, health, mental training (education or occupation), and so on—when trying to understand the kung-fu that occurs during cultivation, and which spiritual exercises are best suited to practitioners. One of the reasons we've expounded upon so many different cultivation methods is to be able to address a wide audience with different needs, capacities, potentials, and inclinations.

In reference to the fact there are differences which the two sexes experience in cultivation, and because most cultivation stories involve men, you might want to research the inspiring stories of several women who succeeded in cultivation. One of the best stories concerns Lady Yeshe Tsogyel, who was the female equivalent of Milarepa. Her story and others can be found in:

Allione, Tsultrim. *Women of Wisdom*. London: Arkana, 1986.
Dowman, Keith. *Sky Dancer: The Secret Life and Songs of the Lady Yeshe Tsogyel*. London: Arkana, 1989.
Edou, Jerome. *Machig Labdron and the Foundations of Chod*. Albany, NY: Snow Lion Publications, 1996.

17. ONE-POINTED VISUALIZATIONS

Unless you're a mathematician, most people don't realize that zero and infinity can both represent the state of emptiness. So by analogy, one can reach emptiness by infinitely expanding the mental scenario that the mind must take in (concentrate upon), or by reducing the scenario until there is nothing left at all.

In either case, one's internal mentation can shut down when concentration is correctly applied to visualizing either of these images. But sometimes this is just clogging the mind rather than reaching a true state of cessation, and as the great Tibetan master Tsongkhapa warned, if you cultivate dullness and ignorance such as a mind that's "blanked" and suppressed rather than open, free, empty and aware, this state of dullness can result in your being reborn as an animal. Cultivation always involves detaching from thoughts, but the mind is always clear, open, wide awake, and free; one does not suppress thoughts, or push them down so that they don't manifest. People who do this to clear their mind are absolutely incorrect. Just let the thoughts go and they'll depart, but remain open and watch them leave. That's correct practice.

Actually, one should never use force to freeze or halt the mind's activities, for you must allow the mind's activities to be freely born. Thus a clogging means of cultivation, such as viewing an entire horizon while walking, as suggested by Don Juan in Carlos Castaneda's books, is also incorrect if it entails jamming. Rather, one must reach some stage where mental activity dies of itself while the mind remains open and free instead of being blocked or clogged by suppression.

Next, one must introspect to investigate the state of clarity produced, which is absent of internal dialogue or mentation and provisionally referred to as "emptiness." One-pointed visualization practices do not directly attain to the true emptiness of cultivation but only lead to an initial stilling of the sixth consciousness. Nevertheless, this achievement provides a foothold for practice from which one can really begin to meditate.

For more information on various aspects of visualization, the reader can reference comments in Nan Huai-Chin's *Tao and Longevity* as well as other works that talk about the correct principles behind such practice. One can also reference various Hindu works, such as:

Aranya, Swami Hariharananda. *Yoga Philosophy of Patanjali.* Albany, NY: SUNY Press, New York, 1983.

Prabhavananda, Swami, and Christopher Isherwood, trans. *How to Know God: The Yoga Aphorisms of Patanjali.* New York: Penguin, 1969.

Rieker, Hans-Ulrich. *The Yoga of Light.* London: Unwin Paperbacks, 1971.

We can't possibly cite all the worthwhile translations of Patanjali's *Yoga Sutras* which have appeared, or the many worthwhile translations of the *Hatha Yoga Pradipika.* However, we can urge you to get at least one translation of both of these texts. It's our firm belief that when you pursue the path of cultivation, and are familiar with the scriptures of many schools, you'll see that as to the initial stages of samadhi, they are all speaking of the same cultivation process and phenomena in different terms and from different cultural backgrounds. Yet because of this variety in expression though commonality in material, there are sure to be one or two sources that can help you understand cultivation better and progress on the path.

18. BHAKTI YOGA

True bhakti yoga is not a cult practice but a very refined form of mindfulness practice. When it turns into a practice of emotional excess, without the requisite understanding of the cultivation path, then it turns into a type of cult practice, or superstition. The emphasis on whipping up the emotion of love that we often see cultivated by bhakti yoga appeals to simple or religious people who can lose themselves in devotional service, and yet people don't recognize that emotional attachment is an obstacle in cultivation.

Because it appeals to the simple folk, bhakti practice was especially popular in medieval Christianity, Islam, and Sufism. Today, Hinduism is the major exponent of bhakti yoga, and in support of this practice the *Bhagavad Gita* often quotes Krishna on this technique.

However, if people lose control of their mind or senses through the practice of bhakti yoga, it's a form of excess rather than true cultivation. Unlike what many teachers may claim, bhakti yoga is not the most suitable practice for today's world, which requires a cultivation path of understanding.

The Hindu sage Sri Ramakrishna is an individual who practiced many forms of bhakti yoga, and his insightful story can be found in *The Gospel of Sri Ramakrishna* (New York: Ramakrisha-Vivekananda Center, 1962), and Swami Saradananda, *Sri Ramakrishna, the Great Master* (Madras, India: Sri Ramakrishna Math, 1956).

One can also investigate the many stories of Sufi and other Hindu saints who traveled the road of bhakti, which you can find in the stories of some Christian saints as well. Why does the method work? Because it is akin to the generation stage yogas of the Tantra school, wherein one cultivates their chi and mai through the devotion to one-pointed visualization of a deity or mandala.

The problem is that individuals following this path are then lacking an understanding of cultivation to proceed to the highest realms. So unless they cultivate prajna-wisdom, and obtain the assistance of a fine teacher, their stage of attainment usually levels off at the lower heavenly realms. Nevertheless, the stories of such saints who have traveled this route can be quite insightful and inspiring. For first-hand accounts of various Indian saints, one should research the many materials written in Bengali.

19. PRAYER

To understand prayer as a form of cultivation, it would be useful to investigate the prayers used by various Christian mystics. Through this investigation you can find that the accomplished saints had transformed prayer into a kind of emptiness meditation. Thus we have the terms "surrendering to God," and books like *The Cloud of Unknowing*.

It's unfortunate that the medieval Christian monks and nuns did not have information about or access to the many higher cultivation techniques other than prayer, or many could have reached much higher levels of spiritual attainment. In cultivation, you need both a sadhana technique and an understanding of the principles behind practice. If these are lacking, it's hard to make progress in cultivation, and an entire culture can be deprived of its highest possible attainments.

20. DREAM YOGA

At the highest stages of cultivation, you don't have dreams anymore because you are always the same whether asleep or awake. In Buddhism, we say that this happens when you break through the skandha of conception, which is akin to "seeing the Tao" described in Zen, or attaining the clear light of the impure illusory body as described in Tibetan Tantra, or the transmutation of shen to emptiness in the Tao school. But for information about how you can actually use dreams as a means of cultivation, please see *Tsongkhapa's Six Yogas of Naropa,* translated by Glen Mullin (Ithaca, NY: Snow Lion Publications, 1996), and W. Y. Evans-Wentz, *Tibetan Yoga and Secret Doctrines* (Oxford: Oxford University Press, 1967). These books deal with the basics of dream yoga practice and seeing the clear light during the dream state.

There are lots of books today on interpreting dreams and omens, but this has little to do with cultivating toward enlightenment to escape birth and death. We didn't cover the topic of how cultivation categorizes dreams, but for reference it is useful to know that cultivation science partitions dreams into five different categories:

1. Mindfulness dreams of actual affairs, which appear as a result of concentrating (thinking too much) on some subject during the daytime. Because of this deep preoccupation, your thoughts are carried over into sleep and appear in your dreams because they've burrowed into the shadow side of the sixth consciousness. Hence certain dreams arise because they correspond to a topic that is always with you, almost like a subconscious obsession. These synchronistic dreams sometimes reflect events in your life as they happen.

2. Memory dreams or dreams of remembrance, which are dreams that echo things of the past, such as reliving things you previously experienced. This includes the events of yesterday or even past lives.

Another type of remembrance dream is the longing dream where you had a connection with an individual in the past, and they come back to you in the dream.

3. Illness or sickness dreams, which provide symbolic indications that your body is suffering some type of organic disturbance. For instance, if the body is too wet you might dream of a flood. If the stomach has indigestion, you might dream that people are running after you. There are many types of this sort of dream. Dreaming of ghosts is another such example because ghosts are of a yin nature, and this indicates that the body is weak or unhealthy.

4. Prognostication or clairvoyant dreams, which show the future. Children seem to have these dreams more often than adults, but they are rare.

5. Outside influence dreams, which manifest outside energies affecting your mind. These are usually bad or uncomfortable dreams, and are rare.

21. MINDFULNESS OF PEACE AND MINDFULNESS OF DEATH

Death comes to everything in existence, no matter how long-lived. Everything in this transient world is subject to birth and death, including our thoughts, so Shakyamuni Buddha told us ages ago that it was useless trying to control thoughts. They'll always continue to spring from nowhere, and will always continue to disappear into emptiness. So why hold on to anything, or worry about some state that is destined to depart?

All phenomena function the same way, which is why they should be viewed in the same manner as dreams. What you have to do is to get around the mental realm that arises, to detach from this realm and see the clear empty awareness within which it arises. That's seeing the ground luminosity, or clear light of mind. To perceive that empty, stainless, formless nature of awareness is to see Tao. It sounds easy, but it's hard to do, which is why we have so many spiritual practices. That realm is where everything comes from, and it's the one thing that will never die even though we will continue going through endless transformations. But all the while, that one thing will never move, while everything it can "know" and perceive will change. Can you find that stainless, empty source of awareness?

In this phenomenal world of transient phenomena that functions like a dream, you can certainly control your actions when you try, but you cannot control their results. So what's the purpose of cultivation? Cultivation is simply a profound means of changing your behavior and learning to master that element of change within this dream. Purifying your behavior is the actual process of the path and, since there's nowhere to go after enlightenment, putting perfect behavior into effect is also the outcome of the path. The basis, process, and result of the path are the same.

Behavior is thoughts expressed, so in cultivation, to cultivate behavior you in turn cultivate the mind of clear awareness. Thus in death practice, you try to achieve this goal. How? By letting go of your mental chatter while remaining clear and aware. If you're really dead, you can really let go of everything, so such a rationale gives you a really strong basis for mastering detachment. That's why this method is so effective in cultivation, and why the Zen school prized it so much. Let everything go, put everything down, don't bother with it. It's not important anymore. Let go of the body and return all your perceptions to the sense organs—what's left? If that which can't be returned to anything else isn't you, then what is it?

Zen cultivation itself is similar to mindfulness of death practice, for you don't do anything about your thoughts or your body, you just leave them alone. You drop everything, cultivating a mind free and open that abides nowhere, and simply remain in this state. This doesn't mean that you're useless to the world, or a hermit, for you fulfill your functions and responsibilities with even greater effectiveness. You simply continue to function in the world while remaining unmoved by phenomena.

22. MEDITATING ON THE WATER , EARTH, FIRE, WIND, AND SPACE ELEMENTS

Before the earth was formed, the universe was just empty space. Empty space still has lots of things in it, but we call it "empty" because it's tremendously still.

As to the creation of the cosmos, eventually the wind element started to arise in this great stillness. That is, wind represents movement, for out of this extreme of yin, movement (yang) started to form. At first the wind element was small, and then gradually it grew larger. The friction of the wind element with itself created the fire element, and the heat of the fire element caused agglomeration so that the water element formed. Eventually the water element cooled and congealed (solidified) to form the earth element, like water transforming into ice, and the earth element contains a little bit of all the elements.

In the same way, before conception we have no body, so we say everything is empty. Since the body's initial cause is a thought on the part of parents, this is the wind element arising. When the egg and sperm come together and unify through the process of intercourse, this is the fire element and then the water element, which represents cohesion. Then, of course, there is the earth element, which is the embryo. As the fetus grows, the wind element exercises its functioning again, and the process continues.

As to the process of death, first we get thinner and feel heavy as the earth element disintegrates. As the water element leaves our body, we become thirsty and have difficulty talking. Next the body begins to cool, which is the fire element leaving us, and when the wind element goes we finally breathe our last. If you study cultivation, you must match its principles with scientific observations such as this. Buddhism does this, as does Taoism to some degree, but ordinary people don't realize it. All the stages of cultivation in purifying the four elements can be found in the external world of phenomena, in the microcosm as well as the macrocosm. If you know this, it will help you with your own cultivation.

The Water Element

Another variation on the water visualization technique is to visualize the whole world transformed into water. Above you, below you, in the front and back—everything is water. Yet another variation is to visualize an endless stream of water coming down from the top of your head and cleansing the body so that only your white skeleton is left. One advantage of this particular method is that you can visualize the water coming from the top of your head washing away any sickness you might have.

This visualized stream of water can serve as a blessing, or internal baptism, to clean the body and mind and wash away disease. In your visualization practice, all your cells are washed by the water and become clean and clear as crystal, after which they disappear. In doing this practice, eventually you'll reach a state where you are the water and the water is you, but you must still match this state with prajna so that there's no such thing as water or self. Thus you'll be able to enter emptiness. This method is really unique and rare. But even if you succeed in this method, you must still return to cultivating the mind.

The Fire Element

As to the fire visualization, people who are sick often use radiation or lasers to become cured, but you can also imagine that you are shining fire or light energy on the part of your body that's sick. Of course, these are just minor offshoots of the basic fire visualization method. In really cultivating the sun's energy, you don't pay attention to these minor techniques.

In esoteric Buddhism, some pictures show a ring of fire around a particular Buddha which may represent the fire of wisdom and the fire visualization achievement. Because the heat of fire is involved, we say this method is related to kundalini accomplishment, but this cultivation technique isn't the kundalini phenomenon or kundalini practice.

The Wind Element

You can use anapana, which is cultivating the wind element, to break open all the obstructions in the body,. Thus anapana is basically a method of chi and mai cultivation. When the mai start to open, you'll feel bliss, and at this time your need for external respiration will decline. As the obstructions in the body are eliminated, you also won't get drowsy anymore because now the chi can flow freely. On the other hand, if the body pains you in a certain location, this is because chi cannot go through that location. So the wind element is very important to master in cultivation.

The Tien-tai school uses the method of cultivating the wind element, and Indian yoga relies on wind cultivation, but they don't know all the important principles. For instance, wind has no specific form. It has no material form, no sound, no structure. Sometimes we say we can hear the sound of wind, but that's not wind. Rather, it's the resistance of wind hitting an obstruction. Wind has no sound or even smell, but smells and scents flow with it, so we can say that the wind is empty. The flow of wind is very significant but to really understand it you need to know lots of science. Only people who cultivate the wind element will really understand it.

If you want longevity you need merit, but when you can merge the mind with your chi, then you can indeed cultivate longevity. Taoism says that when something disintegrates it becomes like chi and that when the chi collects and assembles it has form again, so you must remember this principle when certain cultivation phenomena appear. Emptiness marks the initial start of life and creation. Emptiness is not the nothingness of an absolute vacuum, for there are an infinite amount of things in emptiness and the wind element is the closest element to it. Why tell you of all these miscellaneous principles? Once you know the theory, you can start the cultivation of the wind.

The Earth Element

The most complete description of the method of meditating on the elements can be found in early Hinayana texts on the kasinas. These discuss the meditation methods of concentrating on the elements, and the "counterpart signs" or kung-fu marks that arise when one is successful in their practice. They also discuss the various superpowers that these meditations support.

For instance, mastering the earth kasina enables one to sit on space or on water (through creation of the earth element) and to make duplicates of the physical body. The water kasina is the basis for being able to cause rain, storms, create rivers, and to dive in and out of the earth. The fire kasina is the basis for the ability to burn only what one wants, countering fire with fire, and so on. The air kasina is the basis for causing wind storms and being able to go with the power of the wind. The space kasina is responsible for being able to travel unobstructed through walls, creating space inside rocks, and revealing the hidden. There are also the blue kasina, yellow kasina, red kasina, white kasina, and light kasina. For instance, the yellow kasina is the basis for being able to transmute something into gold. Further information on these practices can be found in Bhadantacariya Buddhaghosa, *The Path of Purification (Visuddhi-magga)*, translated by Bhikkhu Nanamoli (Sri Lanka: Buddhist Publication Society, 1991).

23. MINDFULLY CULTIVATING VIRTUOUS BEHAVIOR

To gain further insight into cultivating the virtues, the reader is referred to the various lists of Hindu, Buddhist, Moslem, Sufi, Christian, and other virtues that have been compiled over the ages, and to match them with their own understanding of the principles and practices of cultivation. This information is readily found in various religious sources and literature. It is also useful to read the works on bodhisattva practices and enlightened behavior, such as found in the *Lotus Sutra* and:

Batchelor, Stephen, trans. *A Guide to the Bodhhisattva's Way of Life*. Dharamsala, India: Library of Tibetan Works and Archives, 1992.

Cleary, Thomas, trans. *Zen Lessons: The Art of Leadership*. Boston: Shambhala Publications, 1989.

Crosby, Kate, and Andrew Skilton, trans. *The Bodhicaryavatara* [of Shantideva]. Oxford: Oxford University Press, 1996.

Wayman, Alex, trans. *Ethics of Tibet: Bodhisattva Section of Tsong-Kha-Pa's Lam Rim Chen Mo*. Albany, NY: SUNY Press, 1991.

One can also reference the Vinaya-pitaka, or rules of discipline, espoused by various schools. Typically there are more religious disciplinary regulations and rules for females than for males, which corresponds to the fact that females represent the (mental) yin principle and males represent the yang. However, female bodies represent the yang principle within (and yin without), while males represent the yin within (and the yang without).

Women have bodies better suited for cultivation than men, who usually succumb to sexual desire that obstructs their progress. However, women usually experience difficulties triumphing over the mental realm, which is an easier feat to accomplish for the male cultivators who can triumph over sexual desire. If a man develops enough wisdom for triumphing over the incredible hurdle of sexual desire, the mental knots and entanglements pose less of a problem in their practice than for women.

Lastly, to understand the road of cultivating behavior, one can do no better than to read Lao Tzu, Chuang Tzu, Mencius, Confucius, Plato's works on Socrates, and the autobiography of Benjamin Franklin, which contains a unique method of altering one's behavior (also see the story of Yuan Huang). In this category, the works of Confucius, who was spiritually enlightened and had attained the various samadhis like Shakyamuni Buddha, also deserve special attention. Confucius taught cultivation through the aspect of harmonious conduct and behavior. His path of cultivation, which also involves cessation and prajna-wisdom, can be found in *The Great Learning*.

In general, the road of Buddhism emphasizes how to cultivate, Taoism emphasizes how to deal with affairs and phenomena, and Confucianism emphasizes how to deal with people, events, and relationships. Of particular note in the Confucian school, besides *The Analects, The Great Learning,* and *The Doctrine of the Mean,* is *Worldly Wisdom: Confucian Teachings of the Ming Dynasty,* translated by J. C. Cleary (Boston: Shambhala Publications, 1991).

It is extremely unfortunate that there are not more published translations of *The Great Learning* and *The Doctrine of the Mean,* as they clearly reveal the spiritual path of cultivation according to the principles we have discussed.

24. CONCENTRATING ON A HUA-TOU, OR MEDITATION SAYING

Koans are overrated today as a type of cultivation technique, mostly because Zen teachers and students don't understand the principles and road of practice. The best translations of koan material, or collections of famous hua-tou cases include:

Cleary, Thomas, trans. *Book of Serenity: One Hundred Zen Dialogues.* New York: The Lindisfarne Press, 1990.
Cleary, Thomas, and J. C. Cleary, trans. *The Blue Cliff Record.* Boston: Shambhala Publications, 1992.
Sekida, Katsuki, trans. *Two Zen Classics: Mumonkan and Hekiganroku.* New York: Weatherhill, 1996.

For further information on dealing with koans, please see J. C. Cleary, *Meditating with Koans* (Santa Clara, CA: Asian Humanities Press, 1992), and *No Barrier: Unlocking the Zen Koan,* translated by Thomas Cleary (New York: Bantam, 1993).

25. JNANA YOGA, OR
ABHIDHARMA ANALYSIS

Jnana yoga, which is the intellectual approach to self-realization (using inquiry and analysis by which the mind examines its own nature), is a difficult road for spiritual attainment as it requires you to be firmly grounded with cultivation progress before you can succeed on this path. One must especially learn the process of stilling the breath and watching the mind (cessation and contemplation practice) so that the mind becomes clear.

Now, there are a variety of means available under the method of jnana yoga. As one example we have abhidharma analysis, where people who study the five skandhas can use their understanding to analyze the various mind events that arise in order to improve their level of samadhi and wisdom. Studying the nature of contact and perception, as done in Kashmiri Shaivism, can also help you to attain a realization of emptiness when you use this knowledge to analyze your most minute activities. Eliminating the concept of name and form, as is done in the Vedanta practice of *abheda-bodha-vakya*, can also lead to a stable mind.

Buddhism also suggests that you study interdependent origination, which helps you detach from the world of phenomena; it shows that nothing has a self-nature of its own because everything is defined through other causes and conditions, which are in turn defined by their own causes and conditions, and so on. Everything exists because of mutual interdependence, or co-dependent arising. Studying Nagarjuna's writings can help convince you of the unreality of phenomena and the fact there is no self, whereupon you can free yourself of clinging and attain an experience of true emptiness. This sometimes happens to people who read Zen meditation cases as well. Then there are the people who get so tied up in what seems to be the logical contradictions in cultivation logic that their internal mentation shuts down. Thus they can arrive at emptiness in this way as well. But no matter how you arrive at emptiness, you must look within to see the empty origin of thoughts, their extinction into emptiness, and the empty nature of mind, which itself is a thought phenomenon. Hence, one must look within to see who is doing the looking. Without this exercise in prajna-wisdom, all your cultivation kung-fu amounts to naught! As we've explained over and over again, this is the correct way to cultivate.

Several important works on abhidharma or vedanta include:

Anacker, Stefan. *Seven Works of Vasubandhu.* Delhi: Motilal Banarsidass, 1994.

Bodhi, Bhikkhu. *A Comprehensive Manual of Abhidharma.* Sri Lanka: Buddhist Publication Society, 1993.

Garfield, Jay L., trans. *The Fundamental Wisdom of the Middle Way: Nagarjuna's Mulamadhyamakakarika.* Oxford: Oxford University Press, 1995.

Gyatso, Lobsang. *The Harmony of Emptiness and Dependent-Arising.* Delhi: Library of Tibetan Works and Archives, 1992.

Kalupahana, David J. *Nagarjuna: The Philosophy of the Middle Way.* Albany, NY: SUNY Press, 1986.

Komito, David Ross. *Nagarjuna's "Seventy Stanzas": A Buddhist Psychology of Emptiness.* Ithaca, NY: Snow Lion Publications, 1987.

Napper, Elizabeth. *Dependent-Arising and Emptiness.* Boston: Wisdom Publications, 1989.

Satchidanandendra, Sri Swami. *The Method of Vedanta.* A. J. Alston, trans. Delhi: Motilal Banarsidass, 1997.

Wood, Thomas. *Mind Only: A Philosophical and Doctrinal Analysis of the Vijnanavada.* Delhi: Motilal Banarsidass, 1994.

Jnana yoga, or abhidharma analysis, is a difficult route to follow, but it will be a prosperous undertaking for many individuals. Regardless of whether you choose to follow this path or not, everyone is encouraged to study basic cultivation principles, such as found in abhidharma texts. Once again, the best sources for the basic principles can be found in our list of recommended books, especially:

Mullin, Glen, trans. *Tsong Khapa's Six Yogas of Naropa*. Ithaca, NY: Snow Lion Publications, 1996.

Nan, Huai-Chin. *Tao and Longevity: Mind-Body Transformation*. Wen Kuan Chu, trans. York Beach, ME: Samuel Weiser, 1984.

————. *To Realize Enlightenment: Practice of the Cultivation Path*. York Beach, ME: Samuel Weiser, 1994.

————. *Working toward Enlightenment: The Cultivation of Practice*. York Beach, ME: Samuel Weiser, 1993.

For mastering this form of jnana yoga practice, you can research the methods of Vedanta as well.

Glossary

ABHIDHARMA: A collection of Buddhist philosophical principles used as the basis for Hinayana studies. They go into the analysis of the composite elements of consciousness, perception, mind and matter in order to help the individual understand the idea of no-self, or absence of an inherently existing ego.

AGNI: Fire.

AMITOFO: A fully enlightened Buddha who resides in a beautiful, majestic Buddha land that he established for the benefit of all beings. This land can be reached upon an individual's death if the person sincerely mantras Amitofo's name during their lifetime. Practitioners wish to be reborn in Amitofo's Pure Land upon his or her death because it offers a more favorable environment for making cultivation progress.

ANAPANA: Buddhist term for various breathing practices, otherwise known as pranayama.

ARHAT: A highly cultivated individual who, because of his cultivation efforts, has freed himself from mental afflictions and desires so as to have gained freedom from being subject to the karmic rounds of transmigration, or rebirth. The stage of the Arhat is the highest accomplishment of the Hinayana path.

ASANA: Physical postures used in meditative or yoga practice.

BARDO: An intercessory period of pause between two dissimilar processes such as in-breathing and out-breathing, the state of wakefulness and sleeping, the state of dreaming and no-dreaming, or the state of being (after death) between an old life and a new life. The typical bardo stage yoga refers to cultivation exercises one employs between death and a new rebirth.

BHAKTI YOGA: A form of devotional practice commonly found in Hinduism; the yoga path of devotion.

BODHISATTVA: Stage of enlightenment on the Mahayana path, and one who therefore has dedicated his or her enlightenment to the benefit of all beings, having vowed to sacrifice themselves for others on the way to full spiritual realization.

BRAHMACARYA: The basic practice of celibacy which is necessary in order to lay the physical foundation that allows for one's jing to transform into chi. Normally this requires at least one hundred days of devoted emptiness practice.

CHAKRA: A psychic energy center in the body which forms at the intersection of various mai or nadi, and which is responsible for certain physiological and psychological functions.

CHI: Chinese term for the life force of the body, also spelled ch'i, qi, or ki. In Indian yoga chi is known as *prana* while in Buddhism it is often referred to as the body's wind element. It is known by a wide variety of alternate terms in many different cultivation schools and cultures, and is basic in cultivation.

CHI-GONG: Chinese practice of playing with the wind element of the body, also known as qi gong. Similar to pranayama practices, most chi-gong practices involve using the mind to connect with bodily sensations of internal wind which practitioners often mistake as the real chi or cultivation.

CLEAR LIGHT: Tibetan term for the original true mind of enlightenment. Realizing the clear light means seeing the Tao. From this point on, the true cultivation process really begins.

DESIRE REALM, FORM REAL, FORMLESS REALM: In the Buddhist world view, the entire universe is divided into three realms. The Desire Realm includes hell beings, hungry ghosts, animals, humans, asuras and certain angelic beings found in celestial heavens. All the beings in this realm are subject to sexual desire, and various cravings. The Form Realm includes seventeen higher celestial realms occupied by gods of Form, and the Formless Realm is comprised of four levels of formless gods. The various upper realms can only be reached through meditation practice and because of great virtue.

DHARMA: A Sanskrit word with multiple meanings such as a doctrine or body of teaching, any phenomenon which makes up existence, or the revealed body of Absolute Truth or Reality.

DHYANA: Four states of meditative concentration, involving emptiness and physical bliss, that correspond to attainment levels in the Realm of Form. Sometimes the word *samadhi* is used interchangeably with dhyana.

EARTH ELEMENT: Refers to the dense physical components of the physical nature, such as bones, nails, hair, teeth, etc.

FIRE ELEMENT: Refers to the heat of the body, and the kundalini phenomenon.

FLOW: A state of mundane samadhi sometimes experienced by athletes due to having achieved an optimal body coordination in conjunction with mental concentration. It is not a spiritual practice as it lacks the aspects of prajna-wisdom, as well as virtue and meritorious service to others.

FORM REALM: See Desire Realm.

FORMLESS REALM: See Desire Realm.

FOUR JOYS/FOUR EMPTIES: In Tibetan Tantra, an individual meditates on the crown, throat, heart and navel chakras in order to experience special states of physical bliss which, when co-joined with the realization of emptiness, constitute the practice of co-emergent emptiness and bliss. While not specifically stated, these states are related to the four dhyanas in Taoism, yoga and orthodox Buddhism.

HINAYANA: Term for "Lesser Vehicle" in Buddhism that refers to any cultivation school, not just Buddhist, that helps the practitioner gain their own salvation without regard to the greater salvation of all beings. The goal of the Hinayana path is to become an Arhat, who is enlightened for himself and thus freed from the chains of transmigration (reincarnation). In Buddhism itself, the Hinayana school is often referred to as the Theravada.

HSI: The state of cessation between the in-breath and out-breath. This gap between the breaths is when the real chi of the body arises. When Patanjali says that the real pranayama is between the in-breath and out-breath, he's referring to the state of hsi which marks the initiation of kundalini.

HUA-TOU: The mind before it's stirred by thought; a question one concentrates on in Zen practice in order to arrive at a state of emptiness, a realm before thought has stirred.

I-CHING: A Chinese book of philosophy, science, moral cultivation and divination with countless uses in a variety of fields.

JAPA: The practice of mantra repetition.

JEN-MAI: An energy channel in the body, present from birth, which passes down along the front of the body. It is the opposite of the Tu-mai which passes along the back of the body.

JING: Chinese term for the seminal essence of the body, which is not to be mistaken with sperm or ova. In Indian metaphysics, the equivalent term is *ojas*. The first basic process in cultivation, according to Tao school terminology, is that one cultivates an empty mind so that there are no obstructions to one's jing transforming into chi. Jing also often refers to the water element of the body, including hormones.

JNANA YOGA: The yogic practice, or path to self-realization, through the study of wisdom texts. Jhana stands for knowledge, intellect or wisdom.

KARMA: The sum total of an individual's past thoughts, words and behavior which determine their experiences of fate in this life and future lives. The conventional realm of reality exists because of the linking of cause and effect. The terms dependent arising or interdependent origination are other descriptive terms for karma.

KARMA YOGA: The cultivation practice of performing charitable acts and other good deeds for the benefits of others as a pathway to enlightenment.

KARMAMUDRA: Certain Tantric sexual practices of cultivation, equivalent to the "left-door" sexual practices of the Tao school.

KUAN YIN: Chinese name for Avalokitesvara Buddha (Kannon in Japanese) who is especially known for the virtue of compassion. Kuan Yin is famous for teaching a special meditation technique for enlightenment that involves entry into the dharma realm through listening to sound.

KUNDALINI: The real chi of the body, or spirit energy of the human organism which is activated through the process of cultivation. See Tumo Fire.

KUNG-FU: A state of physical or mental achievement attained through cultivation practice; the various mind-body changes that occur through the process of cultivation. One's samadhi achievements are one sort of kung-fu, as are psychic powers and physical changes of the body achieved through cultivation. Also known as gong-fu.

MADYAMIKA: A specialized school of Buddhist studies that emphasizes the wisdom road of cultivation, and the middle way between extremes.

MAHAMUDRA: A Tibetan meditative practice similar to Zen. Dzogchen is a similar practice technique.

MAHAYANA: Buddhist term for the "Great Vehicle" whose practitioners aim to become enlightened for the sake of all sentient beings. Practitioners of the Mahayana reach a higher stage of cultivation than Hinayana practitioners because they sacrifice themselves for others, and are therefore known as bodhisattvas until they mature into fully enlightened Buddhas.

MAI: Chinese term for the tiny energy channels in the body, also known as *nadi* in Sanskrit. The modern descriptions of acupuncture energy meridians are examples of chi mai, through which chi runs.

MANJUSHRI: The great Buddha of Wisdom.

MANTRA: A certain sound or sequence of sounds, without or without meaning, whose repetition (*japa*) can lead to the stilling of the mind and thus entry into samadhi.

MUDRA: A special posture assumed by the hands or body.

NADI: See *Mai*.

NIRVANA: A state of profound mental purity and peace where there are no more mental afflictions. This is the state of enlightenment of the Arhats. A higher meaning refers to the perfection of wisdom and awakening to true nature of phenomena.

PRAJNA: Transcendental wisdom, or a mind that realizes emptiness. Prajna-wisdom is non-dual, non-discriminative naked knowing which is directly in touch with the true nature of reality.

PRANAYAMA: Yoga school breathing practices aimed at opening up the body's chi mai, balancing its internal energies, bringing about optimal physical health, and paving the way for entry into samadhi. Many pranayama practices involve breath retention exercises. The purpose of these practices is to prepare the body for the time when the breath naturally stops because of the initial entry into samadhi.

PURE LAND: A realm established by a Buddha and adorned in magnificence through the fruit of the Buddha's merits. Much more pleasant than a human realm, it is a place where many Dharma teachings are available and where beings can more readily mature in practicing to enlightenment.

SADHANA: A form of disciplined cultivation or spiritual practice such as meditation, mantra, visualization exercises, and so forth.

SAMADHI: A heightened state of mental concentration, free of normal mental distractions, that leads to profound serenity, calmness, clarity and awareness. Thus samadhi is a mental state in which normal thoughts seem to have stopped. The basic of cultivation paths are to enable entry into samadhi and from proficiency in samadhi, the awakening to enlightenment which is itself not a samadhi.

SHAMATHA-VIPASHYANA: A spiritual practice common to many religious cultivation schools, also known as stopping and seeing, or cessation and contemplation. Cessation refers to the stopping of random thoughts in the mind, and contemplation refers to silently watching or observing the state produced. Through this practice, one tries to cultivate samadhi (stopping) and transcendental prajna wisdom (observation). In other words, by the practice of *shamatha* one calms the mind to reach a state of concentration, and by the practice of *vipashyana*, one examines the state produced to realize the emptiness of ego and reality.

SAMSARA: The state of conventional reality which is considered unreal from the aspect of the Absolute or fundamental nature, which is Tao.

SEVENTH CONSCIOUSNESS: See Sixth Consciousness.

SHADOW CONSCIOUSNESS: The yin aspect of the Sixth Consciousness, which functions during dreams, sickness and mental illness.

Shen: Chinese term for spirit, or illumination whose equivalent Indian term is *tejas*. The best physical equivalent to shen is light, and shen is cultivated through prajna emptiness meditation as a result of the transformation of chi.

SIXTH CONSCIOUSNESS: In Buddhist Yogacara (Mind-Only or Consciousness-Only) metaphysics, the human consciousness can be divided into eight different types of consciousness. The first five consciousnesses refer to a separate consciousness behind each of the five senses such as hearing, seeing, tasting, etc. The sixth consciousness receives and then interprets the information presented to it by these five sense consciousnesses, and thus stands for our ordinary thinking mind, or mind of mentation. It has a shadow, or yin side called the solitary consciousness that functions during dreaming, illness and states of insanity. The seventh consciousness stands behind the sixth consciousness as its root, and is an ingrained ego consciousness that stains our experiences with ego thinking. Lastly, the eighth consciousness (or *alaya*) is the foundational consciousness.

SKANDHA: In Buddhist metaphysics, all ego experience can be broken down into five categories called the five skandhas. These are the skandhas of form, sensation, conception, volition and consciousness. The skandha of form refers to our physical form and the material world; the sensation skandha refers to agreeable or disagreeable sensations; the conception skandha refers to subtle thought; the volitions skandha refers to subtle stirring impulses of both matter and mind; and the consciousness skandha refers to various realms of consciousness. The topic of the skandhas, or aggregates, is a very detailed subject. The main idea is that the human physical-mental experience is simply a collection of skandha elements, and there is no inherent self or inherent ego factor within them.

SPACE ELEMENT: Refers to the physical separation between objects in the body, such as interstitial spaces, the separations between the joints, and so on.

SUSHUMNA: The central energy channel of the body whose opening leads to samadhi attainments when chi passes through it. See zhong mai.

TAN-TIEN: Abdominal area below the navel, known as the *hara* in Japanese, which often becomes warm in meditation practice. The region contains the navel chakra.

TAO: A word with many meanings such as enlightenment or spiritual realization, the path to enlightenment or realization, the way things naturally work, and so forth.

TATHAGATA: Another term of respect for a Buddha, a fully enlightened being.

TRUE MIND: In cultivation terminology, the original fundamental essence of being possesses the ability for primordial awareness. Since the foundational ground state of being possesses the ability for knowing, the fundamental essence is often called true mind.

TU-MAI: An energy channel in the body, present from birth, which rises from the perineum and runs up the spine (at the back of the body) to the top of the head, and then down the front of the face to the nose.

TUMO FIRE: Another term for the kundalini or warmth element of the physical nature. In several cultivation schools one specifically sets out to cultivate the kundalini energy by envisioning fire in the region of the tan-tien. When the area gets warm this is called the tumo fire or gastric fire in Yoga, and Fierce Woman in Tibet. In Buddhism it is referred to as the fire element of the physical nature and corresponds to the stage of warming in prayoga.

VAIROCANA BUDDHA: The primordial Buddha, also known as the Great Sun Tathagata or Buddha of Great Illumination.

VINAYA PRACTICE: The Vinaya are scriptures concerned with monastic discipline and moral conduct, such as codes of virtuous behavior. Vinaya practice is to live life in such a way as to strictly follow such codes of conduct.

VISAYA: An experiential realm of the mind; some type of mental state or mental experience.

WAI-DAN: Chinese term for external medicines consumed to help change the body and purify it for cultivation. The school of Wai-dan concentrates on ingesting external substances to help cleans the body and quicken the pace of chi-mai cultivation.

Water Element: Refers to the watery elements of the physical constitution, such as jing, blood, hormones, lymph, etc.

WIND ELEMENT: Refers to the chi of the physical body. In some cultivation schools, the various chi of the body are sometimes referred to as winds.

YANG: A Taoist term which symbolizes a variety of characteristics such a movement, brilliance, masculinity, and positive polarity.

YIN: A Taoist term which symbolizes a variety of characteristics such as femininity, quiet, yielding, stillness, responsiveness, rest and negative polarity.

YIN BODY: Taoist term for an invisible body of chi one uses when leaving the physical body to travel to other realms. If an individual dies, this yin body is also called an intermediate body.

YOGA: Any type of spiritual practice or sadhana.

ZHONG MAI: Another term for the sushumna, avadhuti, or central energy channel of the body whose opening often leads to the attainment of samadhi.

ZHUNTI BUDDHA: An ancient, fully enlightened Buddha who is known as the "Mother of the Buddhas" for helping so many achieve perfect, complete, full enlightenment.

Index

A

abheda-bodha-vakya, 234
abhidharma analysis, 161, 234
Aikido, 86
ajna-chakra, 53
alchemy, external, 89, 209
Amitofo, 42
    Namo, 42, 43
    Pure Land of, 42
ananda, 169
ananda-samadhi, 169
anapana, 25, 63, 141
    breathing exercises, 26
    cultivation method, 30
archery, 83
athletic peak performance, 85
avadhuti, 58

B

bardo, 67
    contemplation, 68
    practices of, 67, 202
    state, 76
    state yoga, 77
    yoga, 69, 75
behavior
    mindfully cultivating virtuous,
        145, 231
bhakti devotion, nine types of
    pure, 116
bindus, 53
birth, 131
bliss, 60, 62
bodhicitta, 53
Bodhidharma, 157, 179
bodhimind, 53
body-mindfulness, 21
bones, 39
breath, external, 45
breathing
    exercises, 19
    internal embryo, 27
    practice, 45
breathing exercises, nine-step, 50
bright points, 37
Buddha-mindfulness, 117
Buddha Vairocana, 37

Buddhism, esoteric, 121
Buddhahood, 47
Buddhaghosha, 206

C

celibacy, 104
cessation, 27
   first step of, 28
   respiratory, 46
cessation and contemplation practice,
   13
   preparatory, 14
chakras, 37
   throat, 123
channel, opening the central, 200
chi, 37, 50, 92, 113, 115, 180, 194
   channels, 39
   cultivate, 24, 56, 85, 207
   prenatal, 45
chi-gong practice, 87
Chia-shan, Zen master, 6
Chicken Foot Mountain, 2
chih, 27
chih-guan, 186
child light, 1, 178
Chod practice, 189
Chuang Tzu, 97
clear light, 69, 70
co-emergent emptiness and bliss, 97
color, 82
commandment keeping, 145
Complete Enlightenment Sutra, 135
concentration, 111
   one-pointed, 116
confession, 120
Confucianism, 120
Confucius, 135, 153
consciousness, 133
contemplating mind, 17
contemplation, 27
cultivation, 130, 132, 134, 146
   Hinayana method, 136
   mistakes in, 213

path, 150
practice, 53
sexual, 217
Shakyamuni's ten great roads of,
172
subtraction, methods, 113
cyclical existence, 134

D

dancing, 116
death, initial stages of, 71
decay, 131
deeds, good, 150
Dharanimdhara, 140
dharma doors, 153, 167
dhyana, four, 182, 185
   first, 22, 116, 168
   second, 168
   third, 169
   fourth, 169
diamond earth, 35
Diamond Sow Buddha, 45
Diamond Sutra, 127
Don Juan, 112
dream, 123
   vivid, lucid, 113
dream yoga, 123, 126, 127
dream yoga practitioner, 124

E

Eckhart, Meister, 119, 129
element
   earth, 139, 230
   fire, 138, 229
   five, 133
   four, 45
   space, 143
   water, 135, 229
   wind, 141, 230
emptiness, 6, 29, 110, 112
energy meridians, 37, 45
exercise, physical, 85
existence, 15